SOCIAL CHANGING ENVIRONMENT HOW INFLUENCES

ORGANIZATIONAL STRATEGIES CHANGE CASE STUDIES

JOHN LOK

Contents

Foreword

Preface

Introduction

Management science is a popular business, economic and psychological method to be applied to help any business organizations, societies to solve problems. Whether what are the real functions or advantages that management science methods or strategies can help our societies or organizations to solve any problems ?

Successful organizzational strategy can solve any organizational challenges. Different kinds of business organizations will encounter different kinds of challenges, e.g. cost increasing, staff shortage, reducing customers number or sale etc. challanges. So, when the organization can judge whether which aspects of weaknesses it is experiencing as well as it can know why and how to attempt to implement the most suitable or the best strategy to solve its challenge when it is facing. Then, the organization will have possible to continue to existen. Otherwise, if the organization can not find whether which aspects are its difficuties , it is facing. Then, it can not implement the most suitable strategy to solve its challenges. Then, it will be closed down in possible. In my this book, I shall attempt to indicate some organizational cases and find whether what weakness or difficulties it is facing. Then, I shall recommend the best strategy to attempt to help it to solve the kind of challenge, it is encountering. Any have interesting to learn business strategy students, they can learn new strategic knowledge to help these organizations to solve their challenges.

In my this book first part, I shall attempt to indicate some real social or organizational problems how and why managers can attempt to apply management science methods or strategies to help their organizations or our societies to solve any kinds of common or complex problems. Readers can learn some real management science knowledges to attempt and judge whether some social or organizational problems can be solved by management science knowledge easily.

This book second part brings readers feel you are organizational outsourcing strategic professionals. You need to help your organizational different departments to implement outsource strategy or insource strategy or help government to inplement any human resource , economic development strategies. Although, nowadays, outsourcing is popular strategy to any global organizations. But they neglect outsourcing strategy has also disadvantages to some organizational departments. This book concerns to explain why outsourcing strategy can bring benefits to some organizational departments, but it can also bring disadvantages to some organizational departments. Also, I shall indicate how to implement management strategies to solve social problems.

This book third part concerns how to apply how facility management methods to attempt to explain whether your organization can be influenced to raise your employee individual productive efficiency as well as improve service performance to achieve to let your clients feel more satisfaction by effective human resource training or/and facility management methods. My research question includes:

(1)Can effective human resource training or/and facility management influences your organization's employee individual productive efficiency raising and/or service performance improving?

(2)How and why does organization's facility management in-house department or outsourced department can assist employees to improve its office or warehouse working environment to be more comfortable to let employees to feel in order to influence their productive efficiencies to be raised or improving their service performance to bring customers' more satisfactory feeling?

This part aims to let any organization leaders can attempt to apply psychological methods to predict whether their in-house facility management service is enough or/and human resource management strategy and training course program strategies which both have relationship to influence their employees' productive efficiency and service performance in order to achieve aim to raise more satisfactory feeling to their customers. I believe that effective facility management can improve better workplace environment to influence employee individual productive efficiency raising as well as effective human resource training course program can improve employee individual service performance in order to achieve customers to feel more satisfactory service performance in consequence for the organization's service.

In my this books, I will explain how any why good management science strategy can influence department communication, excellent technological input, effective human resource developement training, good employee motivation strategy and effective performance measurement strategy can influence any organization's overall performance to be more effective. I shall indicate the reasons to explain why above any one of these factors have indirect relationship to influence the organization's overall performance effectiveness. Readers can earn fresh opinions to acknowledge that these any one factors can be possible to influence organization's overall performance effectiveness.

Prologue

Ryanair airline & Easy Jet airline & budget airline

Ethnographic research

Quantitative and qualitative approaches

England wine bar segmentation

P&G (Procter & Gamble) body and
skin product marketing strategy

Mobile phone company marketing
strategy case study

England NHS public hospital patient
price structure strategy

Tesco supermarket supply for fruit
and vegetables supply chain strategy

A national chain of restaurant mobile
advertising strategy

Why social behavior may influence organizational strategy needs to be changed

Human Behavioral network job brings social
economic benefits
       What does human network job mean
       Why human network job behavior may influence economy

Robots take our jobs behavioral and economy influences
       Robot job behavior brings economy influences

Intellectual human economic behaviors
What does intellectual human economic behaviors
mean ?
       The relationship between social change and human
behavior
       How human productive behavior may influence economic development
● New Zealand farmer individual wine productive behavior
● America high technological productive behavior
● China share market investing behavior
Why has any individual country have many people invest share behavior which can influence the country's macro
consumption desire?

Can technology influence human shopping behavioral change?

Why and how human behavior may influence the country's economic growth or recession?

Technology how impacts human behavior changing?

How and why employees behaviors may influence economy development?

Robots invention whether they can help organizations to raise efficiencies or inefficiencies?

Why social behavior may influence organizational strategy needs to be changed ? p.300-339

ONE

INTRODUCTION OF MANAGEMENT

Management Science (MS) can be defined as:

In micro solution level view, "A problem-solving process used by an interdisciplinary team to develop mathematical models that represent simple-to-complex functional relationships and provide management with a basis for decision-making and a means of uncovering new problems for quantitative analysis

Management science encompasses, however, more than just the development of models for specific problems. It makes a substantial contribution in a much broader area: the application of the output from management science models for decision-making at the lower, middle, and top management levels.

A manager's experience, upcoming business conditions, and the output from a mathematical model form the best combination for planning, organizing, directing and controlling the company's activities. Management science is the application of the scientific method to the study of the operations of large, complex organisations or activities. Two disciplines intimately associated with management science are industrial engineering and operations research.

Definition and Concept of Management Science:

In macro solution view, management science (MS) is the broad interdisciplinary study of problem solving and decision making in human organizations, with strong links to management, economics, business, engineering, management consulting, and other fields. It uses various scientific research-based principles, strategies, and analytical methods including mathematical modeling, statistics and numerical algorithms to improve an organization's ability to enact rational and accurate management decisions by arriving at optimal or near optimal solutions to complex decision problems. Management science helps businesses to achieve goals using various scientific methods.

The field was initially an outgrowth of applied mathematics, where early challenges were problems relating to the optimization of systems which could be modeled linearly, i.e., determining the optima (maximum value of profit, assembly line performance, crop yield, bandwidth, etc. or minimum of loss, risk, costs, etc.) of some objective function. Today, management science encompasses any organizational activity for which the problem can be structured as a functional system so as to obtain a solution set with identifiable characteristics.

Management science is concerned with a number of different areas of study: One is developing and applying models and concepts that may prove useful in helping to illuminate management issues and solve managerial problems. The models used can often be represented mathematically, but sometimes computer-based, visual or verbal representations are used as well or instead. Another area is designing and developing new and better models of organizational excellence.

Management science research can be done on three levels:

The fundamental level lies in three mathematical disciplines: probability, optimization, and dynamical systems theory.

The modeling level is about building models, analyzing them mathematically, gathering and analyzing data, implementing models on computers, solving them, experimenting with them—all this is part of management science research on the modeling level. This level is mainly instrumental, and driven mainly by statistics and econometrics. The application level, just as in any other engineering and economics disciplines, strives to make a practical impact and be a driver for change in the real world.

The management scientist's mandate is to use rational, systematic, science-based techniques to inform and improve decisions of all kinds. The techniques of management science are not restricted to business applications but may be applied to military, medical, public administration, charitable groups, political groups or community groups.

Historical Development of Management Science:

The roots of management science extend to the work of F.W. Taylor, the father of Scientific Management. Taylor is known for his systematic development of management techniques which he started at the Midvale Steel Company in Philadelphia around 1880.

(i) Research,

    (ii) Standardization,

    (iii) Control and

    (iv) Cooperation.

When installed at the Link Belt Engineering Company in 1905, the system included cost accounting, time study, inventory control, production control, planning, output scheduling, functional operation, standardized procedures, a mnemonic system of classification, and means for maintaining quality production. Associated with Taylor were other important pioneers of scientific management – Carl Barth, Gantt, Thompson, Hathaway and many others. Barth brought to the work of scientific management the use of research mathematics, which he merged with his extensive knowledge of machine tools. Gantt contributed the recognition of worker psychology, the development of a bonus plan, and the charts used in production scheduling. Out of this came the term Industrial Engineering which today is descriptive of the work of functional staffs responsible for such activities as incentive standards, methods analysis, quality control, production control, cost control and materials handling.

During the ten years just after World War II, a great deal of management science was performed under the name of operations research. The influx of physical scientists many of whom were unacquainted with modern management administration into war technology and the pressures of total war with new and terrible weapons gave rise to a rediscovery of a kind of pragmatic scientific management. This merged with an increasingly popular acceptance of statistical quality control in America and the practical development of high-speed electronic calculators to give impetus to the operations-research approach.

In brief, management science describes an integrated approach to operational control based on the application of scientific research methods to business problems. A systematic approach to problem solving received early impetus from Taylor's scientific management movement and is continued today by Industrial engineers and mathematical business analysts. This approach is characterized by a methodology of sequential investigation steps.

Characteristics of Management Science:

The four major characteristics of management science are as follows:-

(1) Examine Functional Relationships from a Systems Overview:

The activity of any one function of a company will have some effect on the activity of each of the other functions. Therefore it is necessary to identify all important interactions and determine their impact on the company as a whole. Initially, the functional relationships in a management science project are expanded deliberately so that all the significantly interacting parts and their related components are contained in a statement of the problem. A systems overview examines the entire area under the manager's control. This approach provides a basis for initiating inquiries into problems that seem to be affecting performance at all levels.

2) Use the Interdisciplinary Approach:

Management science makes good use of a simple principle, it looks at the problem from different angles and approaches. For example, a mathematician might look at the inventory problem and formulate some type of mathematical relationships between the manufacturing departments and customer demand. A chemical engineer might look at the same problem and formulate it in terms of flow theory. A cost accountant might conceive the inventory problem in terms of component costs (e.g., direct material cost, direct labour cost, overheads etc.) and how such costs can be controlled and reduced, etc. Therefore, management science emphasizes over the interdisciplinary approach because each of the individual aspects of a problem can be best understood and solved by those, experts in different fields such as accounting, biological, economic, engineering, mathematics, physical, psychological, sociological, statistical etc.

(3) Uncover New Problems for Study:

The third characteristic of management science, which is often overlooked, is that the solution of an MS problem brings new problems to light. All interrelated problems uncovered by the MS approach do not have to be solved at the same time. However, each must be solved with consideration for other problems if maximum benefits are to be obtained.

(4) Use a Modeling-Process Approach to Problem Solving:

Management science takes a systematic approach to problem solving. It may use a modeling process approach taking the help of mathematical models.

Other Characteristics of Management Science are:

(5) A primary focus on managerial decision-making.

(6) The application of science to decision-making.

(7) A dependence on electronic computers.

(8) An appraisal resting on criteria of economic effectiveness. Effectiveness may be defined as the extent to which goals are achieved. Effectiveness is evaluated by measures of effectiveness (also known as measures of performance).

The Tools of Management Science:

The tools of management science developed specifically for solving managerial problems are listed below:

(a) Decision Matrices:

Allocation and investment problems involving a relatively small number of possible solutions can be presented in a tabular form known as decision matrix.

(b) Decision Trees:

The extension of decision matrices for situations involving several decision periods takes the shape of a tree.

(c) Mathematical Programming:

It attempts to maximize the attainment level of one goal subject to a set of requirements and limitations. It has extensive use in business, economics, engineering, the military and public service, mainly as an aid to the solution of allocation problems.

(d) Branch and Bound:

It is a step-by-step procedure used when a very large (or even infinite) number of alternatives exist for certain managerial problems.

(e) Network Models:

This is a family of tools designed for the purpose of planning and controlling complex projects. The best known models are PERT and CPM.

(f) Dynamic Programming:

It is an approach to decisions that are basically sequential in nature or can be reformulated so as to be considered sequential. It is a very general and powerful tool.

(g) Markov Chains:

They are used for predicting the outcome of processes where systems or units change their condition over time (e.g., consumers change their preferences for certain brands of commodities).

(h) Game Theory:

It provides a systematic approach to decision-making in competitive environments and a framework for the study of conflict.

(i) Inventory Models:

For certain types of inventory control problems, certain models that attempt to minimize the cost associated with ordering and carrying inventories have been developed.

(j) Waiting Line (Queuing) Models:

For certain types of problems involving queues, special descriptive models have been developed to predict the performance of service systems such as car garages – cars standing in queue for servicing.

(k) Simulation Models:

For the analysis of complex systems when all other models fail, management science uses descriptive-type simulation models.

Specially, five types of models may be employed:

1. Artificial Intelligence.
2. Heuristic programming.
3. Management games.
4. Systems simulation, and
5. Monte Carlo simulation.

APPLY MANAGEMENT SCIENCE METHODS TO SOLVE PROBLEMS STEPS:

Step 1 : Searching or finding what is/are the main problem(s)

We first present a working definition of science. We use that definition along with our review of evidence on compliance with science by papers published in leading journals to develop operational guidelines for implementing scientific principles. We then developed a checklist to help researchers follow the guidelines, and another to help reviewers—those who fund, publish, or use research to assess whether a paper complies with scientific principles.

While the scientific principles underlying our guidelines are well-established, our presentation of them in the form of comprehensive checklists of operational guidance for science is novel. We present evidence that in the absence of such an aid, researchers and research stakeholders will often fail to observe scientific principles. Giving specific and realistic suggestions for addressing our society's pervasive social problems .

Updated with recent issues such as the national debate on health care reform, this Second Edition of How Can We Solve Our Social Problems? gives students a sense of hope by demonstrating specific, realistic steps we can take to solve some of the most pervasive social problems in America today. Author James Crone maintains a sense of sociological objectivity throughout and helps students realize that we can take steps to solve such key social problems as poverty, racial and ethnic inequality, unequal education, and environmental issues. The book's first two chapters define "social problem,," provide a theoretical background, discuss the daunting barriers we face in attempting to solve social problems, and demonstrate how sociology can help.

Research question: Can managers apply management science to solve social problem ?

Problem: The scientific method is unrivalled as a basis for generating useful knowledge, research papers published in the management and social sciences and applied economics fields often violate scientific principles. What can be done to to increase the publication of useful papers?

Methods: Evidence on researchers' compliance with scientific principles was examined. Guidelines aimed at reducing violations were then derived from established definitions of the scientific method.

Guidelines to Problem Solving and DecisionMaking (Rational Approach)

Much of what people do is solve problems and make decisions. Often, stressed and very short for time. Consequently, when they encounter a new problem or decision they must make, they react with a decision that seemed to work before. It's easy with this approach to get stuck in a circle of solving the same problem over and over again. Therefore, it's often useful to get used to an organized approach to problem solving and decision making. Not all problems can be solved and decisions made by the following, rather rational approach. (Note that it might be more your nature to view a "problem" as an"opportunity". Therefore, you might substitute "problem"for "opportunity" in the following guidelines.)

Step 2: Define the problem

This is often where people struggle. They react to what they think the problem is. Instead, seek to understand more about why you think there's a problem.

Define the problem: (with input from yourself and others). Ask yourself andothers, the following questions:

1. What can you see that causes you to think there's a problem?

2. Where is it happening?

3. How is it happening?

4. When is it happening?

5. With whom is it happening? (HINT: Don't jump to "Who is causing theproblem?" When we're stressed, blaming is often one of our first reactions.To be an effective manager, you need to address issues more than people.)

6. Why is it happening?

7. Write down a five-sentence description of the problem in terms of "Thefollowing should be happening, but isn't ..." or "The followingis happening and should be: ..." As much as possible, be specific inyour description, including what is happening, where, how, with whom and why.(It may be helpful at this point to use a variety of research methods.

Step 3: Defining complex problems

If the problem still seems overwhelming, break it down by repeating steps 1-7 until you have descriptions of several related problems. Verifying your understanding of the problems: It helps a great deal to verify your problem analysis for conferring with apeer or someone else.

Step 4: Prioritize the problems

If you discover that you are looking at several related problems, then prioritizewhich ones you should address first. Note the difference between "important" and "urgent" problems.Often, what we consider to be important problems to consider are really justurgent problems. Important problems deserve more attention. For example, ifyou're continually answering "urgent" phone calls, then you've probablygot a more "important" problem and that's to design a system thatscreens and prioritizes your phone calls.

Step 5: Understand your role in the problem

Your role in the problem can greatly influence how you perceive the role ofothers. For example, if you're very stressed out, it'll probably look like othersare, too, or, you may resort too quickly to blaming and reprimanding others.Or, you are feel very guilty about your role in the problem, you may ignorethe accountabilities of others.

Step 6: Look at potential causes for the problem

• It's amazing how much you don't know about what you don't know. Therefore,in this phase, it's critical to get input from other people who notice theproblem and who are effected by it.

• It's often useful to collect input from other individuals one at a time(at least at first). Otherwise, people tend to be inhibited about offeringtheir impressions of the real causes of problems.

• Write down what your opinions and what you've heard from others.

• Regarding what you think might be performance problems associated withan employee, it's often useful to seek advice from a peer or your supervisorin order to verify your impression of the problem.

• Write down a description of the cause of the problem and in terms of whatis happening, where, when, how, with whom and why.

Step 7: Identify alternatives for approaches to resolve the problem

At this point, it's useful to keep others involved (unless you're facing apersonal and/or employee performance problem). Brainstorm for solutions to theproblem. Very simply put, brainstorming is collecting as many ideas as possible,then screening them to find the best idea. It's critical when collecting theideas to not pass any judgment on the ideas -- just write them down as you hearthem. (A wonderful set of skills used to identify the underlying cause of issuesis Systems Thinking.)

Step 8: Select an approach to resolve the problem
·When selecting the best approach, consider:
· Which approach is the most likely to solve the problem for the long term?
· Which approach is the most realistic to accomplish for now? Do you havethe resources? Are they affordable? Do you have enough time to implement theapproach?
· What is the extent of risk associated with each alternative?
   (The nature of this step, in particular, in the problem solving process iswhy problem solving and decision making are highly integrated.)

Step 9: Plan the implementation of the best alternative (this is your action plan)
1.Carefully consider "What will the situation look like when the problemis solved?"
2. What steps should be taken to implement the best alternative to solvingthe problem? What systems or processes should be changed in your organization,for example, a new policy or procedure? Don't resort to solutions where someoneis "just going to try harder".
3. How will you know if the steps are being followed or not? (these are yourindicators of the success of your plan)
4. What resources will you need in terms of people, money and facilities?
5. How much time will you need to implement the solution? Write a schedulethat includes the start and stop times, and when you expect to see certainindicators of success.
6. Who will primarily be responsible for ensuring implementation of the plan?
7. Write down the answers to the above questions and consider this as youraction plan.
8. Communicate the plan to those who will involved in implementing it and,at least, to your immediate supervisor.
   (An important aspect of this step in the problem-solving process is continuallyobservation and feedback.)

Step 10: Monitor implementation of the plan
   Monitor the indicators of success:
1. Are you seeing what you would expect from the indicators?
2. Will the plan be done according to schedule?
3. If the plan is not being followed as expected, then consider: Was the planrealistic? Are there sufficient resources to accomplish the plan on schedule?Should more priority be placed on various aspects of the plan? Should theplan be changed?

Step 11: Verify if the problem has been resolved or not
   One of the best ways to verify if a problem has been solved or not is to resumenormal operations in the organization. Still, you should consider:
1. What changes should be made to avoid this type of problem in the future?Consider changes to policies and procedures, training, etc.
2. Lastly, consider "What did you learn from this problem solving?"Consider new knowledge, understanding and/or skills.
3. Consider writing a brief memo that highlights the success of the problemsolving effort, and what you learned as a result. Share it with your supervisor,peers and subordinates.

Step 12: Rational Versus Organic Approach to ProblemSolving
   Rational person
A person with this preference often prefers using a comprehensive and logicalapproach similar to the guidelines in the above section. For example, the rationalapproach, described below, is often used when addressing large, complex mattersin strategic planning.
1.Define the problem.

2. Examine all potential causes for the problem.

3. Identify all alternatives to resolve the problem.

4. Carefully select an alternative.

5. Develop an orderly implementation plan to implement that best alternative.

6. Carefully monitor implementation of the plan.

7. Verify if the problem has been resolved or not.

A major advantage of this approach is that it gives a strong sense of orderin an otherwise chaotic situation and provides a common frame of reference fromwhich people can communicate in the situation. A major disadvantage of thisapproach is that it can take a long time to finish. Some people might argue,too, that the world is much too chaotic for the rational approach to be useful.

Organic person

Some people assert that the dynamics of organizations and people are not nearlyso mechanistic as to be improved by solving one problem after another. Often,the quality of an organization or life comes from how one handles being "onthe road" itself, rather than the "arriving at the destination." The quality comes from the ongoing process of trying, rather than from havingfixed a lot of problems. For many people it is an approach to organizationalconsulting. The following quote is often used when explaining the organic (orholistic) approach to problem solving.

A major advantage of the organic approach is that it is highly adaptable tounderstanding and explaining the chaotic changes that occur in projects andeveryday life. It also suits the nature of people who shun linear and mechanisticapproaches to projects. The major disadvantage is that the approach often providesno clear frame of reference around which people can communicate, feel comfortableand measure progress toward solutions to problems.

Examples of solution of Teaching Social Problem steps

The teaching social problem suitation

Kids and young adults need to be able to problem-solve on their own. Every day, kids are faced with a huge number of social situations and challenges. Whether they are just having a conversation with a peer, working with a group on a project, or dealing with an ethical dilemma, kids must use their social skills and knowledge to help them navigate tough situations. Ideally, we want kids to make positive choices entirely on their own. Of course, we know that kids don't start off that way. They need to learn how to collaborate, communicate, cooperate, negotiate, and self-advocate. Social problem solving skills are critical skills to learn for kids with autism, ADHD, and other social challenges. Of course, all kids and young adults benefit from these skills. They fit perfectly into a morning meeting discussion or advisory periods for older kids. Not only are these skills that kids will use in your classroom, but throughout their entire lives. They are well worth the time to teach!

Here are 5 steps to help kids learn social problem solving skills:

Step 1:

Teach kids to communicate their feelings. Being able to openly and respectfully share emotions is a foundational element to social problem solving. Teaching I statements can be a simple and effective way to kids to share their feelings. With an I statement, kids will state, "I feel ______ when _____." The whole idea is that this type of statement allows someone to share how their feeling without targeting or blaming anyone else. Helping kids to communicate their emotions can solve many social problems from the start and encourages positive self-expression.

Step 2:

Discuss and model empathy. In order for kids to really grasp problem-solving, they need to learn how to think about the feelings of others. Literature is a great way teach and practice empathy! Talk about the feelings of characters within texts you are reading, really highlighting how they might feel in situations and why. Ask questions like, "How might they feel? Why do you think they felt that way? Would you feel the same in that situation? Why or why not?" to help teach emerging empathy skills. You can also make up your own situations and have kids share responses, too.

Developing Empathy

Step 3:

Model problem-solving skills. When a problem arises, discuss it and share some solutions how you might go forward to fix it. For example, you might say, "I was really expecting to give the class this math assignment today but I just found out we have an assembly. This wasn't in my plans. I could try to give part of it now or I could hold off and give the assignment tomorrow instead. It's not perfect, but I think I'll wait that way we can go at the pace we need to." This type of think-aloud models the type of thinking that kids should be using when a problem comes up.

Step 4:

Use social scenarios to practice. Give a scenario and have kids consider how that person might feel in that situation. Discuss options for what that person might do to solve the problem, possible consequences for their choices, and what the best decision might be. Kids can consider themselves social detectives by using the clues and what they know about social rules to help them figure out the solution. These are especially fun in small groups to have kids discuss collaboratively. Use these free social problem solving cards to start your kids off practicing!

Social Problem Solving Task Cards

Step 5:

Allow kids to figure it out. Don't come to the rescue when a child or young adult has a problem. As long as it's not a serious issue, give them time to think about it and use their problem-solving skills on their own. Of course, it's much easier to have an adult solve all the problems but that doesn't teach the necessary skills. When a child comes to you asking for your help with a social problem, encourage them to think about it for five minutes before coming back to you. By that point, they might have already figured out possible solutions and ideas and might not even need you anymore. If you are interested in helping your kids learn social problem solving skills right away, consider trying out these Social Problem Solving Task Cards. They highlight real social scenarios and situations that kids can discuss. The scenarios include a variety of locations, such as in classrooms, with family, with friends, at recess, and at lunch. This set is targeted for elementary-age learners.

TWO

MANAGEMENT SCIENCE PROBLEMS SOLUTION CASES

Case 1

How reduces transport cost of shipping or road transportation to the most minimum level in warehouse, factory locations

linear programming management science solution method :

Researching the main shipping or /and road transport problem to bring cost rising to between either warehouse or/ and factory or both and the goods transfer transport destinations.

Inventory Models management science method helps warehouse, factory locations to reduce road or shipping transporation cost between goods transfer locations. For certain types of inventory control problems, certain models that attempt to minimize the cost associated with ordering and carrying inventories have been developed.

Transportation problem is a particular class of linear programming, which is associated with day-to-day activities in our real life and mainly deals with logistics. It helps in solving problems on distribution and transportation of resources from one place to another. The goods are transported from a set of sources (e.g., factory) to a set of destinations (e.g., warehouse) to meet the specific requirements. In other words, transportation problems deal with the transportation of a single product manufactured at different plants (supply origins) to a number of different warehouses (demand destinations). The objective is to satisfy the demand at destinations from the supply constraints at the minimum transportation cost possible. To achieve this objective, we must know the quantity of available supplies and the quantities demanded. In addition, we must also know the location, to find the cost of transporting one unit of commodity from the place of origin to the destination. The model is useful for making strategic decisions involved in selecting optimum transportation routes so as to allocate the production of various plants to several warehouses or distribution centers.

Suppose there are more than one centers, called 'origins' , from where the goods need to be transported to more than one places called 'destinations' and the costs of transporting or shipping from each of the origin to each of the destination being different and known. The problem is to transport the goods from various origins to different destinations in such a manner that the cost of shipping or transportation is minimum. Thus, the transportation problem is to transport various amounts of a single homogenous commodity, which are initially stored at various origins, to different destinations in such a way that the transportation cost is minimum.

Inventory Models Management Science Solution Method

A tyre manufacturing concern has many factories located in many different cities transport cost case

For certain types of inventory control problems, certain models that attempt to minimize the cost associated with ordering and carrying inventories have been developed. The objective of the transportation model is to determine the amount to be shipped from each source to each destination so as to maintain the supply and demand requirements at the lowest transportation cost.

For example: A tyre manufacturing concern has many factories located in many different cities. The total supply potential of manufactured product is absorbed by retail dealers in different cities of a country. Then, transportation problem is to determine the transportation schedule that minimizes the total cost of transporting tyres from various factory locations to various retail dealers.

The transportation model can also be used in making location decisions. The model helps in locating a new facility, a manufacturing plant or an office when two or more number of locations is under consideration. The total transportation cost, distribution cost or shipping cost and production costs are to be minimized by applying the model. How do you calculate the cheapest way to ship goods between several warehouses and stores? In this lesson, you will explore the transportation problem and its solutions.

Searching What Is The Transportation Problem to cholocate retail stores case
Mathematical Programming Management Science Solution Method:
It attempts to maximize the attainment level of one goal subject to a set of requirements and limitations. It has extensive use in business, economics, engineering, the military and public service, mainly as an aid to the solution of allocation problems.

Imagine yourself owning a small network of chocolate retail stores. To run a successful business, you will also have to own or rent a warehouse where you will store the goods ready to be delivered whenever the stores need them. If you have only one warehouse, it will be supplying all your stores. However, as soon as you expand and open a second warehouse, you will have to make an important decision: which warehouse will deliver which goods to each of your stores? Depending on the choice you make, you might save or spend a significant amount of money.

The transportation problem is a distribution-type problem, the main goal of which is to decide how to transfer goods from various sending locations (also known as origins) to various receiving locations (also known as destinations) with minimal costs or maximum profit. As long as the number of origins and destinations is low, this is a relatively easy decision. But as the numbers grow, this becomes a complicated linear programming problem. Think about Walmart. In 2016, it had 5,229 stores and 166 distribution centers in the US! It would be impossible to calculate the optimal shipping routes without a computer algorithm.

General transportion problem types
Transportation problems can be classified into different groups based on their main objective and origin supply versus destination demand. Transportation problems whose main objective is to minimize the cost of shipping goods are called minimizing. An alternative objective is to maximize the profit of shipping goods, in which case the problems are called maximizing.

In a case where the supply of goods available for shipping at the origins is equal to the demand for goods at the destinations, the transportation problem is called balanced. In a case where the quantities are different, the problem is unbalanced.

When a transportation problem is unbalanced, a dummy variable is used to even out demand and supply. A dummy variable is simply a fictional warehouse or store. For example, if total supply at all warehouses is 50 units, but total demand at all stores is only 40 units, we create a fictional store with an additional demand of 10 units. The cost of shipping to the fictional store is usually zero. Now, the transportation problem becomes balanced. It is worth noting that sometimes problems that are solved using the transportation method have nothing to do with an actual movement of goods. What is crucial for applying the method is to recognize the network of connected elements.

Case 2
Management science solves public transport passenger queue problem
Waiting Line (Queuing) Models: solution imbalanced taxi and passenger queue in urban public transportation service case
The Four Problems Of Urban Transportation (And The Four Solutions)
The fixed-route bus and the bicycle solve at least one urban problem better than new technologies urban transportation problem case. There are four main problems in urban transportation that require four separate solutions. Some urban transportation design recommendion argued that technology can solve some problems, but

not the same problem that public transit solves."The city has four separate problems of urban transportation which have four separate kinds of solutions, and it is very important to not mistake the solution for one problem for the solution for a different problem."

The first solution :

Bus stop time real -time information technology and apps solution method

Friction arises between a transit system and its users when the users don't have the information they need when they need it. That problem has been largely solved, Walker said, by information technology and apps. "That has been a fantastic transformation. Some of you may not be old enough to remember what life was like without real-time information, when you just went right out into the snow and wondered when the bus was coming."

The second solution:

Innovation method

The innovation method solves the city has four separate problems of urban transportation may include: Emissions and Energy Efficiency: "for which we're currently working on electric vehicles, and that's fantastic." Labor and Safety: The cost of labor is the primary driver of operation costs for passenger transport, Walker said. "It is why your bus doesn't come more often, and it is also why Uber can't make money." Autonomous vehicles will address that and the accident rate. "There is a problem with the efficient use of labor, and also a colossal problem of safety for which we are talking about autonomous vehicles, and that's fantastic." Space: "And there is a fourth problem which is the efficient use of space, for which the solution is on the one hand, cycling and walking, and on the other, public transit provided by big vehicles."

The third soution:

The fixed-route bus or train solutione method is the best solution reason

The fixed-route bus or train is the vehicle of the future, because it remains the most efficient way to move large numbers of people through the congested space of a city. In his critique of public transit, Musk pointed out that people prefer "individualized transport, that goes where you want, when you want," like the Tesla Model S. But Walker contends individualized transport that goes where you want when you want can't move people through a congested city as efficiently as a fixed-route bus.

"We are always going to need vehicles sized to the appropriate capacity requirement, which means big buses in big cities," he said. "Our friends in the tech industry, including many of you here, and I love what you're doing, are always trying to sell us stories about how everything will fit together into a magnificent fusion. They want us to mix it up, to think about how it combines. And I'm always saying, but wait a minute, if you're going to be a smart customer you have to think about how they work separately as well."

Instead of above technological methods to solve public transport problem. The queue control management method will be one good solution

How do I conduct queue management of passengers in waiting taxi or bus area for Public transportation Vehicles?

Are there existing design projects and studies that a public transportation vehicle (Taxi or Bus) would know the number of passenger in waiting area/shed through long range network? I am conducting a design project for buses in my country that would know the number of passenger in waiting area and this information will be sent to the terminal or bus which will they used to pick up these passengers. Thus, congestion of buses and passenger can be lessen

I think that there are 2 technical issues: a) how to collect and transmit information, b) how to manage public transportation to minimize queue. About the 1st question you probably need either to do it manually (operator sitting at every station and making phone calls like "please send one more bus urgently, we have 100 of people waiting here", but this may be too expensive, at least for city buses) or to do it automatically (video camera, some image recognizing software that calculates people and then sends a message to the center) in this city has four separate problems of urban transportation concerns taxi and bus queue case.

Conclusion of the best solution method

As I know, there is not such a system design yet. but you may devise one by using the queue theory and optimizing the performance of the system by the following pattern:

- defining a objective function corresponding to the total passengers awaiting time.
- optimizing the objective function by finding the best set of assigning the available buses to the stations (considering the routes)

Case 3

Waiting Line (Queuing) Models: solution imbalanced taxi and passenger queue in airport case

Predicting Imbalanced Taxi and Passenger Queue Contexts in Airport management problem

For certain types of problems involving queues, special descriptive models have been developed to predict the performance of service systems such as car garages – cars standing in queue for servicing.

The taxi and passenger queue contexts indicate the various states of queues related to taxis and passengers (i.e. taxis are waiting for passengers, passengers are waiting for taxis, both are waiting for each other, none is waiting). Predicting these queue contexts in a future time is very important for better airport ground transport operations. However, queue context prediction at the airport is a challenging problem due to the presence of different contextual factors i.e., time, weather, taxi trips, flight arrivals and many more. Also these taxi and passenger queue contexts at the airport are imbalanced since some of the contexts are very infrequently occurring compared to others. In this paper, we address the problem of predicting imbalanced taxi and passenger queue contexts at the airport. First, we investigate different contextual factors, including time, taxi trips, passengers and weather for queue context prediction. Then we propose a detailed step by step solution to address this problem. To support the effectiveness of our detailed approach, we generate a queue context dataset by fusing three real world datasets including taxi trip, passenger wait time and weather condition that represent the taxi and passenger queue contexts at any major international airport in any country City. The experimental results demonstrate that our developed queue context prediction framework provides detailed solutions to deliver higher accuracy in queue context prediction.

Therefore, context-aware mobility analytics enables the provision of intelligent analysis on mobility contexts considering different user perspec- tives. The success of many applications such as transport management and location recom- mendation requires the discovery of valuable knowledge through extensive analysis of related factors . For example, an airport can be regarded as the first and last impression of a city. Since a longer passenger wait time for a taxi ride can diminish the satisfaction rating of an airport , the authorities try hard to maintain a higher customer satisfaction rating by providing various mobility services such as easy and comfortable airport transfer to the city using taxicabs. However, the demand-supply equilibrium of taxis is highly dependent on the taxi drivers' decisions to make airport trips. The ubiquitous data can help with managing the mobility of airport users by detecting different mobility contexts (i.e. situa- tions of the concurrent queues related to passengers and taxis) . The intelligent analysis and prediction of different mobility contexts can help with making mobility decisions for airport passengers and taxis at different times of the day.

We argue that by incorporating the temporal deviation of taxi drivers' moves as the feature importance score can identify good quality neighborhoods and thus significantly boost the taxi-passenger queue context prediction accuracy. We utilize a real world queue context data set that includes information from taxi trip logs, airport passenger arrivals and weather conditions which are relevant to the different queue contexts. Then we propose a temporal driver-knowledge deviation based feature importance scheme to select a quality neighborhood for predicting taxi and passenger queue contexts.

As we extract more features by computing the deviations of all feature values from its hourly mean along with the current features of the queue context dataset , it is necessary to check the relevancy of all features. The reason is that the use of all these features may degrade the prediction performance significantly due to the inclusion of some irrelevant and redundant features. Also, for different stations, the configurations such as lane numbers, and maximum queue length of taxis and passengers can affect the solution of the passenger-taxi queue problem.

The proliferation of pervasive devices in smart cities has enabled the development of many smart mobility applications . Smart parking is one of the innovations that provides easy to use parking services to the urban commuters by leveraging pervasive sensors and flexible payment systems.

Inferring a situational awareness map using clustering methods has become a popular research topic in recent years.

GPS trajectory has been utilised in smart mobility applications. In this section, we briefly review the related work which can be separated into two categories: points clustering and trajectory clustering. For example, intelligent reminders of user activities and notifications for major transporta- tion delays due to the current situation of the users. This outcome can also be leveraged for the applications of discovering user rou- tines based on personal contexts of mobile users. In an intelligent healthcare scenario, a robust and simultaneous recogni- tion of multiple user contexts would be important to be considered for elderly and disabled people, while travelling through various accessible paths .

Case 4

Management games model solves salespeople emotion problem in store environment

Any organizations can let salespeople feel happy to sell their products. Then their sale performance will also raise. The question concerns that how to make them to feel happy to help the organization to sell their products? I shall explain how to apply managment games or management psychological methods to solve this organizational problem as below:

How to manage sales for predictable revenue?

In order to hold salespeople sale psychology whether they feel happy or unhappy, executives need to understand the essential activities, sales managers must focus on to be analysts for change, foster continuous improvement and create a sales culture that drives results. Sale executives need to know how to achieve top objectives of sales management is to drive sales, capture new revenue and exceed monthly sales and margin objectives, e.g. performing sale straregy development with each salesperson on Monday morning at a minimum, and in a formal one-on-one meeting during the week;using strategy tools and questioning techniques to ensure the prospects are qualified and the strategy is valid; knowing the ratio between future values and future monthly quotos to raise sale opportunities; six month on-going sale plan aims to make sure there are coordinated to achieve sale to various market segments; developing on ongoing series of networking events to build market awareness in order to ensure all salespeople attend specific events involved in networking by salespeople to, understanding the market how to influence salespeople sale method to sale number, understanding trends and seeking some channels to raise additional sales opportunities; how to create trained or warm sale environment to let sales teams feel happy to sell.

How to design and utilize efficient control sale procedures?

The sale cycle procedure may include these market activities, such as advertising, sales promotion, market research, physical distribution, pricing , sale place, sale staffs seeking. SO, any organizations need have good sale planning, direction and control of the personnel, selling activities of a business with including recruiting, selecting, training, rating, supervising, paying or reward system, motivating strategy , as all these tasks apply to the personnel sales-force.

The factors may influence salespeople psychology, they may include fair income reward system, or appreciation methods and sale career development plan to every salesperson. It aims to encourage them to achieve the highest sale effort. Anymore, methods to train sale managers have the right direction to guide, lead and motivate their salespeople, e.g. knowledge of salespeople psychology needs how to satisfy them, understanding why they choose to do or act themselves sale behaviors in order to improve their weakness to motivate salespeople to achieve company's sale target goal every month easily, e.g. raising profitability, sales volume, market share, growth and corporate image building raise clients' confidence to choose to buy this company's any products more easily.

The sales organization is required for the following purposes, they may include: enabling top-management, to devote to more time in policy making for the growth and expansion of business to divide and fix authority among the subordinates , so that they may shirk work, to avoid repetition of duties and functions, so that there may not be any confusion among them to locate responsibility of each and every employee , so that they can complete the whole work in stipulated time, if not then the particular person must be responsible, to establish the sales effort to enforce proper supervision of sales force.

What does the concept of salespeople replacement value mean?

What is a sales force turnover management tool?

Sales force turnover is defined as the rate at which salespeople leave an organizations, resignations, retirements or dismissals. So, if the organization can raise the sales force turnover ratio, because many salespeople can be promoted or the retirement, or the sales force turnover ratio raising reasons as well as they are not resignation or dismissal reasons. I believe that the organization ought have good sale environment and reasonable reward and welfare strategy to let its salespeople feel happy to help this company to sell its products every day.

However, sales management's actions have direct or indirect effects to impact on turnover. Direct effects may include the firm's firing or dismiss policy. The indirect effects on sale turnover may include new salesperon recruiting and selecting policies affect the quality and performance of the sale force as well as the speed at which salespeople are replaced. The same policies have an impact on the sales force turnover rate through the characteristics of the newly recurited salespersons and the promotion , training, retraining policies, support, supervision, compensation. ALl of those factors have an impact on salesperson's personal satisfaction or dissatisfaction absolutely. So, any sale organizations need to concern how and why whether any one of above these factors may influence their salespeople how to perform or act sale behaviors in order to excite their sale number more effective in long term.

How to achieve sale force management effectively?

Sale management is one strategy to many organizations, because organizations expect their salespeople can only raise product sale number. So , they will consider whetther how to implement the sale management strategy to be the most suitable to themselves sale organizations in order to excite their sale teams to sell their products to achieve sale growth aim effectively. So for organization's long term sale growth development, it seems that one excellent sale management strategy can help the organization has stable sale number growth in long term possible.

However, the term " selling" includes a variety of sales situations and activities. For example, those sales positions where the sales representative is required primarily to deliver the product to the customer on a regular or periodic basis. The emphasis is this type of sales activity is very different to the sales position where the sales representative is dealing with sales of capital equipment to industrial purchasers. IN additions some sales representatives deal only in export markets whereas others sell direct to customers in their homes. So, sale organizations need to sell to local or overseas market as well as its target customer is businessmen or individual consumer or both in order to implement to choose their most suitable sale management strategy to train their salespeople more effective or achieving sale growth objective only. Because these its sale major target and where sale market place both factors will influence how it ought train its salespeople, so any organization's training method ought be influenced to change by whom is its major sale target and where is its major sale market location factors.

How to know the psychology of salesmanship?

When the organization can predict or find reasons to explain why its salespeople feel unhappy to help this organization to sell its products. Then, it can attempt to improve its weaknesses in order to let its salespeople to feel more sale service satisfactory feeling to continue to help this organization to sell its products. Then, it won't need not often to train or recruit new salespeople to replace its old salespeople in consequence.

How to know what its salespeoples' real need in order to raise their sale service satisfactory feeling ?

Psychology means that " science of the mind" and psychology plays to important part in business and it is quite worth to bring to influence any organization salespeoples' posivitive or negative sale emotion in their every sale process between themselves and their every client in personal. For example, if the salesperson often have negative emotion or he feels unhappy in every sale process, then he will encounter or increase many times of sale failure possibilities. He will feel that he is one poor verbal advertiser or seller or promotor to help his organization to promote its products to sell again as well as he will lose confidence to sell any products next sale chance, because his failure sale experiences are accumulated to influence his sale emotion to be poor or difficult sale.

Hence, the poor performance salesperson needs have more successful sale experiences to compensate his / her prior many sale failure times feeling, if the organization hopes this poor performance salesperson can raise sale number easily. Overall, any organizations need to concern how to improve or raise the more failure times of sale experience salespeoples' sale techniques or methods or attitudes more than choose to fire or dismiss them as well as finding another new salesperson to replace him/her. Because it is possible that the salesperson 's poor sale performance that is not due to himself/herself poor sale effort and sale knowledge or lacking sale experience to the product, it may be due to the poor sale team cooperation relationship , feeling poor or not comfortable sale physcial shop environment, poor sale manager and other salespeople working relationship, the sale manager lacks leadership effort, poor family relationship etc. external factors more than himself/herself personal poor or negative emotion or poor health etc. personal factors. Hence, the organization ought enquire him/her why he/she feels unhappy to sell its products and it needs to attempt to find methods to solve his/her challenges immediately. If his/her challenges can be solved. It is possible that his/her sale efforts can be also raised for. So, if the organization can know how to utilize positive sale emotion psychological methods to predict or know why and how every salesperson perform his/her sale behavior in whose daily sale tasks, then it can concentrate on implementing effective and the most suitable sale training to raise their sale abilities more easily.

However, the sale training may include: How to build or improve long term good salesperson and his/her customer sale service relationship between every salesperson and every client in every buying and selling cycle process, how to using right communicating styleds for better understanding every client's real needs, powers and negotiating, e.g. every salesperson needs to review why there are many clients do not choose to buy any products from his sale presentation or promotion, finding every time sale failure reasons can let the salesperson makes himself/herself sale failure reasons evaluation or judgement in order to find what is the major reason influences his/her sale failure, e.g. lacking product knowledge, he/she often let many clients to feel that he lacks patience to listen the client's enquiry or feedback, his sale presentation is not attractive to let many clients like to stay longer time to listen his sale presentation in whole sale process, the salesperson himself/herself emotion is negative and he /she can let many clients feel he / she is not happy or does not enjoy to sell this product from himself/herself face impression or sale behavior impression easily, lacking enough sale techniques to persuade his/her clients why he/she ought choose to buy this product in whole sale process etc. these factors may influence the salesperson's sale failure chance to be raised. Hence sales manager ought need to spend long time to meet the poor sale performance salesperson to discuess what his/her sale challenges are the most major to influence his/her every sale successful chance in order to improve his/ her sale performance more successfully.

In conclusion, the reasons why salespeople often encounter sale failure possibilities. The factors may include these aspects, such as they lask the desire to help customers to make satisfactory purchase decisons, they only concern how to achieve sale final objective or aim only, it will cause clients feel they do not real concern their real needs. They only concern to sell the product in success. They do not know how to describe the product whether what characteristics or features it owns accurately in order to increase sale chance to persudade them to make final decision to by the product, they do not attempt to participate the whole sale process to help them to choose the most right product in order to satisfy their any purcahse needs, they ought avoid deceptive or manipulative influence tactics, avoid the use of high pressure sales techniques etc. Thus, if any organizations can spend time to investigate what factors cause why any one of salespeople choose perform his/her sale behavior often in order to know or understand their salespeople' sale psychology absolutely. Then, I believe that their sale number will only grown more easily.

Case 5
Markov Chains Management Science Method : Persuading or exciting property buyers' property purchase choice in preference
Markov Chains Management Science Method means that it is used for predicting the outcome of processes where systems or units change their condition over time (e.g., consumers change their preferences for certain brands of commodities).

Something Behavioral (e.g., Prospect Theory) excites to property buyer preference choice to the property developer
What Is the Prospect Theory?
Prospect theory assumes that losses and gains are valued differently, and thus individuals make decisions based on perceived gains instead of perceived losses. Also known as the "loss-aversion" theory, the general concept is that if two choices are put before an individual, both equal, with one presented in terms of potential gains and the other in terms

of possible losses, the former option will be chosen.

How the Prospect Theory Works ?

Prospect theory belongs to the behavioral economic subgroup, describing how individuals make a choice between probabilistic alternatives where risk is involved and the probability of different outcomes is unknown. This theory was formulated in 1979 and further developed in 1992 by Amos Tversky and Daniel Kahneman, deeming it more psychologically accurate of how decisions are made when compared to the expected utility theory.

The underlying explanation for an individual's behavior, under prospect theory, is that because the choices are independent and singular, the probability of a gain or a loss is reasonably assumed as being 50/50 instead of the probability that is actually presented. Essentially, the probability of a gain is generally perceived as greater. Although there is no difference in the actual gains or losses of a certain product, the prospect theory says investors will choose the product that offers the most perceived gains.

Tversky and Kahneman proposed that losses cause a greater emotional impact on an individual than does an equivalent amount of gain, so given choices presented two ways—with both offering the same result—an individual will pick the option offering perceived gains. For example, assume that the end result is receiving $25. One option is being given the straight $25. The other option is gaining $50 and losing $25. The utility of the $25 is exactly the same in both options. However, individuals are most likely to choose to receive straight cash because a single gain is generally observed as more favorable than initially having more cash and then suffering a loss.

Types of Prospect Theory

According to Tversky and Kahneman, the certainty effect is exhibited when people prefer certain outcomes and underweight outcomes that are only probable. The certainty effect leads to individuals avoiding risk when there is a prospect of a sure gain. It also contributes to individuals seeking risk when one of their options is a sure loss.

The isolation effect occurs when people have presented two options with the same outcome, but different routes to the outcome. In this case, people are likely to cancel out similar information to lighten the cognitive load, and their conclusions will vary depending on how the options are framed.

·The prospect theory says that investors value gains and losses differently, placing more weight on perceived gains versus perceived losses.

·An investor presented with a choice, both equal, will choose the one presented in terms of potential gains.

·The prospect theory is part of behavioral economics, suggesting investors chose perceived gains because losses cause a greater emotional impact.

·The certainty effect says individuals prefer certain outcomes over probable ones, while the isolation effect says individuals cancel out similar information when making a decision.

Prospect Theory Example

Consider an investor is given a pitch for the same mutual fund by two separate financial advisors. One advisor presents the fund to the investor, highlighting that it has an average return of 12% over the past three years. The other advisor tells the investor that the fund has had above-average returns in the past 10 years, but in recent years it has been declining. Prospect theory assumes that though the investor was presented with the exact same mutual fund, he is likely to buy the fund from the first advisor, who expressed the fund's rate of return as an overall gain instead of the advisor presenting the fund as having high returns and losses.

How and why behavioral economic method can predict house buyers house purchase need or desire whether the country's house buyers their house purchase need or desire will increase or decrease in the year. I shall explain the reasons as below:

Supply-side economists say that increasing business growth, not consumer demand, will boost the economy. They agree the government has a role to play, but fiscal policy should target companies. They rely on tax cuts and deregulation. So, supply-side economists believe that raising house buyers' house purchase or long term renting or instalement payment desires. Government or business organizations will play a important role, e.g. decresing salary tax, banks can charge low interest to encourage many people to borrow much long term loan or money to spend long term expenditure, e.g. buying house. So, it seems that other parties will encourage house buyers' house purchase more more than themselves psychological feeling influence. Otherwise, demand-side economists say that any house buyer individual psychological living need desire is more influential to encourage they choose to buy house in preference. On one hand, in demand-side economists view, I shall apply behavioral economic concept to explain why and how causes house buyer individual house purchase choice in preference than rent choice . On the other hand, in supply-side economists view, I shall apply demand and supply economic concept to explain why and how casues house buyer individual house purchase choice in preference than rent choice in property market.

What does behavioral economy mean ?Think about supposing you plan to buy a house. You may have decided to simplify your decision making by opting for the house price, living environment, such as air and noise pollution, income level, school, public library, public park, public swimming pool, transportation facilities etc. different factors to influence you house purchase decision in the location. You may then have visited the house location to view its environments before you decide to choose the location to buy the house to live. But the decision making process did not stop there, as you now had to customize your model by visiting from different house location . You aim to compare whether anywhere location(s) can let you to feel the location is better to let you feel to live.) Instead the house location and environment factor, you were still considered the house appearance and design and comfortable feeling features you really needed. At this stage, most property developers will show a base model with options that can be changed according to whether the house buyers their preferences are environment, house design, house price, facilties before they decide to buy the house to live. The way in which these different location of house choices are presented to house buyers will influence the final house purchases made and illustrates a number of concepts from behavioral economic (BE) theories.

First, the base model shown in the customization engine represents a rational choice to any house buyers' purchase decision usually. Usually, house buyers, they will visit the house location to feel its living environment, entertainment facilities supply, transport facilities supply and house design and comfortable feeling to decide to buy the house to live, instead of income factor in house market. The more uncertain house customers are about their rational house feeling , such as comfortable living, environment and facility and house design decision, instead of income factor influences can change their earlier first house purchase decision if they feel the house price is more expensive to compare the other houses choices.

Second, the house developer can frame options differently by employing either an 'add' or 'delete' customization mode (or something in between). In an add mode, house buyers start with a base model and then add more or better options. In a delete frame, the opposite process occurs, whereby house buyers have to deselect options or downgrade from a fully-loaded model. Such as this house market case, past research suggests that house buyers end up choosing a greater number of features when they are in a delete rather than an add frame (Biswas, 2009). Finally, the option framing strategy will be associated with different house price anchors prior to customization, which may influence the perceived value of the house. If the final house ends up with one million house price bid, its cost is likely to be perceived as more attractive if the initial default configuration was two million house price (fully loaded) rather than one million house price. Why does the more expensive house price will still attract some house buyers to choose to buy in preference—an option framing strategy that maximizes sales, but set at a default house price that deters a minimum of potential house buyers from considering a purchase in the first place. When the house buyers group is high and stable income group, they won't consider the more expensive house price issue to influence them to change to buy the one million house price houses to live easily. Instead of after they view the house location to let them to feel that there have less transport facilities, e.g. bus, taxi, underground train, tram etc. public service transport tools are close to their living location, or tehy feel the natural environment is polluted to let they feel the can not breathe fresh air , or there are many factories are close to their houses to cause they feel dirty air, or traffic jam is serious to cause air pollution and noise pollution , or they feel that the two million house design is poor, they can not let them to feel comfortable to live in the appartments, it means that the house price is under value to be accepted to same to two million price. Then, the stable and high income house buyers will change their earlier house purchase first choice to accept the other house opitions to decide to buy in preference.

● Rational Expectations And Rational Theories excite or raise property market buyers ' perference property choice desires to the property developer method

●

What are Rational Expectations?

Rational expectations is an economic theory that states that individuals make decisions based on the best available information in the market and learn from past trends. Rational expectations suggest that people will be wrong sometimes, but that, on average, they will be correct.

Understanding the Concept of Rational Expectations

The idea of rational expectations was first developed by American economist John F. Muth in 1961. However, it was popularized by economists Robert Lucas and T. Sargent in the 1970s and was widely used in microeconomics as part of the new classical revolution.

The theory states the following assumptions:

·With rational expectations, people always learn from past mistakes.

·Forecasts are unbiased, and people use all the available information and economic theories to make decisions.

·People understand how the economy works and how government policies alter macroeconomic variables such as price level, level of unemployment, and aggregate output.

The rational expectations theory comes in weak and strong versions. The "strong" version assumes that actors are able to access all available information and make rational decisions based on the information.

The "weak" versions assume that people lack the time to access all relevant information but make decisions based on their limited knowledge. For example, if they buy cornflakes, it is "rational" to keep buying the same brand and not worry about getting perfect information about relative prices of other cornflakes brands.

Most macroeconomists today use rational expectations as an assumption in their analysis of policies. When thinking about the effects of economic policy, the assumption is that people will do their best to work out the implications.

The rational expectations approach is often used to test the accuracy of inflation forecasts. For example, Pet is an individual's forecast in year t-1 of the price level in year t. The actual price level is denoted by Pt. The difference between the actual price level and individual's forecast is the forecast error for year t. Pt – Pet = rt is the individual's forecast error in year t. With rational expectations, the forecast errors are due to unpredictable numbers. However, if people systematically under-predict or over-predict numbers, the price level expectations are not rational.

Under rational expectations, what happens today depends on the expectations of what will happen in the future. But what happens in the future also depends on what happens today. Many macroeconomic principles today are created with the assumption of rational expectations. The theory is also used by many new Keynesian economists because it fits well with their assumption that people want to pursue their own self-interest. If people's expectations were not rational, the economic decisions of individuals would not be as good as they are.

Adaptive Expectations

While individuals who use rational decision-making use the best available information in the market to make decisions, adaptive decision makers use past trends and events to predict future outcomes. This is also known as backward thinking decision-making.

Adaptive expectations can be used to predict inflation. If inflation increased in the previous year, people expect an increased rate of inflation in the following year. The formula for adaptive expectations is Pet = Pt -1. It shows that people expect the trend of inflation to be the same as last year.

People will change their expectations of any variable if there is a difference between what they were expecting and what actually occurred. However, if their expectations turned out to be right, their future expectations likely will not change.

Limitations of Adaptive Expectations

While adaptive expectations allow us to measure expected variables and actual variables, they are not as commonly used in macroeconomics as rational expectations because of their limitations. The adaptive model is simplistic because it assumes that people base their decisions based on past data. However, in the real world, past data is just one of the factors that influence future behavior. Rational expectations incorporate many factors into the decision-making process.

What is house buyer individual Rational Choice ?

In an ideal house market world, defaults, frames, and house price anchors would not have any bearing on consumer choices. House purchaser decisions would be the result of a careful weighing of costs and benefits and informed by existing preferences, such as whether the house future price will appreciate to raise value or reduce under value, the house living location will increase public transport facilities, public entertainment facilities, build more schools, offices to close to the house location. We would always make optimal decisions. In the 1976 book The Economic Approach to Human Behavior, the economist Gary S. Becker famously outlined a number of ideas known as the pillars of so-called 'rational choice' theory. The theory assumes that human actors have stable preferences and engage in maximizing behavior.

Mental Accounting management science method

The economist Richard Thaler, a keen observer of human behavior and founder of behavioral economics, was inspired by Kahneman & Tversky's work (see Thaler, 2015, for a summary). Thaler coined the concept of mental accounting. According to Thaler, people think of value in relative rather than absolute terms. They derive pleasure not just from an object's value, but also the quality of the deal – its transaction utility (Thaler, 1985). In addition, humans often fail to fully consider opportunity costs (tradeoffs) and are susceptible to the sunk cost fallacy. Why are people willing to spend more when they pay with a credit card than cash (Prelec & Simester, 2001)? Why would more individuals spend $10 on a theater ticket if they had just lost a $10 bill than if they had to replace a lost ticket worth $10 (Kahneman & Tversky, 1984)? Why are people more likely to spend a small inheritance and invest a large one (Thaler, 1985)? Such as this property market case, if the house living needer , he/she does not choose to pay all money to buy the house, although he/she has enough money to buy the house. He/she chooses to pay instalement or rent the house to live. If he/she own visa card. Then, he/she will choose to use visa card to pay rent or pay month instalement to the property developer's house in order to earn accumulated money reward or any benefits after he/she use the visa to pay the house rent or instalement every month. So, the visa card can encourage the house buyer to achieve the house rent or instalement payment house purchase long term transaction easily.

According to the theory of mental accounting, people treat money differently, depending on factors such as the money's origin and intended use, rather than thinking of it in terms of the "bottom line" as in formal accounting (Thaler, 1999). An important term underlying the theory is fungibility, the fact that all money is interchangable and has no labels. In mental accounting, people treat assets as less fungible than they really are. Even seasoned investors are susceptible to this bias when they view recent gains as disposable "house money" (Thaler & Johnson, 1990) that can be used in high-risk investments. In doing so, they make decisions on each mental account separately, losing out the big picture of the portfolio.

Another concept related to mental accounting captures the fact that people don't like to spend money. We experience pain of paying (Zellermayer, 1996), because we are loss averse. The pain of paying plays an important role in consumer self-regulation to keep spending in check (Prelec & Loewenstein, 1998). This pain is thought to be reduced in credit card purchases, because plastic is less tangible than cash, the depletion of resources (money) is less visible and payment is deferred. Different types of people experience different levels of pain of paying, which can affect spending decisions. Tightwads, for instance, experience more of this pain than spendthrifts. As a result, tightwads are particularly sensitive to marketing contexts that make spending less painful (Rick, 2018). Hence, such as this property market purchase case, because some house buyers do not hope to spend much money to buy one house to live. They will feel to use visa card, it can replace money to let them to feel they won't lose much money to spend in the moment. So, in mental spending feeling view, they will feel visa card will help them to reduce to spend much money to rent or pay instalement to live the house in long time. So, in psychological view, visa card is one good spending money replace tool to influence these non- accepted spend money buyers to make final house rent or paying instalement decision to live the house decision more easily.

Choice Overload managment science method

Humans' bounded rationality is particularly well illustrated by the concept of choice overload. Also referred to as 'overchoice', this phenomenon occurs as a result of too many choices being available to consumers. Overchoice has been associated with unhappiness (Schwartz, 2004), decision fatigue, going with the default option, as well as choice deferral—avoiding making a decision altogether, such as not buying a product (Iyengar & Lepper, 2000). Many different factors may contribute to perceived choice overload, including the number of options and attributes, time constraints, decision accountability, alignability and complementarity of options, consumers' preference uncertainty, among other factors (Chernev et al., 2015). Choice overload can be counteracted by simplifying choice attributes or the number of available options (Johnson et al., 2012). Hence, such as this property market case, when the month has too many properties are supplied to let house buyers to choose in the country's property market. Then, it will bring properties choice overload effect to cause the increasing houses number of options to cause the country's house buyers feel need to spend long time to make the house purchase preference decision in order to avoid any loss after they bought the under value houses to live. So, Choice overload usually cause long time choice process to any consumers, such as this property market consumption case.

Limited Information: The Importance of Feedback management science method
Bounded rationality's principle of limited knowledge or information is one of the topics discussed in the 2008 book Nudge. In the book, Thaler and Sunstein point to experience, good information, and prompt feedback as key factors that enable people to make good decisions. Consider climate change, for example, which has been cited as a particularly challenging problem in relation to experience and feedback. Climate change is invisible, diffuse, and a long-term process. Pro-environmental behavior by an individual, such as reducing carbon emissions, does not lead to a noticeable change. The same is true in the domain of health. Feedback in this area is often poor, and we are more likely to get feedback on previously chosen options than rejected ones.

Information Avoidance
Behavioral economics assumes that people are boundedly rational actors with a limited ability to process information. While a great deal of research has been devoted to exploring how available information affects the quality and outcomes of decisions, a newer strand of research has also explored situations where people avoid information altogether.
Information avoidance in behavioral economics (Golman et al., 2017) refers to situations in which people choose not to obtain knowledge that is freely available. Active information avoidance includes physical avoidance, inattention, the biased interpretation of information (see also confirmation bias) and even some forms of forgetting. In behavioral finance, for example, research has shown that investors are less likely to check their portfolio online when the stock market is down than when it is up, which has been termed the ostrich effect (Karlsson et al., 2009). More serious cases of avoidance happen when people fail to return to clinics to get medical test results, for instance (Sullivan et al., 2004). While information avoidance is sometimes strategic, it can have immediate hedonic benefits for people if it prevents the negative (usually psychological) consequences of knowing the information. It usually carries negative utility in the long term, because it deprives people of potentially useful information for decision making and feedback for future behavior. Furthermore, information avoidance can contribute to a polarization of political opinions and media bias.
The impact of smoking, for example, is at best noticeable over the course of years, while its effect on cells and internal organs is usually not evident to the individual. Traditionally, generic feedback aimed at inducing behavioral change has been limited to information ranging from the economic costs of the unhealthy behavior to its potential health consequences (Diclemente et al., 2001). More recent behavior change programs, such as those employing smartphone apps to stop smoking, now usually provide positive and personalized behavioral feedback, which may include the number of cigarettes not smoked and money saved, along with information about health improvement and disease avoidance.
Predictably Irrational and Nudge alerted the public to a new breed of economists influenced by the study of behavioral decision making that was pioneered by Kahneman and Tversky's work (sometimes referred to as 'choice

under uncertainty'). The psychology of homo economicus—a rational and selfish individual with relatively stable preferences—has been challenged, and the traditional view that behavior change should be achieved by informing, convincing, incentivizing or penalizing people has been questioned (Thaler & Sunstein, 2008). The field associated with this stream of research and theory is behavioral economics (BE), which suggests that human decisions are strongly influenced by context, including the way in which choices are presented to us. Behavior varies across time and space, and it is subject to cognitive biases, emotions, and social influences. Decisions are the result of less deliberative, linear, and controlled processes than we would like to believe.

Hence, such as this property market case, if the property developer can not provide more property advertisement to the property buyers to receive to let them to feel whether what benefits or enjoyment benefits that they can enjoy after they lived the property developer's houses to live. Due to lacking clear property information message to let many property buyers to know the property developer's property sale advertisement from property magazines, newspapers, TV, wesbite etc. channel. Then, it will influence the property developer's houses , they won't be many property buyers' choices, before they make final property purchase decision at the moment. So, property market purchase need desire change will be influenced by the time and space external unpredictable factor , such as visa card promotion , unemployment ratio rises up or falls down, the property advertisement attractive effort etc. unpredictable factors to excite any property buyers' living need desire in any time indirectly.

Dual-System Theory applies to property buyer market

Daniel Kahneman uses a dual-system theoretical framework (which established a foothold in cognitive and social psychology of the 1990s) to explain why our judgments and decisions often do not conform to formal notions of rationality. System 1 consists of thinking processes that are intuitive, automatic, experience-based, and relatively unconscious. System 2 is more reflective, controlled, deliberative, and analytical. Judgments influenced by System 1 are rooted in impressions arising from mental content that is easily accessible. System 2, on the other hand, monitors or provides a check on mental operations and overt behavior—often unsuccessfully.

Example 1: Availability and Affect

System 1 is 'home' of the heuristics (cognitive shortcuts) we apply and responsible for the biases (systematic errors) we may be left with when we make decisions (Kahneman, 2011). System 1 processes influence us when prior exposure to a number affects subsequent judgments, as evident in the anchoring effects discussed previously (Tversky & Kahneman, 1974). One of the most universal heuristics is the availability heuristic. Availability serves as a mental shortcut if the possibility of an event occurring is perceived as higher simply because an example comes to mind easily (Tversky & Kahneman, 1974); for instance, a person may deem pension investments too risky as a result of remembering a family member who lost most of her retirement savings in the recent recession. Readily available information in memory is also used when we make similarity-based judgments, as evident in the representativeness heuristic.

Finally, another 'general purpose' heuristic is that of affect, namely good or bad feelings that surface automatically when we think about an object. Applying the affect heuristic can lead to black-and-white thinking, which is particularly evident when people think about an object under conditions that hamper System 2 reflection, such as time pressure. For example, consumers may consider food preservatives' benefits as low and costs as high, thus leading to a significant negative risk-benefit correlation (Finucane, Alhakami, Slovic, & Johnson, 2000).

The role of affect in risky or uncertain situations is also evident in the risk-as-feelings model (Loewenstein, Weber, Hsee, & Welch, 2001). 'Consequentialist' accounts of decision making tend to focus on expectations along with the likelihood and desirability of possible outcomes. The risk-as-feelings perspective explains behavior in situations where emotional reactions to risk differ from cognitive evaluations. In these situations, behavior tends to be influenced by anticipatory feelings, emotions experienced in the moment of decision making.

Example 2: Salience

Availability and affect are processes internal to the individual that may lead to bias. The external equivalent of these processes is salience, whereby information that stands out, is novel, or seems relevant is more likely to affect our thinking and actions (Dolan et al., 2010). For example, a technological device can be framed as being 99% reliable or having only a 1% failure rate, thereby emphasizing either positive or negative information. Salience also underlies heuristic judgments that rely on external cues. Some psychologists have derived effort-reducing heuristics that simplify consumer decision making. The brand name heuristic, for example, suggests that salient cues in the form of brand names can be used to infer quality (Maheswaran, Mackie, & Chaiken, 1992). In terms of degrees of visual salience, one study found a congruence effect between price and font size, where showing a lower sale price in a small print size relative to the regular price resulted in greater purchase likelihood than presenting the sale price in a relatively large font (Coulter & Coulter, 2005). Finally, the salience of options can also be manipulated by rearranging the physical environment; for instance, a change as simple as moving water bottles closer to the cashier in a cafeteria has been shown to increase the salience and convenience of this healthier drink choice and thereby significantly boost water sales (Thorndike, Sonnenberg, Riis, Barraclough, & Levy, 2012).

Hence, such as this property market case, if the propety buyer feels that the property developer's house price won't be influenced to decrease easily in long time , even there are many property buyers still choose to buy the property developer's houses to live as well as the property developer's houses number supply won't increase in the long time. So, in Dual-System Theory explains if the house buyer felt that the property developer's house number supply won't increase, even decrease after there are many property buyers still chooce to buy its properties to live in preference in the country's property market. Then, the property developer's house high price and limited house supply factors will not influence the house buyer's prefer house choice decision more easily.

Property market demand and supply view

How can demand and supply determine property market price ? Property price is arrived at by the interaction between house buyers demand and property developers' houses number supply. Property price is dependent upon the house design and environment and facilities characteristics of both these fundamental components of a property market. Any properties demand and supply represent the willingness of house consumers and property developers to engage in properties buyers buying needs or desires. An exchange of a house purchasetakes place when properties buyers and properties sellers can agree upon a agreed property price. This module will look at property price in a competitive market. When imperfect property market competition exists such as with a property developer monopoly or single peoperty selling firm, property price outcomes may not follow the same general rules.

Equilibrium Price in property market

When a property exchange occurs, the agreed upon price is called an "equilibrium" property price, or a "market clearing" price. This equilibrium property price occurs at the intersection of house demand and house supply as presented are in balance at the moment in property market short time, e.g. one month.

Property price determination depends equally on the moment house buyers' living demand and the moment house number supply. It is truly a balance of the two market components. To see why the balance must occur, examine what happens when there is no balance, for example when the moment property market price is below than the past property market price, the property quantity demanded is greater than the property quantity supplied. In such a situation, property consumers would be clamouring for a property that property developers would not be willing to supply; a property shortage would exist. In this event, property consumers would choose to pay a higher price in order to get the property they want, while property developers would be encouraged by a higher price to bring more of the properties onto the property market.

The end result is a rise in property price, when the moment has many proprety buyers feel living desire needs. where the property supply and demand are in balance. Similarly, if a property price is above were chosen arbitrarily the property market would be in shortage properties are supplied, too less properties supply are relative to high living desire demand. If that were to happen, properties developers would be willing to take a higher price in order to sell, and property consumers would be induced by higher prices to increase their property purchases desire , because they feel afraid that there will have less properties to be supplied to sell later and their prices will continue to raise in long time.

Hence, a property market price is not necessarily a fair price, it is merely an outcome. It does not guarantee total living satisfaction on the part of house buyer and property seller. Typically some assumptions about the behaviour of property buyers and property sellers are made, which add a sense of reason to a property market price. For example, property buyers are expected to be self-living comfortable interested and, although they may not have perfect property living and house price knowledge, at least they will try to look out for their own living interests. Meanwhile, property sellers are considered to be profit maximizers. This assumption limits their willingness to sell to within a price range , high to low, where they can stay in business.

Change in Equilibrium Price of property market

When either property demand or supply shifts, the property equilibrium price will change. Look at the modules on understanding property number supply for a discussion of why of that property market component may move. So, what factors can influence the property equilibrium price to be raise.

Example 1: Unusually environment and facility factor

When the property's location , it's environment and facilities are improved to let property buyers feel to compare before. With no immediate change in property consumers' willingness to buy the property developer's houses to live in the location at the moment because they feel that its environment and facilities can not let them to feel enough and comfortable to live in the location, there is a movement along the reducing demand curve to a new low equilibrium market price. Property consumers will buy more but only at a lower house price, becaue they feel poor environment and not enough facilities supply to influence they do not choose the property developer's houses location in preference. Otherwise, if the property demand curve in this example were more vertical (more inelastic, it means that the property developers raise their price won't influence less property buyers because their living desire is increasing), the property price-quantity adjustments needed to bring about a new equilibrium between property demand and the new property supply would be different. Then compare the size of property price-property quantity changes in this with the first situation. With the same shift in property supply, equilibrium change in property price is larger when property demand is inelastic than when property demand is more elastic. The opposite is true for property quantity. A larger change in property quantity supply will occur when property demand is elastic compared with the property quantity change required when property demand is inelastic.

How Does Property Developer Supply and House Buyer Demand Affect the Housing Market?

Real estate is a tangible asset made up of property and the land on which it sits. Like other assets, real estate is also subject to supply and demand. The prices of homes, like stocks and bonds, depend heavily on the law of supply and demand. But just what kind of relationship does the housing market have to this law? I suppose house supply number and house demad number , they must have close relationship to influence their house price changes in any time. Although, houses are expensive and fixed tangible asset, but they are still similar to general cheap product price changes to be influenced by demand and supply as below:

·The housing market relies very heavily on supply and demand.

·Housing demand and low supplies normally cause prices to rise.

·Prices drop when there is low demand and a larger supply of homes on the market.

·Low interest rates generally impact demand, while natural disasters, changing lifestyles, and the lack of available lots affect supplies.

The law of supply and demand is a basic economic principle that explains the relationship between supply and demand for a good or service, and how their interaction affects the price of that good or service. When there is high demand for a good or service, its price rises. If there is a large supply of a good or service but not enough demand for it, the price falls. The theory of supply and demand is one of the most basic principles in economics. Supply and demand work against each other until the point at which the equilibrium price is achieved—that is the price where supply is equal to demand in the market, such as property market case.

The law of demand dictates that people will have low or no demand for a good that has a higher price. That happens, of course, when all other factors remain equal. People tend to sacrifice something that comes at a higher cost, which curbs demand. Similarly, lower prices drive demand, meaning consumers value and purchase something more when it's cheaper. In fact, general property buyers' preference house purchase decision will be influenced by price factor in earlier. It is such as general cheap product demand and supply factor to influence its house price changes in any time. When it comes to the law of supply, prices drop when there is an increase in the supply of a good or service in the market. But when prices increase, the number of goods and services tend to drop. That's because it tends to cost more to produce and sell goods at a higher price.

Real Estate Supply and Demand economic theory

The housing market relies very heavily on supply and demand, which is why it is very prominent in the industry. Each housing transaction involves a buyer and a seller. The buyer places an offer on a property, leaving the seller to accept or reject the offer. The law of supply and demand dictates the equilibrium price of a property. Hence, supply and demand work against one another until the point at which a property's equilibrium price is reached.

A low property supply may drive prices up, which is what tends to happen with bidding wars. A specific property may be in demand by multiple parties who try to outbid each other by increasing their purchase price offer. The bidding war ends—depleting the supply—when the seller accepts one of the offers. When there is high demand for properties in a particular city or state, and a lack of supply of quality properties, the prices of houses tend to rise. When a weak economy and an oversupply of properties leads to low or no demand for housing, the prices of houses tend to fall.

Factors Affecting Housing Supply and Demand

Supply and demand is never an easy thing to measure in the real estate market. That's partly due because it takes a long time to construct new homes and fix up old ones to put back onto the market. Similarly, real estate is not like other industries in that it takes a lot of time to buy and sell homes and other properties. Some of the factors that influence housing demand include lower interest rates or borrowing costs in economic environment view. When interest rates are low, people are generally willing to take on more debt. They may be able to finance the purchase of a home because the amount of interest they have to pay isn't burdensome. If more buyers flood the market, demand for housing increases. And if there's a limited supply of housing inventory, that makes people in a low interest rate environment want to purchase even more.

Meanwhile, the supply of housing is in a constant state of change. Inventory may increase when people are moving—some may downsize, others may be try to make more room for an expanding family, while others may purchase their first home. Similarly, there may be an increase in development and new home construction, adding to the existing inventory. On the other hand, housing inventory decreases during times of natural disaster—such as floods and earthquakes—and when existing properties are demolished. Land is also a finite resource, so the amount of new developments is generally limited. It is unpredicted environmental factor to influence property price changes in the moment.

Economic environment factor influences property price changes

One of the major causes of the Great Recession that followed the financial crisis in the mid-2000s was the housing market crash. It was a direct result of the law of supply and demand. During the lead up to the financial crisis, consumers were enjoying relatively low borrowing rates. Banks began to offer low rates on mortgages, and were encouraged to relax their lending standards. People who weren't otherwise able to afford a home now found themselves able to realize their dreams. These consumers, called subprime borrowers, were able to snag a home with low down payments and low credit scores.

During this time, speculative buyers also began entering the market, driving up demand for housing and, at the same time, cutting in to the available supply. All of this, in turn, drove prices up to very lofty levels. The market couldn't keep up, and investors who were merely in the market to make some money—many were buying and flipping homes in a very short period of time—began pulling out of the market. Demand started to drop and, so did prices. The collapse of the real estate market in 2007 created an oversupply of houses and decreasing properties prices. Real estate prices depend on the law of supply and demand. When the demand for property is high but property is scarce, prices skyrocket and it becomes a seller's market. When the number of available properties increases to glut the market, prices typically drop. Supply and demand in real estate aren't easy to balance. Creating more saleable properties takes time, considerable work, and a lot of effort. It's not possible at all in some cases, and even when it is, it might not be possible for supply to increase in time to meet consumer demand. So, salespeoples' house sale experiences can also influence the property developer's house sale number.

Understanding this basic economic principle can help consumers decide the best time to buy or sell their properties.

Property market Over-Supply Or Under-Supply factor

You can usually expect a drop in prices when there is an over-supply of homes or land in a given area. You can't move the overage to another area to keep prices stable. Scarcity causes prices to rise when there isn't enough land or if there aren't enough homes in a given area. Even if land is available on which to build more homes, the time it takes to construct them cannot meet immediate property needs, so demand will remain constant or rise. Many forces that might have little or no impact on other regions influence local markets and vice versa. Pay attention to the factors that influence your local market. Watch local businesses and make note of upsizing and downsizing trends if you do business in a market that has jobs and many workers relocating there. You'll also want to keep an eye on these issues if you're a homeowner looking to sell in such an area or if you're looking for property to purchase.

Things like divorce rates, death rates, and demographics can factor in. Factors that can greatly impact property market supply and demand—and by extension your business—might include local weather trends, an aging population, and investment trends if you do business in a resort area that includes vacation homes. Trends that impact discretionary income have more of an influence on this type of market than others. Trends in interest rates, national home prices, new housing starts, and many other economic indicators can influence real estate markets as well. These national events might not typically move real estate supply and demand directly, but they can render it less or more important. The mood and sentiments of the buying public cannot be overlooked. Supply and demand don't exist in a vacuum. But few could afford to pay those prices in a worsening economy and even those who could were understandably reluctant to part with their money at that time. So properties sat on the market, unsold. Worried homeowners in financial distress put their homes up for sale rather than risk foreclosure. Remember, almost 9 million jobs were lost during the Great Recession. Now what happens? Supply begins surpassing demand by leaps and bounds. The housing market is glutted and those healthy prices evaporate—which has little to do with local factors except as they're an extension of national woes.

Land Parcels Are Finite factor to influence property market price

If the country has high population, but land supply is less to let property developers to find lands to build houses easily. Such as Hong Kong is one high population and small city. So, its property prices must be higher to compare other countries, and it causes that its rooms and houses size or area is small , but house sale price or rent is still high. Such as Hong Kong house market case, Hong Kong people cannot fill a real estate supply shortage by manufacturing more units of land. It's a finite supply, not a manufactured commodity. Hong Kong people might be able to create more units within a given space, such as condos or townhouses, but the land itself is unique and cannot be duplicated to accommodate a short supply. When a shortage of land for homes exists in a given area, Hong Kong people can't simply move in more land to alleviate the shortage. Real estate is where it sits. It will always be a local commodity influenced by local conditions. In short, keep up with the big picture but narrow your primary focus to your region. Supply and demand in real estate will always be foremost a local issue.

As with many other types of business market, the property market is driven by supply and demand. Property prices fluctuate depending upon the factors that influence both supply and demand. Knowledge of these factors equips you with the capability of knowing when to rent/buy and, perhaps just as importantly, when to sell. At the most basic level, when property supply is greater than demand, prices fall. That's the nature of almost every product. Similarly, when the demand for properties is greater than the available supply, prices rise. Even though property markets have these principles in common with many other types of products or business services, there are some differences worth mentioning. For example, the real estate market also takes into consideration factors such as location, seasonality, and durability. There are also different types of real estate – residential, industrial, commercial and land – each of which has their own factors that influence market supply and demand. "Real estate" is defined as more than just property. It also includes natural resources and land, too. So, Hong Kong property market's price is influenced by land supply factor more than other factors, such as facilities , environment , transport etc. factors influence.

Local factors that influence property rates include:

1 – Restrictions on property production – for instance, in the case of Manhatten, there is not much space for added supply. As a result, demand remains high and prices even higher.

2 – Credit access – this often depends on where individuals live. Rural communities may have less access to bank credit, for example – reducing demand.

3 – Job market – the more jobs, the greater the demand for properties.

4 – Transport – better transport translates into greater desirability for people to move – increasing demand.

5 – Retired persons – retired people often decide to downsize and opt for a smaller property in a different locality, thereby increasing supply.

6 – Families – as families begin to grow, they need greater sized properties. This increases the demand for larger homes, whilst decreasing demand for smaller homes.

7 – Meteorology – destinations with more favorable weather profiles and ones that avert the extremes of weather are preferable. Demand in places such as San Diego is significantly higher than the tornado alleys of Alabama.

8 – Income – if income levels in a locality are generally high, there is more money in the market to purchase homes, decreasing supply and increasing prices.

9 – Construction market – the greater the degree of construction of new properties, the greater the supply in the market.

Understanding the factors that drive market supply and demand, and hence property prices are important. The more informed about these nine factors, the better purchasing/selling decisions you can make. For example – designs and styles and fads come and go into "fashion", and what design/style/fad factors elevate a property price one-year can diminish the price of a property the following year. If you are managing a property, you can factor these decisions when determining optimum rent or a selling value.

When borrowing rates are lower, properties become more affordable. This, too, influences demand. Tax credits, for example – for first-time buyers – can encourage more buyers to seek interest in the property market. As well as this, there are various social factors involved, too – such as the social status afforded to people who own their own homes. Age can come into play here, too, depending on the city and what social expectations young professionals have.

What drives property market supply and demand, then, is an interweaving network of factors, many of which playoff on one another. It's important to appreciate the impact that each of these individual factors has and how they influence property prices throughout the country.

How to Analyze Supply and Demand For Apartment Buildings

One of the most important ways to use all of the data gathered in a real estate market analysis is to examine the supply and demand factors for a particular type of real estate. For example, an investor considering the construction or purchase of a new multifamily residential property uses the market analysis to determine what cash flows they can expect to receive given the expected demand for units. The demand must be high enough to generate cash flows that provide a rate of return high enough to make the investment feasible.

In order to estimate the demand for multifamily housing units, it is necessary to understand recent population growth trends for the city. Then, it's important to consider the major industries in the market area and the forecasted growth for those industries over the next few years. You can then put this information together to forecast multifamily housing demand and compare that demand to the existing and proposed supply of multifamily units. This case study takes data about population and industrial activity in the Orlando, Florida region and analyzes supply and demand of multifamily residential units in the region.

Population Trends and Apartment Building Demand

Recent data from the U.S. Census Bureau and the Orlando Economic Development Commission lists the total population of the Orlando metro area at 2,387,138 (2016). Between 2015 and 2016, the population of the Orlando metro area grew by 2.6%. That made Orlando the fastest growing region in the United States. The Orlando Economic Development Commission estimates that population growth in the region since 2000 equates to a gain of 138 people per day. Population growth is mostly fueled by domestic migration. Americans moving to Orlando for retirement in warmer weather or for new career opportunities account for about 40% of the population increase. International migration (mainly from Central and South America) accounts for 34% of the increase in population. People have been moving to the Orlando area due to the region's comparative advantages (climate, entertainment and lifestyle, and economic growth). Without these advantages, Orlando would not be one of the fastest growing regions of the country. With an average household size around 2.5, that means there are an estimated 954,855 households in the Orlando metropolitan area. Data from the American Consumer Survey indicates that about 43% of the population is renters. So, 43% of households would give an estimated demand of 410,588 multifamily units. In reality, not all renters live in multifamily units since many rent single-family homes. Therefore, it is necessary to estimate how many of those renters occupy multifamily units. A 2016 report from Fannie Mae estimated that there were 156,000 multifamily units in the Orlando metro area with a 5.75% vacancy rate. So, in 2016 there were around 147,030 occupied multifamily units (156,000 x (1-.0575) = 147,030). This means an estimated 35.8% of the households that are renters occupy multifamily units while the remaining 64.2% of renters occupy single-family homes.

Economic Trends and Multifamily Housing Demand

Employment data from the Bureau of Labor Statistics confirms that economic growth is driving the population growth in the Orlando metro area. In fact, job growth from 2015-2016 in Orlando was over twice the national average. A strong economy and growth in the number of jobs indicates that the population should continue to grow over the next few years unless there is a major shift to the national economy or a natural disaster. Furthermore, the job growth rate of 4.22% exceeded the population growth rate of 2.6%. If the major industries in Orlando continue to grow at this pace, more new workers will need to move into the region to fill these new jobs. So, forecasted population growth may be higher than the average of 2% seen over the past 10 years. It might be more appropriate to estimate population growth of at least 3% annually.

As with commodities traded on the market, housing prices continually fluctuate, sometimes with drastic changes over a short period of time. Availability is a huge factor affecting prices within a set region, such as in a specific suburb of a metropolitan area. Likewise, demand for homes in that market also plays into that price, which is why two nearly identical homes in different cities may sell for vastly different prices. When buying a home in a seller's market, limit your contingencies and make your offer as favorable to the seller as possible.

For houses and virtually anything else available for purchase, supply and demand play into the ultimate selling price. When an item is in short supply and many people want it, prices tend to rise. When the market is flooded with an item or there's no demand for it, prices fall. Sporting event ticket prices tend to rise when a team reaches the championship level, yet tickets to the same team's events a few years later, when the team isn't doing well, cost far less. Prices on holiday decor are another great example: At the peak of any holiday's shopping season, some shoppers are willing to pay a premium for the decor. Three days after the holiday, the leftover stock of these items is marked down to clearance prices due to little demand.

Housing supply and demand works in exactly the same way. Sometimes there are so many single-family homes available in the same region that there aren't enough buyers for all of them. In this housing oversupply, prices drop to draw more attention from potential buyers. A lowered price may influence an interested buyer to choose one home over a similar house in the same general area. Without a lowered price, a house may sit on the market for months due to the abundant number of similar homes for sale nearby at the same time.

On conclusion, property price change can be influenced by house buyers living need and land and house number supply factor, but any house buyer individual rational will influence his/her prerference property choice decision before he / she decides to choose what kinds properties or anywhere locations to live. So, house buyer individual psychological factor will influence his/her properties choices.

Case 6

Management science classical theory solves internet invention to raise smart phone sale number increases

Why does internet can influence smart mobile phone consumers' purchase desire? Has internet have direct relationship to influence smart mobile phone buyers' purchase desires ? Can the smart mobile phone talking product still attract phone buyers' preference choice, if it lacks internet function? Can internet raise smart phone sale number and create many mobile phone inventors and manufacturer occupations to raise GDP real GDP when smart phone buyers number and smart phone related occupation needs increase. I shall apply behavioral economic theory to attempt to explain the reasons how and why internet has direct relationship to influence smart mobile buyers' preference talking product choice in this traditional home telephone talking product market as below:

Is the internet putting up a barrier between people, even in bed? Does internet influence mobile phone consumers have not choose to buy because they are influenced to use mobiles when they use mobile to link internet to see any movies, or phones or news and influence their sleeping time in habit and they won't have nervous to work or learn on day time. We compulsively carry our smartphones with us wherever we go. The classroom, the bathroom, the bedroom, the outdoors — our phone is always in hand as if it were some magic self-defense tool capable of protecting us from all that is evil in the world. It all happened so fast. We didn't have the time to set any boundaries for smartphone usage, and now we find ourselves unable to save our relationships and form meaningful interactions with those dear to us.Smartphones are very useful in many circumstances. However, although not ruining your relationships per se, they can harm it in devious ways.

A smartphone is a modern day distraction that is so common, it's hardly noticed any more. It accompanies us wherever we go, demanding our attention multiple times a day. A phone call, a Facebook notification. We become irrevocably immersed in our digital lives, prioritizing the virtual world over anything else. Is it really that important to Instagram your dinner, rather than actually savoring it and sharing your impressions – or maybe a forkful of the dish – with the person next to you?Smartphones get in the way of our relationships, making it impossible for us to wholeheartedly devote our attention to the present moment. As a result, we lose many moments of wonder that are unique and never to be lived again.

Addiction to smartphone usage is a common problem among adults worldwide. It manifests itself in the excessive usage of their phones, while engaged in other activities such as studying, driving, social gatherings and even sleeping. However, many people fail to realize that addiction to smartphone usage is a serious issue that can have a negative effect on the person's thoughts, behavior, tendencies, feelings, and sense of well-being. In particular, it can be a risk factor for depression, loneliness, anxiety and sleep disturbances. As per the Mental Health Foundation in the United Kingdom, people with depression experience an unhappy mood, loss of interest or pleasure, feelings of guilt or low self-worth, disturbed sleep or appetite, low energy, and poor concentration. Depressive and anxiety disorders are two main common disorders that are highly prevalent globally, as over 300 million people are estimated to suffer from depression, which is equivalent to 4.4% of the world's population. It is speculated that not only addiction to smartphone usage can affect one's mental and behavioral status, but also that those with mood disorders are more likely to become addicted to using their smartphones .

Numerous tools have been utilized in literature to assess the same phenomenon, but with different terms such as excessive smart phone usage, smartphone addiction, dependency on smart phones, internet addiction, problematic mobile phone usage, and so on. Remarkably, there was a tendency to use a non-pathological terminology, such as "Problematic Smartphone Use," rather than the term smartphone addiction. Addiction manifests itself in various forms such as preoccupation, tolerance, lack of control, withdrawal, mood modification, conflict, lies, excessive use and loss of interest. Several studies have found that women are more likely to develop an addiction to smartphone usage than men. This was viewed as a positive way for people to stay connected in social relationships. One study clarified that women like to show affection to their families using their smartphones while men use phones for efficiency and practicality . Though there are several studies on this topic, no study has proven this connection so far. Smartphone addiction has been found to be correlated with various physical and psychological issues, as indicated in a number of studies that tested this relationship among various age groups. For example, one study found that people with depression, social anxiety and loneliness had different uses for their smartphones compared to others. People with social anxiety made fewer outgoing calls, as well as, fewer text messages than those without social anxiety. It was reported that high levels of smartphone addiction were correlated with low self-esteem, loneliness, depression and shyness.

Although, internet can bring smart mobile phone users to spend sleeping time to use this kind of mobile product to watch movies, watch TV, listen music, social media communication, searching etc. non-talking communication behaviors. It seems that internet may influence smart phone users to change their phone purchase choice to buy the kind common mobile product more. But, in behavioral economic view, internet can bring smart mobile phone product has more attractive strengths to influence common mobile phone kind product users to chooce to use smart mobile phone products in preference. Internet can also bring these positive emotion to persuade the common mobile users to choose to use them.

Convenient applying: Any smart phone users can apply smart phone to link to internet to replace home computers to link to internet to watch movies, watch TV, listen music, social media communication, searching etc. non-talking communication behaviors in anywhere and any time conveniently. It is one kind of small size and light talking communication tool, but it can also help any mobile users to apply smart phone product to apply internet to do the same computer tasks in any time and any places. Hence, smart mobile can bring many computer users to feel that they can apply computer to do similar internet search behaviors at home. Convenient internet search function is one attract function to influence traditional computer users to choose to apply smart phone tools to replace computers tools to apply internet to search information, news, watch TV, movie, lisen music etc. social media communication behaviors at homes. When they bring smart phone to any where, then they can apply this tool to click to internet to do the same computer and internet link tasks in order to enjoy their entertainment needs. So, they do not need to apply computer tool to link to internet to enjoy their visal entertainment at homes. They can bring smart phone to go to anywhere to link to internet to enjoy their visal entertainment in any time conveniently. So, smart phone can be replaced to home computer tool to solve any visal entertainment enjoyers' needs.

● Internet brings smart phone users to feel more visal entertainment enjoyment

The Internet has revolutionized direct communication, lead to the digitization of books and film, as well as made convenience even more important. Companies have developed strategies that capitalize on the growing desire for easily accessible goods and services in only a few mouse clicks. As technology grows increasingly local and more connected to all aspects of the customer purchasing process, small business owners need to be more efficient in how they target their markets. Understanding why convenience plays such a large role in the purchasing process is vital in growing a successful business. Here are five trends that have popped up in recent years as businesses looked for ways to help their customers take advantage of well-timed opportunities. Internet can bring more attract to smart phone users, instead of visal enjoyment needs, the reasons may include as below:

1. Prior Consumer Knowledge

In today's digital world, consumers are looking for retail solutions which allow them to maximize their free-time and to stretch their disposable income. Due to this economic climate, small businesses which are able to provide their customer with a more convenient experience than a large retailer, are cashing in. H.M Cole, a custom clothier, offers its customers an entire planned wardrobe for the upcoming year after an hour's consultation. Other convenience services such as Trunk Club and Stitch Fix, personalized styling sites for men and women respectively, take that one step further in creating a complete look. These levels of convenience take a simple fitting and turn it into a way for consumers to spend less time deciding outfits, and more time doing other things they value.

2. Direct-to Store Delivery

Due to the "larger-than-life" nature of big box stores, they have begun to develop strategies which combat the convenience of a smaller retailer. The newest trend among these chains is to offer direct-to store delivery. Shoppers are able to find what they are looking for online, and purchase directly on the site. Rather than having to wait the 3-5 days for delivery, chains are making their purchases available (sometimes at discounted rates) for pick up at their local store. Essentially, customers are taking part in shopping services where the store physically groups together the inventory, saving the individual time in their purchases.

3. Personalized Billing, Shipping Info

Customer profiles across frequently visited webpages allow for consumers to not only keep their billing information in one place, but also have access to similar products or content. Businesses are able to not only track purchases, but to specifically target an individual with the information provided for convenience sake. A user does not usually choose to re-enter billing or shipping information on a site they frequent, and so by saving this information, a company is removing an obstacle that might otherwise influence the purchase.

4. Time is Money

Fast food and drive-thru options have changed the world's nutritional demands, creating a society of cheap convenience foods. Although the nutritional value of these highly-processed foods is lacking, the demand for them has been on the rise across the globe. While these types of businesses are growing at a record rate, the pressure to remain affordable and convenient has driven them online.
Some innovative restaurant chains have transitioned to online ordering which provide an easy, personalized interface for their customers to select and buy all from the website portal. A restaurant receives the order digitally, packages the food, and then sends it out to delivery, often for an additional fee. Both Google and Amazon , as well as many startups, have launched services that deliver meals and groceries to your home. Time has shown that customers are willing to spend a little more for the convenience of having food arrive at their doorstep.

5. Subscription Services

Another recent convenience service trend is through subscription services. This can include streaming goods such as TV shows, movies, audio books, or music tracks. Companies charge their customers a fee to have access to a database of content whenever, wherever they want. Some providers have included commercials as a means to generate more income. Other subscription services include coffee of the month clubs, or deliver gift boxes. These companies charge a monthly (or yearly) subscription fee and compile a box of themed goodies for their customers.While some very big companies have struggled to make convenience a larger part of their customers' experiences, many small businesses that offer niche products and services have an advantage in this area. The Internet is helping them to level the playing field in a way. It provides a platform for small businesses to capitalize on the demand for goods by using convenience to win fans and new customers.
On conclusion, internet can bring smart phone users to do any activities when they need to apply computer tools at home in any time and anywhere. So, internet has direct relationship to persuade mobile phone or computer users to choose to buy mobiles for communication uses or internet uses in preference nowadays as well as internet can bring the different kinds of new or unique mobile phones design needs increase to achieve the creating mobile phone inventors and mobile phone manufacturers occupations need. So, it seems that internet can influence mobile phone product's occupations needs and mobile phone consumers number increase to raise real GDP growth to the smart phone maufacturing and sale country really.

Reference

Bigne, Enrique (2005). The impact of internet user shopping patterns and demographics on consumer mobile buying.

Falk, Louis, K. et. al (2005) " E-commerce and consumer's expectations: What makes a website work". Journal of website promotion, 1(1), 65-75.

Parasuraman, A., Zeithaml, V.A. and Berry L.L. (1988) SERVQUAL: A multiple-item scale for measuring consumer perceptions of

service quality. Journal of retailing, 64, 12-40.

Case 7

GAME THOERY SOLUTION IBM AND MICROSOFT COMPUTER LARGE COMPANIES COOPERATION MANAGEMENT PROBLEM CASE
Economics is just as much about consumer and producer behavior as it is about finance or the allocation of resources. With that in mind, game theory will explain one of the most fundamental tools economists use to frame competitive decision making. It provides a systematic approach to decision-making in competitive environments and a framework for the study of conflict.

Game theory solves the Prisoner's social criminal behaviors

Two small-time criminals are out breaking into cars, stealing what they can. They are working together in the same area of town. Fortunately, they get caught and booked down at the station. The detective goes in to question them separately and offers them both the same deal: they can either confess or stay silent. Their punishment will be determined by what action they take and what action the other perp takes. Here's what could happen:

a) If both perps confess, they each get 3 years.

b) If both perps stay silent, they each get 1 year.

c) If perp #1 stays silent and perp #2 confesses, perp #2 serves NO time and perp #1 serves 10 years.

d) If perp #2 stays silent and perp #1 confesses, perp #1 serves NO time and perp #2 serves 10 years.

So, if you were perp #1, what would you do? You could stay quiet and count on only getting one year, hoping that your friend stays quiet as well, and you'll both only serve 1 year. But, what if you admit to being involved and they admit being involved as well, then you'll both get 3 years. Or, what if you stay silent but your friend admits? Then you'll get 10 years; that wouldn't be good! Well, it is if your friend stays quiet.

The lesson to be learned from the prisoner's dilemma described above is how difficult it is to make an optimal decision when two competitors - and that's what these two perps are right now - can't collaborate. Typically, the economic man (or woman) is someone who makes decisions based on their own self-interest and chooses that which maximizes their own benefits. The entire idea behind game theory is that the result of your decision isn't known to you until you find out what your friend (or competitor) is going to do, so you have to make the best decision you can based on the information you have.

Game Theory in Real Life

We know how game theory works in a fictional situation that would never really happen, but what about how game theory applies to real life? Well, we can talk about that, too. Think about any strategic decision a business might make. The success or failure of that decision may very well depend on how the competition reacts. Perhaps a fast food restaurant wants to build a new location on the corner of a popular intersection. They complete their analysis of traffic flow, demand, other options in the area, etc., and ultimately decide it's a good idea. Then, once construction begins, another restaurant opens up a new location across the street, with a new building plan that includes drive-through ordering. What does our first restaurant do now?

Technology marketing cooperative strategy

Future when the thinking capabilities of computers approach our own is quickly coming into view. Raid process in coming decades will bring about machines with human –level intelligence capable of speech and reasoning, with a myriad of contributions to economics, politics and warcraft. The birth of true artificial intelligence will profoundly affect humankind's future. In our future technological development market, what it will bring much influences to economy. I shall indicate these several aspects, they may include as below:

On artificial intelligent invention brings high unemployment to low skill employees aspect, from the time the last artificial intelligence break through was reached in the last 1940s, scientists around the world have looked for ways of this " artificial intelligence" to improve technology, raising efficiency and productivity beyond what even the most sophisticated of today's artificial intelligence programs can achieve. Even now, research is ongoing to better understand what the new AI programs will be able to do, when remaining within the intelligence such as human brain. Most AI programs currently programmed have been limited primarily to making simple decisions or performing simple operations on relatively small amounts of data.

AI technological invention will bring much contribution to influence our future economic development. It had unique characteristics to compare common machines and it can help many industries to raise efficiency, productivity and improve performance as well as consumer individual self use. Such as the network is not taught to understand prose in any human sense. Instead, during its training phase, it adjusts the internal connections in its simulated neural networks to best anticipate the next word. It can be applied to read any article and understand any meaning to write any article as same to authors' mind and writing ability. For example, in the future, any one entered the first few sentences of any article, you are reading, the algorithm spewed out two paragraphs that sounded liked a freshman's effort to recall the gist of an introductory lecture on machine learning during which she was daydreaming. The output contains all the right words and phrases , not bad. So, (AI) technology can be applied to become just one more example of programs that do things thought to be uniquely human playing the real-time strategy game, translating text, making personal recommendations for books and movies, recognizing people in images and videos. But with the invention, of deep neural networks and the massive computational of the tech industry, computers improved until their outputs to longer appeared . In the future, algorithms can best humans, (AI) can help human to do any things in possible. Then, our society will encounter one automobile machine working environment. Does (AI) innovation will low skill employees lose their jobs because robotic can replace to any human to do simple jobs in any industries.

Whether machines can become sentient matters for ethical reasons. If computers experience life through their own senses, they cease to be purely a means to an end determined by their usefulness to us humans. Then our society will have many jobs which are needed to be worked by human, due to (AI) or robotic invention, it can replace human to do many simple jobs, e.g. factory manufacturing jobs, warehouse deliver jobs, public transportation , e.g. tram, train, ferry, underground train, bus etc. driving tasks, they are replaced by robotic auto driving, even pilot flying job will be also replaced to drive air planes by (AI) driving on sky impossible. Although, (AI) can help businesses to raise efficiency, increase productivity and improve performance, but it also bring these jobs to be replaced by (AI) and it will cause many people lose jobs when (AI) is invented to be applied in popular in our future societies. On business benefits aspect, (AI) can bring working efficiency and productivity improvement, but it can also bring unemployment ratio raises as the same time when employers accept to apply (AI) to replace human to any simple or difficult tasks.

So, we need to limit or prohibit (AI) invention to exceed human's extent in possible. I mean that we do not need to limit to invent any (AI) skill, but we need to concern human need to work in the same time. If (AI) was real replaced to do any simple jobs in any industries, then there are many low skill workers , such as factory workers, clean workers, drivers ,even high skill workers, such as lawyer, teacher, pilot. They will lose their jobs in possible. So, how to invent (AI) technology will influence our future global employment chance to provide us to continue to work in any organizations. So, (AI) will may bring high unemployment ratio, if it is applied to any low skill , even high skill jobs aspects to different industries in global.

On conclusion , in economist view, technology market development must need, such as (AI) invention because it can help any industries to raise efficiency, productivity and improve performance, but we need to know how it can be applied to avoid human to lose jobs, due to (AI) is replaced to do their tasks for any industries in possible. Whether (AI) invention can create jobs or bring job lose? (AI) scientists must need to consider how to invent their skill to be applied to which tasks aspect if they hope human won't lose many jobs to do in future one day.

● How to apply robotic to raise efficiency and productivity and improving performance for manufacture as well as bringing long term productive economic benefit to manufacturers?

It is one good question. Can scientists only concentrate on researching artificial intelligent for raising productivity, efficiency and improving performance to businesses aspect, so neglecting on research other scientific researching aspects? Technological marketing economy is as a play between independent individual subjects. However, it has also become clear that the notion of play has to be interpreted within a different framework than that of classical functionalism. In mainstream classical economics, interaction or exchange is understood as the effect of the ends-means rationally of individuals. Smith's sympathy —based view of man and society avoids this functionalistic reduction of interaction and exchange. For example, the utilitarian or functional aspect of , the social process of producing and distributing wealth through free exchange, is in Smith's view on part of the value and belief system which people in ordered and prosperous societies employ to give sense and meaning to their experiences.

Hence, in our business society, technology can bring marketing economic change to be better. One free technology marketing economic society must have these advantages to bring to influence our living, such as below:

It interprets and explains improving social processes of producing and distributing to business, such as (AI) skill invention , it can help businesses to improve performance and efficiency and productivities for their manufacturing aim only, but (AI) ought not be applied to replace to do all low skill workers' jobs in any positions in any factories or warehouses. So, any employers ought not dismiss all workers and they are replaced by all robotics. They will need to consider overall economic benefit. I mean that avoiding low skill workers unemployment ratio raises. For example, one factory can still keep 50% workers and 50% robotics to cooperate to work together. Because some human workers can be such as assistants to do any simple tasks in factory every teams. Human workers can discover any errors to let manager to know in order to improve in their cooperation process with robotics. So, human workers and robotics cooperation , it is more efficient manufacturing method to compare any manufacturing process is needed to finish from robotics only in any future factory or warehouse working environment. So, robotics and human workers cooperation can bring the most efficient production and distribution benefits to future manufacturers in any factories or warehouses because human can help robotics to find any error in order to improve. Otherwise, if the factory or warehouse has only all robotics to work. Although, they may bring raising productivities or improving performance and efficiencies. But they can not know whether how to improve their errors or revises their every time productive performance to be better every day. SO, the most efficient manufacturing method is that human workers and robotics cooperate to work together in any factories or warehouses.

On innovation and information economic influence aspect, one of the most important topics in economics is the economics of information. Information includes things as varied as e-mail, and even the text book you are reading. Information is a very different kind of commodity from things like pizza and shoes because information is expensive to produce , but cheap to reproduce. Because of the unusual nature of information, it is subject to market failure, so we need to develop different kinds of public politics to regulate it, the law of " intellectual property".

We are encountering the essence of economic development is innovation and that monopolists are in fact of innovation in a capitalist economy. What does the economics of information mean ? Who do we need to develop information economy? Modern economics emphasizes the special problems involved in the economics of information. Information is a fundamentally different commodity from normal goods. Because information is costly to produce , but cheap to reproduce, markets in information are subject to serve market failures.

For the production of software program industry example, the windows software, developing this program took several years and cost Microsoft many money of dollars. You can purchase a legal copy for $5. The same phenomenon is at work in pharmaceutical, entertainment and other areas where much of the value of a good comes from the information it contains. In each of these areas, the research and development to software on the product may be an expensive process that takes years. But once, the information is recorded on paper, in a computer or on a compact disc, it can be reproduced and used by a second person essentially for free.

The inability of firms to capture the full monetary value of their invention is called inappropriability. Inventions are not fully appropriable because other firms may imitate an invention, in which case the other firms may derive some of the benefits of the inventive investments. Sometimes, imitators may drive down the price of the new product, in which case consumers would get some of the rewards. Information consumers can earn these benefits when the value of an invention to all consumers and producers is many times the appropriable private return to the inventor (the monetary value of the invention to the inventor).

However, information is expensive to produce but cheap to reproduce. To the extent the rewards to invention are inappropriable, we would expect private research and development to be underfunded, with the most significant underinvestment in basic research because that is the least appropriable kind of information. The inappropriability and high social return on research can lead most governments to subsidize basic research in the fields of health and science and to provide special incentives for other creative activities. Thus, special laws governing patents, copyrights, business and trade secrets and electronic media create intellectual property rights. The purpose is to give the owner special protection against the material's being copied and used by others without compensation to the owner or original creator.

On the Internet information economic market influence hand, inventions that improve communications are hardly limited to the modern age. But the rapid growth of electronic storage, access and transmission of information highlights of providing incentives for creating new information. Many new information technologies have large sunk costs but virtually zero marginal costs. With the low cost of electronic information systems like the internet, it is technologically possible to make the large amounts of information available to everyone, everywhere, at close to zero marginal cost. Perfect competition is nowadays different e-commerce internet information business competitive feature, and any e-commerce merchants can not survive here because a price equal to a zero marginal cost will yield zero revenues and therefore no viable firms.

Hence, the economics of the information economy highlights the conflict between efficiency and incentives. On the one hand, all information ,might be provided free of charge, e.g. free e-book download, e-song download e-movie download from internet. Free provisions of information looks economically efficient because the price would thereby be equal to the marginal cost, which is zero. But a zero price on intellectual property would destroy the profits and therefore reduce the incentives to produce new books from authors, movies and songs from creators would earn little rewards from their creative activity. But with the costs reproduction and transmission so much lower for electronic information than for traditional information, so the future any electronic publishing industry 's products, e.g. e-books, e-songs , e-music, e-movies prices will be lower than traditional paper books, pack of songs and movies price, either consumers go to shops to buy them or consumers pay visa card to enter websites to buy any e-books , songs, e-music , e-movies from internet channel. Then, it will cause these traditional publishing and entertainment industries' competition to be raised because these e-publishers or e-entertainment can reduce their price to sell from their websites when their costs are nearly to zero. Hence, information technology can raise competition to the traditional publishing and entertainment industries. The traditional paper book, music, movie business merchants need to any authors or creators to help them to create any unique movies, songs, paper books to sell from their shops and they need to ensure their authors or music , movie creators won't give these creative book, song, movie products to any e-music, e-publisher, e-movie merchants to sell from their websites absolutely.

On conclusion, information technology influence any music, publish, movie creative product competitive raising to the traditional paper book publishers, music or movie publishers when many book publishers or music or movie creators choose e-commerce to replace traditional shop visiting sale method. So ﹐ it is possible to influence overall publishing and music and movie creative industries will change to e-commence consumption model. Then the traditional book and music and movie visiting stores will disappear and the online websites to these merchants will increase and their price also will reduce in global e-publishing and e-creative product consumption environment. So, information technology will bring some traditional store visiting number decreases and online merchant e-store number increases and consumers can pay less price to buy these creative products from internet.

New trade game theory explains IBM and Micro software both compaines cooperative advantages
New trade theory (NTT) suggests that a critical factor in determining international patterns of trade are the very substantial economies of scale and network effects that can occur in key industries.

These economies of scale and network effects can be so significant that they outweigh the more traditional theory of comparative advantage. In some industries, two countries may have no discernible differences in opportunity cost at a particular point in time. But, if one country specialises in a particular industry then it may gain economies of scale and other network benefits from its specialisation.

Another element of new trade theory is that firms who have the advantage of being an early entrant can become a dominant firm in the market. This is because the first firms gain substantial economies of scale meaning that new firms can't compete against the incumbent firms. This means that in these global industries with very large economies of scale, there is likely to be limited competition, with the market dominated by early firms who entered, leading to a form of monopolistic competition.

Monopolistic competition is an important element of New Trade Theory, it suggests that firms are often competing on branding, quality and not just simple price. It explains why countries can both export and import designer clothes. This means that the most lucrative industries are often dominated in capital-intensive countries, who were the first to develop these industries. Therefore, being the first firm to reach industrial maturity gives a very strong competitive advantage. (some may say unfair advantage)

New trade theory also becomes a factor in explaining the growth of globalisation. It means that poorer, developing economies may struggle to ever develop certain industries because they lag too far behind the economies of scale enjoyed in the developed world. This is not due to any intrinsic comparative advantage, but more the economies of scale the developed firms already have.

Examples of New Trade Theory
·Specialisation of IT in Silicon Valley – the US. Hewlett and Packard started their computer business. Success attracted more IT firms to that area. Not because of any particular intrinsic benefit but new firms start to get the network

benefits of being around other IT setups.'

·Globalisation has led to increased variety for consumers. The proliferation of brand clothing labels. Firms competing in the model of monopolistic competition and heavy branding. Neither UK or Italy has a particular comparative advantage in producing clothes, but consumers are attracted to brand image of Italian and British fashion labels.

Moral hazard influences to Macrosoft or Microcorp and IBM software cooperational success problem

Moral hazard is when one party can take risks knowing the other party will bear the consequences. It describes the risk present when two parties don't have the same information about actions that take place after an agreement is in place. The situation creates a temptation to ignore the moral implications of a decision: doing what benefits you most instead of doing what is right.

Example of Moral Hazard in Insurance

Moral hazard is a term that originated in the insurance industry and spread to the financial sphere. To illustrate the concept, imagine you rent a car and opt for the maximum insurance coverage possible. Damaging the vehicle does not have significant negative consequences for you, because the insurance company pays for repairs—or a replacement car—if something happens.

The insurance company uses statistics to estimate how likely the vehicle is to suffer damage, and they price their services accordingly. You pay much less for insurance than it would cost to repair a car because, in most cases, the insurance company won't have to pay for any repairs. But there are times when you might have an unfair information advantage over your insurance company. That's where moral hazard comes in.

You plan to drive into the mountains on rough, narrow roads. So, you get the most generous insurance coverage possible, and you don't worry about bouncing over rocks or scratching the paint in thick brush along the side of the road. You might even have a perfectly good car available at home, but there's no way you're going to drive your vehicle up that road—so you rent a car and buy insurance. The low cost of insurance means you have no incentive to protect the car you rented, but the insurance company doesn't know you're driving it under such conditions.

Moral hazard happens when you have an incentive to take risks that somebody else will pay for. You get to do whatever brings you the greatest potential benefit, and you don't suffer the consequences. In this example, the insurance company bears the risk: the cost of repairing or even replacing the car. The more insulated you are from risk, the more temptation you face.

Examples of Moral Hazard in Lending

Moral hazard became a significant factor during (and after) the financial crisis that began in 2007. The concept can apply to both lenders and borrowers.

Lenders were eager to approve loans before the mortgage crisis. Some mortgage brokers encouraged "subprime" borrowers to lie on loan applications, or they altered documents to make it appear that borrowers were able to afford loans that they really couldn't afford. For example, sometimes they reported inaccurate income numbers or the brokers did not require documentation that would demonstrate a borrower's ability to repay the loan.

Why would lenders hand out money when they don't know if the borrower can afford the payments—especially if they have to commit fraud to get the loans approved? In many cases, the lenders were only originating, or selling, the loans. After approving and funding loans, lenders would sell the loans to investors, who eventually suffered the losses. In other words, the lender took little or no risk. But lenders had an incentive to keep making new loans because that's how originators generate revenue.

When things turned sour, lawmakers and the public got scared. They worried that if major banks collapsed (some of them were loan originators, while others held risky investments), they would bring down the U.S. economy—not to mention the global economy. Because these banks were considered "too big to fail," the U.S. government provided funding to help some of them to weather the economic storm. If those banks suffered significant losses, the government promised to protect deposits (in some cases through the FDIC). Of course, taxpayers fund the U.S. government, so the taxpayers were ultimately bailing out the banks. The moral hazard was the lenders and investment banks taking risks that had consequences not for themselves, but for taxpayers and others.

Borrowers

Moral hazard can occur in almost any agreement, whether it's an informal understanding or a formal contract. If one party has the opportunity to benefit from taking "risks"—while risking almost nothing—moral hazard is at play.

During the financial crisis, as millions of homeowners struggled to pay their mortgages and loan defaults skyrocketed, government programs offered relief. People could avoid foreclosure thanks to money and guarantees from the U.S. government.

The moral hazard in these cases was that borrowers, increasingly underwater on their home loans, would be tempted to walk away from their mortgage rather than repay it. Such an action would put risk back onto the lender. The hazard is that the borrower no longer had an incentive to do the right thing—to pay back the mortgage as agreed.

Hence, such as moral hazard applies to Macrosoft or Microcorp and IBM software cooperational case . If Macrosoft and Microsorp and IBM do not decide to co-operate to help themselves to expand their software strengths to achieve the aim to improve their software quality and feature and function, then they can not bring any software innovation to let future software users to raise any new softwares invention or improvement useful benefits. Then, global software market can not be improved to let any software users to raise high techological software products choices number. Because they are competitors, they won't hope themselves softwares' quality, feature and function and improvement are worse to compare other softwares companies among them. So, global software users will have moral hazard to enjoy any kinds of new softwares products invention in short time. But, if they can cooperate to buy and sell themselves both shares, then they both will be another softwares owners, they won't hope the another software company loses many software customers because itself new software inventions to attack the another software company. They must hope themselves any new software invention products , they can still attract many new software products customers together. Then, global software users won't have moral hazard to enjoy any new software invention products in short time, because they must cooperate to help themselve to improve their any new softwares ' qualities , features and functions in order to they can have many software customers share in these software market when they are global large software firms.

What are Principal-Agent Problems to Microsoft and IBM both large computer companies cooperation?

For example, a company's stock investors, as part-owners, are principals who rely on the company's chief executive officer (CEO), as their agent, to carry out a strategy in their best interests. That is, they want the stock to increase in price or pay a dividend, or both. If the CEO opts instead to plow all the profits into expansion or pay big bonuses to managers, the principals may feel they have been let down by their agent. There are a number of remedies for the principal-agent problem, and many of them involve clarifying expectations and monitoring results. The principal is generally the only party who can or will correct the problem.

Understanding the Principal-Agent Problem

The principal-agent problem has become a standard factor in political science and economics. The theory was developed in the 1970s by Michael Jensen of Harvard Business School and William Meckling of the University of Rochester. In a paper published in 1976, they outlined a theory of an ownership structure designed to avoid what they defined as agency cost and its cause, which they identified as the separation of ownership and control.The trend has been towards contracts with the agent that link compensation directly to performance measurements set by the principal.

This separation of control occurs when a principal hires an agent, The principal delegates a degree of control and the right to make decisions to the agent. But the principal retains ownership of the assets and the liability for any losses.

Factoring in Agency Costs

Logically, the principal cannot constantly monitor the agent's actions. The risk that the agent will shirk a responsibility, make a poor decision, or otherwise act in a way that is contrary to the principal's best interest, can be defined as agency costs. Additional agency costs can be incurred while dealing with problems that arise from an agent's actions. Agency costs are viewed as a part of transaction costs.

Agency costs may also include the expenses of setting up financial or other incentives to encourage the agent to act in a particular way. Principals are willing to bear these additional costs as long as the expected increase in the return on the investment from hiring the agent is greater than the cost of hiring the agent, including the agency costs.

Examples of the Principal-Agent Problem

The principal-agent problem can crop up in many day-to-day situations beyond the financial world. A client who hires a lawyer may worry that the lawyer will wrack up more billable hours than are necessary. A homeowner may disapprove of the City Council's use of taxpayer funds. A home buyer may suspect that a realtor is more interested in a commission than in the buyer's concerns. In all of these cases, the principal has little choice in the matter. An agent is necessary to get the job done.However, there are ways to resolve the principal-agent problem.

Solutions to the Principal-Agent Problem

The onus is on the principal to create incentives for the agent to act as the principal wants. Consider the first example, the relationship between shareholders and a CEO. The shareholders can take action before and after hiring a manager to overcome some risk. First, they can write the manager's contract in a way that aligns the incentives of the manager with the incentives of the shareholders. The principals can require the agent to regularly report results to them. They can hire outside monitors or auditors to track information. In the worst case, they can replace the manager.

Contract Clauses

In recent years, the trend has been towards employment contracts that connect compensation as closely as possible with performance measurements. For managers of businesses, incentives include performance-based awards of stock or stock options, profit-sharing plans, or directly linking management pay to stock price. At its root, it's the same principle as tipping for good service. Theoretically, tipping aligns the interests of the customer, or the principal, and the agent, or the waiter. Their priorities are now aligned and are focused on good service.

Hence, such as this IBM and microsoft large both companies, if they hope to cooperate , they need to solve which company can have more management authority and which company can have more share owming or investing authory. If IBM can have more management authority to control their both companies, but IBM has less shares number to Microsoft, e.g. IBM has 30 % shares to Microsoft, whether IBM ought earn more profit or less profit to 30% profits from Microsoft, if IBM have more management authory, but IBM can not cooperate to Microsoft to assist it to raise more computer buyers number. So, agent problem will cause IBM and Microsoft cooperation more easily together in nowadays computer market. But, if IBM can help Microsoft to increase computer buyers number after IBM participates to manage Microsoft's internal organizational management , then IBM can increase Microsoft computer buyers number in long time. Then, their cooperation can be more success, it means that their principle and agent problem will solve between them.

Management Science Dependency Theory Solves Macrosoft and IBM software cooperational success method

● Macrosoft or Microcorp and IBM software cooperational strategy

What is information technologic game strategy? How and why information technological game strategy can influence economic growth? I shall explain as below:

Nowadays, Macrosoft and Microcorp are the global information technological big companies. They own much market share in global information technological industry. Whether what factors influence they can still be global information technological products leaders. Why does computer software consumers still choose their products to compare other software products in preference? I suppose that Macrosoft and Microcorp, their hypothetical any software games have developed a clever new computer game that is certain to be very popular. Although Microcorp have the unique competitive advantage with its own software game engineers and compete against Macrosoft, but it can so it cheaper and better if it can hire any Macrosoft's software game engineers. So, in economic view, it needs to pay high salary (higher cost) to hire Macrosoft's engineers (labor), but Macrosoft's engineers can help Microcorp to invent any new kinds of software games to compete Macrosoft. Although, Microsorp needs to pay higher labor cost, but when it can raise its any software games' design and game playing methods to attract any game players. Then, these new and exciting software games can help it can bring many game entertainment players and then it can sell cheaper price to raise more attractive effort to win its competitor (Macrosoft). So, higher software game designing engineers (skill labor), their game designing effort will be the major factor to influence any one information technological companies in success. If one software designing company can employ one high software game designing effort profession to help it to design any kinds of attractive software games. Although, it may pay high salary (labor cost), but it have much chance to attract many software game buyers to compare that if it pays less salary to employ one poor game software designing profession. Because the poor software game designing profession may need to spend long time to research how to design any kinds of attractive game software to excite game players' playing desires in this playing software game industry market. Long time research to the poor software game designer may be one none any reward to compensate to the software game designing firm when it needs to pay long time salary to employ him. Otherwise, if the software game designing firm can accept to pay higher salary to the higher software game designer, he will have higher chance to help it to design any more attractive software games to influence game players' playing game entertainment desires. So, any software game designing companies their game designers (labor) must be the major factor to influence their business succeeds or fails in this software game entertainment market.

On the employing method hand, Microcorp can choose to include in its contracts with its software engineers that from working for another Macrosoft software company for a certain period of time if they resign from Macrosoft. A move such as this is sometimes called a preeptive move. Its propose is to alter its rivals' payoffs in order to alter their employing strategies. Preemptive moves are usually costly (high slaary), and this one is no exception. In its employment contracts makes Macrosoft a less attractive to let its old game software engineers want to leave their current employer, such as Macrosoft. As a result, Macrosoft must pay its software game designing engineers above the going market salary if it hopes their employment contracts can be continue between Macrosoft and its software game engineers.

Should Macrosoft must need to decide how to react. It can choose to fight Microcorp by aggressively advertising its game, which is costly high, but gives it a larger market share in the game player entertainment market, when Macrosoft had any one profession game software engineer(s) leave(s) his company and he/they change(s) to the another Microcorp software game designing company to work, or it can forego the expense of an advertisement campaign and simply share the market 50/50 with its major competitor, Microcorp to be partners.

Their competition has close relationship to influence economic growth because it will have many game players number to be increase if they can cooperate to be partners in success when they can design any new kinds of software game products to satisfy software game players' entertainment feeling. Otherwise, if they can not be one good partners and they only consider their every business benefits and neglect themselves business benefits. Then, their software playing games sale price can either to be reduced in order to attract any software game players when their software games can not be designed to have much new playing methods to attract many game players. Consequently, the GDP income to this software game entertainment market must reduce because any kinds of entertainment software games prices are reduced as well as the game players number is also decreasing. Due to they are the major software entertainment game suppliers in global. Any game players will only choose either Microcorp or Macrosoft to buy their any kinds of entertainment software game products to play majorly. So, their software game manufacturing and sale number must influence global GDP income increases or decreases in macro economy view. It implies that any countries technological software game industry's GDP income will depend on these both Microcorp and Macrosoft software game's cooperation relationship whether they have good or bad cooperation relationship. If their cooperation relationship is good, then they can manufacture high quality and attractive entertainment software games as well as raising sale price and exciting many game players' entertainment desires to achieve the increase to game players number aim more easily.

How to achieve their cooperation relationship more easier. I suppose that, in the software game entertainment industry, over its lifetime, the computer game will generate $500,000 in new income (income minus production cost) for all the firms producing it or its clones. Macrosoft must pay its software engineers an additional $100,000 to get them to agree to accept a contract containing an anticompetition clause. It costs Microcorp $100,000 to develop the software if it can hire Macrosoft's engineers and $200,000 otherwise. Aggressive advertising costs Macrosoft $70,000 and has the effect of giving it a 80% market share if it restricts its engineers' employment and a 72% market share if it does not. So, the fall in total market share is caused by the fact that without some of Macrosoft's advertisements. If however, Macrosoft passively acquiesces to Microcorp's entry and shares the market, then both firms can still achieve a 50% market share fairly. Hence, they must need to achieve 50/50 market share if they hope to achieve the cooperation relationship in success. Otherwise, they will not achieve cooperation relationship in success.

However, the spending advertisement factor will also their cooperation chance in success. For example, it would be more realistic to recast the Software Game as one in which Macrosoft chooses how much to spend on advertising with sales depending continuously on the amount spent. Other examples of continuous cooperation choices may include: the productive capacity of an electrical power plant; the salary to offer a prospective employee; or the insurance premium to charge a prospective policyholder. So, the amount to any of these expenditure factor will influence whether they will decide to cooperate to sell their software games products in global game entertainment market.

How and why Macrosoft and Microcorp's cooperation can influence global economic growth? It is significant that Macrosoft and Microcorp both technological software game designing companies are global the largest firms, they are doing international software game trade business to many countries and they have large market share in the software entertainment game sale market. Aside from trade based on technological gaps and software game product cycles, software game entertainment industry is dynamic in nature or game players' entertainment taste will change any time in completely static in nature. That is, given the nation's game players' playing taste and game entertainment factor, such as game playing designing technological method and game player individual playing game taste both. We proceeded to determine the nation's comparative advantage and the gains from the different kinds of entertainment software game designing supply factor and the game player individual game taste changing factor. So, any nation's software game players number will depend on these both factors to influence whether their number will either increase or decrease in the year in this global software game entertainment market. However, these factors can be changed by time, technology usually can improve any software game playing methods and game player individual playing taste will also change any time. As a result, the nation's comparative advantage also changes over time, such as when the nation has many game players lose their interest to buy any software games to play, then the nation ought not only consider how to develop its software entertainment game in the technological industry, it is right time to research any other new technological industries to develop if it still hopes its GDP income can rise in the technological industry overall aspect. Such as dynamic trade theory is still in its infancy. However, our comparative statics analysis can carry us a long way in analyzing the effect on international trade resulting from changes in factor technology, and tastes over time, such as entertainment software game case.

The growth of factors of production will also influence the software game entertainment industry development, through time, a nation's population usually grows and with its size of its labor force , such as China and India. Similarly, by utilizing part of its resources to produce capital equipment, e.g. India needs to utilize its technological resources, technological engineers and technological material can need to be used to manufacture either new software game products or computers. But, its technological resources will be shortage (both labor and technological material). So, many technological companies choose to apply more technological material and technological engineers to use much time and money to manufacture any new software game products. Then, these labor and material resources will be reduced to be spent time and material to manufacture any new computer products in the year. In this technological industry case, capital refers to all the man-made means of production, such as machinery, factories, communication and education and training of labor force, all of which greatly enhance the nation's ability to produce either computer products or software game products. So, the national will also continue to assume that it can experiencing economic growth is producing two commodities, such as software game and computer both kinds of technological products under the constant returns to scale. So, if India can not raise the rapid technical process to skill labor and supply technological material supplying number to satisfy to manufacture the enough software game and computer products to supply them to sell to any countries' playing game players and computer users every month. Then, its technological industry will lose many clients, due to it can not supply enough software games and computers number to sell to any countries.

Several empirical studies have indicated that most the increase in real per capita income in technological industrial nations is due to technical progress and much less to capital accumulation. However, the analysis of technical progress is much more complex than the analysis of factor growth because there are several definitions and types of technical progress, and they can take place at different rates in the production of either or both commodities, such as software game and computer.

Technical progress is usually classified into neutral, labor saving , or capital saving. All technical progress , regardless of its types reduces the amount of both labor and capital required to produce any given level of output. So, if India could have good technical progress to raise its technological labor skill and reducing the technological material to be used to manufacture the software games and computers. Then, it will have chance to keep the maximum manufacturing level number to software game and computer products as the same time.

THREE

ORGANIZATIONAL MANAGEMENT STRATEGIES CASES STUDIES

How to apply marketing theories to predict marketing behavior

Body Shop case study -Applying experiment to predict consumer behavior

1. Critically assess the extent to which whether Body Shop to be a truly marketing oriented organization throughout its 30 years history.

Body Shop Background

The body shop international power line carrier (the body shop) was founded by Dame Anita Roddick in the England in 1976. It sold personal beauty care products, such as baby and child specific products, bath and shower and colour cosmetics, deodorants, skin care, hair care, fragrances, sun care etc skin health products to provide human body benefits. Nowadays, the body shop was skin and body care manufacturer and retailer operating in 55 countries with over 2,100 stores. It had 42 exclusive outlets in Hong Kong. It's missions were to dedicate to pursuit of social and environment change to meaningfully contribute to local, national and international communities in which trade to passionately campaign for the protection of the environment, human and civil rights and against animal testing and to make fun, passion and care part of our daily lives (Adrian, P. 2012).

What is the difference between production orientation and societal marketing orientation and sales orientation

There are five main marketing orientations of which a company will adopt one. This will determine the way it interacts with the customer. Such as product orientation suggests that a company focuses inwards looking at what it is capable of, rather than the needs and wants of the client; sales orientation is based upon selling existing products with a turnover sale numbers relationship marketing orientation recognizes the value of repeat business over, not only with customers but suppliers as well; societal marketing orientation is relatively new in the scheme of things but suggests on top of meeting the needs and wants of the customer and the organization there is the societies interests to be looked and marketing orientation is based around the needs and wants of a customer to meet business objectives and it assumes that a sale depends on a customer's decision to purchase a product or provide a service.

What is marketing two levels meaning ?

Marketing can be seen at two levels, the first level is such as a business philosophy, marketing puts customers at the center of an organization's consideration and which is reflected in basic values , such as the requirement to understand and respond to customers' needs and the necessary to search constantly for new market opportunity. In a truly marketing oriented organization, these values are instilled in all employees and should influence their behavior without any need for prompting. The personnel manager would have a selection policy that recruited staff who could fulfil the needs of customers rather than simply minimizing the wage bill in any marketing oriented organization. The other level is techniques of marketing also include pricing, the design of channels of distribution and new product development.

What are the three components of market orientation ?

The assessing the nature and importance of market orientation for large firms, such as body shop. The three components of market orientation could be analytically separated. The components of market orientation organization include the first component is the customer orientation, it means an organization must have a thorough understanding of its target buyers, so that it can create a product of superior value to give client benefits ; the second component is the competitor orientation, it means any firm should look at how well its competitors are able to satisfy buyers' needs. It should understand the short term strengths and weaknesses and long term capabilities and strategies of current and potential competitors as well as the third component is to develop marketing plans that are not acted upon by people who are capable of delivering promises made to customers and a marketing orientation organization requires that the organization draws upon and integrates its human and physical resources effectively and adapts them to meet client's needs. Otherwise, a production and sales orientation may be appropriate to firms at certain stages in the evolution of markets. Where the dominant business environment is based on the need for good production planning above all, the company that does this best will achieve the greatest overall business success. It is either production orientation, it means organizations that produce what they imagined consumers wanted, rather than what they actually wanted. Planning for full utilization of capital equipment are often seen as more important than ensuring that equipment is used to provide goods and services that people actually wants. Production-oriented firms generally aim for efficiency in production rather than effectiveness in meeting customer's needs . It is either or selling orientation, it means advertising, sales promotion and personal selling techniques are used to emphasize product differentiation and brands and it does not focus on satisfying client needs or desire new product offerings and production led. Hence, one market orientation organization needs to focus on satisfying clients' needs profitably by these marketing mix, such as product, price, place, physical evidence, processed, people and promotion. Anyway ,Market orientation implied that body shop , which ought seek information about clients, such as current and future needs and took action based this information (client orientation); it ought seek information about competitors' current strengths and weaknesses and their long term strategies and took actions based on these information (competitor orientation) ; it ought coordinate the actions taken by sharing clients and competitors information internally (intra-firm communication).

What is the three components of market orientation ?

The three components of market orientation meant social marketing and understanding boarder concerns and ethical environmental, legal and social context of marketing activities and programs. The cause and effects of marketing clearly beyond the company and the consumer to society as whole. New terms humanistic marketing and ecological marketing were suggested to societal marketing concept.

What is the social marketing concept ?

The social marketing concept holds that the organization's task is to determine the needs, wants and interests of target markets and to deliver the desired satisfactions more effectively and efficiently than competitors and the society's welling being, such as body shop had achieved sales and profit gains by adopting and practicing a form of the societal marketing concept called cause related marketing.

DISCUSSION

Body Shop is marketing orientation organization in 30 years. Critically assess the extent to which I consider Body Shop to be a truly marketing oriented organization throughout its 30 years history . It seemed body shop had achieved cause-related marketing as an opportunity to enhance their corporate reputation, raised brand awareness, increased customer loyalty and built sales. It's corporate values were composed of five core values. The first one was to oppose animal testing. The opposing animal testing for both cosmetic products and ingredients began in 1976 years.

In the 1980 year and 1990 year, who successfully campaigned with animal protection groups to change the UK and European laws to support the development products were tried on human
volunteers. Along with the development of technology testing had played a leading role to protect the rights of both human and animals . The second one was to support community trade, it initiated the trade not aid objective of creating trade to help people in the third world utilizing their resources to their own needs. This reflects communities

needed a fair price for natural ingredients who purchased from these often marginalized countries. The third one was to activate self esteem. Women were the main customers and employees in the body shop. The fourth one was to defend human rights. The body shop had long campaign on human rights, highlighting abuses and increasing the global awareness of issues by making full use of the geographic advantages of their shops and supporting other human rights organizations. The last one was protect our plant. In 2001 year, huge campaign against global warming was hosted by the body shop and green peace, who advocated the use of recyclable source and materials (Adrian, P. 2012). Although profits were an essential element of long run survival in body shop and it was likely to be overall corporate and marketing objectives, but body shop seemed more to be required level of profits rather than profit that there were many other objectives, which might pursue through its pricing strategies . For example, if body shop wanted to maximize market share or simply survive, a different set of prices would be delivered than if the objectives were to maximize profits. Hence, body shop ought to see viewpoint the marketing side of pricing and it ought not to see viewpoint the production / supply side of pricing if it was a truly marketing oriented organization. The key inputs for body shop to make pricing decision whether it was marketing oriented or productive / supply oriented included production objectives or marketing objectives, demand or supply numbers were considered cost or sale price and competitors or clients consideration factors, such as beauty skin care products in competitive markets demand, i.e. To decide the price whether customers are willing and able to pay is a major consideration in the selection of pricing strategies and levels of demands . Hence, body shop ought to consider demand numbers , it ought not consider production / supply numbers if it was a truly marketing oriented organization. For example, since most of the body shop's factories were still located in the UK, where wages and salaries were much higher than in Asia, so UK itself sale product prices were higher than that from Asia itself sale product prices.

I think Body Shop was a truly marketing oriented organization more than production/supply oriented organization throughout its 30 years history. In fact, Body Shop was experiencing market level growth. It could expand its sales market in Europe, America, Middle East, Asia and Africa etc different countries. It seemed that it had attempted to carry on marketing research to decide to choose which countries would have more client numbers to demand to buy its personal care products, then it would follow the countries' estimated client numbers to produce its products to sell to the countries. So, it was why some Asia countries sold its bath and shower and skin and hair care and colour cosmetics products more than its fragrances products, such as Hong Kong young people were more acceptable to use bath and show and color cosmetic and skin and hair care products more than fragrances products . It seemed that Hong Kong Body Shop sold fragrance products numbers were less than bath and shower and color cosmetics etc. products. Nowadays, I think the personal beauty care products new businesses which planned to entry this market was more difficult. It was possible than Body Shop was a famous personal beauty care products sale company, it had owned many clients too many years. So , it caused barriers to any new personal beauty care product competitors felt difficult to entry this market .Furthermore, Body Shop had build strong buyer and seller power to increase clients had more confident to use its products, it was possible that who felt its different kind of products could give more health to their skin or body more than other similar personal beauty care products. Moreover, I believe Body Shop had attempted to carry on technological experimenting to aim to build different countries' clients had more confident to use its products forever.

In conclusion, it seemed that Body Shop was truly marketing oriented organization more than productive/ supply oriented organization oriented organization throughout its 30 years history.

To what extent are the pursuits of profit and meeting the needs of wider groups of stakeholders incompatible? Whether Body shop pursuits social responsibility aim or profit aim more.

Any companies need to consider the social responsibility during which are the pursuits of profit and meeting the needs of wider group of stakeholders incompatible. Without this self interest, there will be little motivation for firms to provide better services, workers couldn't earn better salaries and clients couldn't aspire for a high level of consumption. Hence, self interest which helps markets work more effectively for the benefits of all. Hence, companies should adopt a code of behavior and conduct and ethical behavior which would not influence any stakeholders groups' benefits to pursuit their profit honestly.

Corporate social responsibility is a form of corporate self regulation integrated into a business model. It aims to give responsibility for corporate actions and to encourage a positive impact on the environment and stakeholders including consumers, employees, investors, communities and others and it is titled to aid an organization's mission as well as guide to what the company can give the best benefits to serve its customers. I shall use body shop company as one example to judge whether what extent are the pursuits of profit and meeting the needs of wider groups of stakeholders will be incompatible. Factually, body shop could adopt a code of behavior and conduct and ethical behavior which would not influence any stakeholders groups' benefits to pursuit their profit honestly. Such as, one of the major and most successful initiatives which body shop used an effective supply chain for their products and body shop made use of their sustainable chain supply strategy to ensure that there was the promotion and the maintenance of the social ethical behavior in its business. Hence, it seemed that body shop could be compatible to achieve an effective supply chain to deliver to different countries' stores to meet clients who had more need to buy different kinds of skin care products to provide them to choose to buy in the reasonable price choices in the short time. It is therefore in the best practices and interests for body shop to reach out to the communities in their businesses to provide raw materials to help the manufacturers of the beauty products. It also partook in the development of the market for such small scale suppliers. In many cases the body shop tried to outsource its raw materials to its customers. This had ensured the sustainability of its customer base this included it's sensitivity to its environment and the required standards of the labor practices of its partners. Hence, it seemed that body shop could be compatible to help its partners to earn profits and any countries' partners could provide more job chances to unemployed people to work from body shop's outsourcing strategy. Hence, this had been developed by the body shop by including strategies, such as third party logistic providers and intermediaries in which who had no ownership. The body shop was a multinational company also adopted trading to purchasing approach where it shifted from short term where focus of buying articles to long term focus of fewer suppliers. This was an attempt of it to develop quality products where prices were also fair and affordable to sell to different countries' clients. It seemed that body shop could be compatible to sell reasonable prices of products to it's clients. Moreover, it had included in its strategies the aspect of business promotion using catalogues. For the same reason, it had been involved in printing of catalogues which were given out to the clients with their purchases. It was important to note that it' catalogues always contained all it's information descriptions and any person who purchased it's products was bound to receive the explanation of all it's product. This was an attempt of it to develop quality products where prices were also fair and affordable to sell to different countries' clients. It seemed that body shop could be compatible to provide clear information description in catalogues to let whose clients to know what it's different kinds of style body skin care products ingredients and benefits were , then who could compare it's products to other competitors to decide to buy or not buy fairly.

Experiment to predict consumer behavior: In Oct. 2007 the campaign for safe cosmetic products, in which 25 multinational companies participated, tested 33 brand name lipsticks and found one-third of the sampled exceeded the limit of lead allowed in confectionery. The affected brands included L'Oreal and Christian Dior. A definite effect would be that consumers would be more concerned regarded the ingredients of products who used, which was likely to have an effect on cosmetics and skin care products were released to capture share. It seemed body shop needed to consider its beauty personal care products were the most ensure to own organic ingredients to let any countries clients (stakeholder) to meet their body health care needs (Adrian, P. 2012).

On the health and natural aspect, body shop had health and safe responsibility to consumers. Although, I felt who had considered this issue because it had 30 years history to operate this business and it had not received any serious negative complaints damage its health product image from clients before. However, with consumers were increasingly informed and were educated, who were now more demanding for more information regarding products and were becoming more aware of health issue. Products with organic ingredients and natural ingredients, such as tea and plants were gaining popular. Furthermore, consumers were looking for healthier substitutes to seemingly unhealthy products, such as color cosmetics. Hence, body shop began to sell the reducing numbers, it was possible due to clients compared it's body care products quality to the other competitors and who felt it's product's ingredients existed some poor ingredients to cause every one's body to be unhealthy. Hence, it's productive processing was very important. It seemed that body shop could be compatible to consider its individual client body skin health issue whether after who had used it's body skin care products to have skin hurt or skin pain feeling. In conclusion, to judge what extent are the pursuits of profit and meeting the needs of wider groups of stakeholders incompatible for any individual business, it is depended on whether the company's any stakeholders, such as employees, clients, suppliers, partners, society (communities) etc. who will have positive or negative influence from it. I feel that it will be incompatible if the company give negative influence to any one of its stakeholder. Hence, if any one company's at least one stakeholder who felt who had negative influence due to it did business to relate to whom unwillingly, then it's pursuit of profits aim would be incompatible to meet it's needs of its any one of stakeholder. Such as body shop will give positive influence to its all stakeholders. Hence, I feel it is compatible extent to pursuit of profit and meeting the needs of its wider groups of stakeholders definitely.

What companies, if any have managed to sustainable reconcile these two aims?

I feel that Nestle company has managed to sustainable reconcile to pursuit profits and meeting the needs of its wider groups of stakeholders two aims compatibly. Nestle was the world's largest food and beverage company. Nestle in the United States, which represented seven operating across the USA country and it was the first expanded effort in USA and achievement tied to Nestle 's global sustainability principle and commitment. Nowadays, It served 97% of American householders and Nestle 's mission was to lead the industry in nutrition, health and wellness and to create a more sustainable future. Instead of it's mission was to pursuit of profits aim, it had also achieved specific sustainability commitment and progress in the categories of nutrition, environmental impact and water use, social impact, rural development and responsible sourcing to meet the needs of it's wider of groups of stakeholders' aim. On the nutrition, health and wellness aspect, Nestle met the needs to its stakeholder (clients), such as, Nestle rolled out new portion guidance tools and launched an educational campaign and balance your plate to help consumers build nutritious and delicious and convenient meals that met the dietary guidelines for Americans; Nestle also reduced sodium content in many of its most popular brands, such as Stouffer's and DiGiorno and committed to further reduce sodium content by 10 percent in products that did not meet the Nestle; Nestle also reduced sugar content, such as ninety six percent of Nestle 's children's products met the Nestle criteria for low sugar and by the end of 2014 year, 100 percent of children's products would meet these criteria as well as Nestle also removed trans-fat content, such as Nestle committed to reach zero food and beverage products with trans-fat originating to use as functional ingredients by 2016 year. It seemed that Nestle had considered its food and beverage production content whether these content would have negative influence to its stakeholder (clients) nowadays (Adrian, P. 2012). On the environmental impact aspect, Nestle reduced waste during it's food and beverage products were producing. As part of its commitment to eliminate all forms of waste, Nestle reduced 44 percent of waste per ton of product since 2010 year in the USA five factory locations reached zero waste to landfill status by the end of 2013 year; Nestle also considered responsible packaging responsibility, such as Nestle Waters North America led the USA bottled water industry in light weighting packaging, in part by reducing the plastic content of its 1/2 liter bottles by 60 percent since 1994 year. Since 2003 year alone, more than 3.3 billion pounds of plastic had been saved by Nestle as well as Nestle also adopted responsible sourcing, such as Nestle Purina Pet Care implemented responsible sourcing guidelines for seafood that align with Nestle 's global responsible sourcing guidelines, working with experts to track suppliers and contribute to healthier ecosystem. In 2013 year, Nestle also reached an important target for palm oil, with 100 percent of palm oil now Round table on sustainable palm oil certified. It seemed that Nestle also considerate whether environment would have negative influence occurrence during it's production (Adrian, P. 2012).

Experiment to predict consumer behavior : On social impact aspect, Nestle supported local communities, such as Nestle in USA donated more than $2.3 million dollars to support local United Way organizations; It also provided disaster relief, such as Nestle waters donated more than 685,000 bottled of water and Nestle Purina contributed more than 60,000 pounds of pet food and 41,000 pounds of cat little to local shelters across the USA for disaster relief as well as it grew supplier diversity, such as Nestle works with over 4,100 small, minority, women and veteran owned businesses to help to spur local economies. It seemed that Nestle also considerate social needs. Thus, it is seemed Nestle company have managed to sustainable reconcile these two aims to pursuit profit as well as it also could gave positive influence to its stakeholders. Such as consumer could feel safe to enjoy to eat Nestle company's health foods; societies could be reduced unemployment from its outsourced assistance job to partners; natural environment could be reduced pollution from its productive protection. Hence, it was not actually neglect its shareholders' benefits during it was doing business as the same time (Adrian, P. 2012).

What are basic lessons in marketing that the Body Shop might have taken on board in its early years in order to improve its chances of long term success?

The body shop is a global manufacturer and retailer of naturally inspired , ethically produced beauty and cosmetics products. Founded in the UK in 1976 year by Dame Anita Roddick, who now have 2,133 stores in 55 countries with a range of over 1,200 products in Europe, America, Middle East, Asia and Africa. However, the body shop has not entered the China market. It takes a strong position on activism, ethical business, human rights and environmentalism in a global perspective. The body shop is banned in China because cosmetics sold there have to be tested on animals, according to Roddick. In, 2006 when it was bought by the French cosmetics company L'Oreal which is a big player in China. China has launched scientific developing strategy for future the current policies of advocating. Hence, it is the perfect time for the body shop to enter China market. However, prior to that, as an independent member of the L'Oreal family, the body shop has to make decisions on differentiation marketing strategies, market segmentation and marketing position (Adrian, P. 2012). It might have taken two purposes to body shop marketing in its early years in order to improve its chances from short term to long term success. The short term objective was to generate more sales for the body shop. Through, the introduction of a new service, the market up class, it was hoped that clients could try and experience the body shop cosmetic products. Positive experience of using its products could then be developed through their trial using the market up class. It was estimated that this positive experience could push up the sales.

The long term objective was to educate the belief of the body shop to the young potential clients, so that who would become those who preferred natural cosmetic products and were loyal to the body shop in the future. Objectives could provide the starting point for marketing plans and strategies and should be specific targets that are obtained but also challenging. Specific, measurable, agreed, realistic and time related objectives might be taken to body shop to improve early years in chances in long term success. It seemed that Hong Kong was one good market for body shop to satisfy an unfulfilled customers needs to pursue body shop investment chance. Therefore, the objective were to push up sales and built a loyal customer basis for the future. For example, Hong Kong was one young student clients growth market to body shop. In the past, one cosmetic products market statistic was indicated that the colour cosmetic retail value had been increasing from 2002 year, HK$938.3 million dollars to 2007 year, HK$1,132,3 million dollars, so percentage was increased to 5.12% . (Adrian, P. 2012).

It seemed Hong Kong might be one good skin cosmetic care products developed market to this body shop in early years. The another factor might improve body shop long term success factor was whether body shop had attempted to analyze direct competition. The body shop's direct competition was not from the name brand like Dior, Chanel or Olay, but rather the less well known brands, from Japan or Korea. Along with the great impact of Korean fashion, many Korean cosmetics brands like Missha and the Face shop had already established shops in China. These two brands also promoted their natural ingredients and target the young customer segment as what the body shop products competition concept could be offered to a market to satisfy a want or need and offered five levels, which were the core benefits, basic product, expected product, augmented product and potential product.

Each level added more customer value and the five constitute client value hierarchy products of these three brands were all using natural ingredients and simple and natural in packaging. (Experiment result) The body shop , however, differentiated itself at the top levels of the five product and transformations the products might undergo in the future.

Marketing management and planning was essential to body shop, it was the implementation of strategies to achieve long run profitability to body shop and growth. When body shop was looking at how it would achieve this in early years in order to improve the chances long term success, its two keys points to consider are: What was body shop man activity at a particular time? And how it would reach its goals? It might design a strategy that insured a consistent approach to offer its skin care products to raise competition in mind the skin care products changing market. These included product line, distribution methods, marketing communication and pricing. For example, achieving marketing research to Hong Kong and China skin care products market to analyze what were these factors to influence these country people who felt needs to buy its skin care products: Such as internal factors include personality, motivation, learning, perception and attitude; external factors included culture, social class, reference groups , family and personal influences and situational factors included time, income, mobility and availability. The reason was because due to consumers bought skin care products to protect whose skin (core benefits) and their expectations if who were willing to pay more basic product. To enhance the product level, body shop skin health product needed emphasize that skin products were natural. Products of the body shop offered the same effective and natural and flavor and unique corporate values. Body shop was mostly natural (augmented level). Far more than the visible products, the shop shop's unique corporate values create the potential value to fulfil customer's desire of making a better health world. It's good corporate desire citizenship went beyond supplying rational and emotional benefits. Body shop might enter China market to improve long term success. The body shop divided its markets to include overseas Pacific Europe, America , Australia and New Zealand, Middle East, Africa and local UK countries. Adrian, P.(2012) indicated that a sampling questionnaire survey was conducted among 200 consumers, ranging from 18 to 50 ages in May 2006, a total of 170 valid responses that were used for analysis. Among the 170 responses, 66% were females. The findings were:

(1) About 60 % hoped that cosmetics could be a symbol of being environmental friendly.

(2) 90% would choose products made of natural ingredients.

(3) 90% spent less than 300 RMB on cosmetics and skin care products quarterly.

(4) 83% Chinese youth (age range from 18 to 25 ages) were innovators and conscious of environment.

Hence, the body shop might take a share of potential market in China. It should launch its products among younger cosmetic industry were young females who chased beauty and were willing to spend money on it. So, packaging was one of the vital factors in attracting client. The body shop took a unique approach by choosing simple packaging. The package was not made for mature women. It was made for young female students, who could enjoy on international brand at an inexpensive cost. The body shop was not only to meet young people's demand for beauty , but the demand of being responsible to environment and human rights. Hence, the target market of the body shop should focus on young people ageing from 15 ages to 30 ages. Hence, body shop might take marketing research in Hong Kong and China market to have more confident to invest in these market to improve more success. Next, Whether body shop might achieve price strategy to improve to raise success chance. An assumption is when the individual client is considering the price of any a body shop's beauty skin health product. Economic theory suggests that the customer will act in a totally rational economic manner, such that body shop's every client total utility (or satisfaction) is maximized. In deciding whether try or not try body shop's product, which totally rational consumer will carefully equate whether ought to buy or ought not buy body shop's product at the asking price set will maximizing whose utility. In making judgment, the economist assumes that the consumer has perfect information about both the prices and utility of all the other competitive products in the market and that price is the only consideration in choice. Clearly there are unrealistic assumptions. Price could be determined easily when a target market was identified. (Adrian, P. 2012)

Survey predicts consumer behavior: From survey indicated 64% of the 170 responses spent less than 1000 RMB on cosmetics and skin care every quarter and 24% of their expenditure was between 100 RMB and 300 RMB on cosmetics an skin care. This number could not be ignored if a cosmetics company wanted to enter this large market and be a leader. For the younger generation, the prices of the products could not be high. The price of these main competitors ranges from 10RMB to 200 RMB. The prices in Hong Kong have higher than that in the USA or the UK. And the consumer's purchasing power in mainland China is much lower than that of Hong Kong . Hence, body shop should adopt a price range in China which was similar to that of the USA or the UK rather than of Hong Kong. Once the body shop established greatly reduced and the capability of price adjustment would be achieved accordingly.

Further, body shop might have chain stores selling channel strategy to attempt to achieve long term success. Sample survey revealed that supermarket was for Chinese to purchase skin care and cosmetics. 120 out of the 170 responses hoped that who could choose products from the chain stores in the future, which suggested that the body shop should build up its own stores was regarded as cares about corporate culture and corporate image. It insisted on selling in its own stores rather than setting up counters in a shopping mall.

The stores of body shop could be found easily worldwide because of stores were importance in this competitive buyer. Hence, in China, its appearance should be same as worldwide. Some housewives joined the body shop as sales agent and hold sales parties for other housewives. The sales channel allowed the body shop to reach out to more clients by bringing the store directly into client's homes. This would be a totally new method of marketing in China, but it offered a good opportunity for women to choose products and share feedback in a relaxed atmosphere. This fresh concept could attract female consumers. Nowadays, students in China could only obtain famous skin care products and cosmetics brands from campus agents, as who could not afford the products sold over the counters. It was a major problem that agents could not guarantee the ingredients and the quality of the goods. If the body shop could hold small parties to share products and opinions, that would be a good way to boost sales among students. Hence, body shop might take price strategy to Hong Kong and china market to predict whether what price who could accept to raise more confident to invest to this market to improve more success. Further, body shop might also have promotion strategy to attempt to achieve long term success. The body shop adopted environmental friendly manufacturing, opposed abuses of human rights and was accountable for its actions. The unique values attracted numbers of media groups in many countries. This results in its establishing a good reputation without any advertisements. The body shop also joined numerous social causes, which substitute advertisements. In China, however, it was totally different. In this brand new market, most people were out aware of this company. If it carried on a marketing promotion of no commercials it was impossible to reach a high market share. Hence, commercial advertisements were needed in China. The body shop could use this advertisement to give on impression that women should care about their well being both mentally and physically and it had created a sexy grand with simple packaging and without objectifying women. Many brands reach customers directly by colorful commercials and show their products in movies and TV play series. For the sakes of brand image, some movies about human rights , environmental protection and animal protection could be chosen by the body shop as carriers for particular commercial as most of the audiences were well educated, well paid and environmentally concerned. The target consumers of the body shop aged from 20 to 40 ages were energetic , knowledgeable and environmentally concerned. The body shop could give some lectures on makeup or skin care on campuses to raise feeling among students. To reach brand awareness and high brand loyalty , some samples should be given to students by experience marketing approach. Hence, body shop might take promotion to Hong Kong and China schools to let many young people to know why who needed to buy skin care products to protect their body skin to persuade who felt more needs. In conclusion, the body shop was famous for creating a niche market sector for naturally inspired skin care and cosmetic products through it's unique corporate values worldwide. The significance of the body shop's early entry into China market were strongly proposed. Once the body shop decided to enter the China market, the relevant marketing strategies and management should be implemented, such as the market segmentation and market positioning with the proper consideration of Chinese consumers should be studied in order to win the mind share of potential Chinese customers with the right marketing strategies. Overall, the findings of market survey and theoretical analysis strategy support the feasibility of the body shop's early entry into China market.

Case study change in the marketing environment on sales of ready meals to supermarket, such as Walt Mark-applying consumer segment concept to predict consumer behavior

Using an appropriate framework of analysis, briefly summarize the effects of change in the marketing environment on sales of ready meals.

Although, previously dismissed and a poor substitute for real cooking and ready meal sales have grown rapidly in recent years in many western developed countries, such as UK, France or Germany. But, Ready meal manufacturers ready to respond to a changing marketing environment. Due to one big change in recent year has been growing demand for ready prepared meals bought from a supermarket. An analysis of the reasons for the growth in the ready prepared meals markets indicates the effects of boards factors in the marketing environment on the size of a particular market. In fact, this food market is changing to drive the growth in the ready meals market, but there are differences in the food market potential between countries. The effect of change in the marketing environment on sales of ready meals, such as technology has played a big role in the growing take up of ready meals and new technologies have allowed companies to develop ready meals which preserve taste and texture, which still making them easy to use by the consumer. Furthermore, great advances in distribution management, in particular the use of information technology to control inventories, has allowed fresh, chilled ready meals to be effectively and efficiently distributed without the need for freezing or added preservatives. Ready meals particularly appeal to single householders, which individual family members tend to eat at different times, so family meals together remains stronger in many continental European countries than in the UK individual ready meals. Young people have lost the ability to cook creatively, as cookery has been reduced in importance in the school, so young clients group will rise to buy ready meals from supermarket. Marketing can be seen as a system that must respond to environmental change.

A food market can be defined as a meeting place for stakeholder (consumers) and sellers. Food market can be set up in a supermarket or restaurants. A food market consists of the individual's target taste, such as older group, family group, young group or business clients who are actual or potential caters of a restaurant meals or supermarket package of foods. Grocery stores (supermarkets) have an influence of meals (fast cooked food) outlets in low income urban areas, which has contributed to the income in access to healthy foods. An organization's marketing environment means the individuals, organizations, and forces external to the marketing management's ability to develop and maintain successful exchanges with its customers.

The marketing environment to ready meal manufacturers had three levels. (marketing segment predicts consumer behavior)

Firstly, it includes the micro environment, it describes those elements that impinge directly on the ready meal manufacturers themselves, so the micro environment of ready meal manufacturers which include business clients who have direct contact, such as restaurants, supermarkets and individual clients who have direct contact. Otherwise, supermarket shoppers, restaurant clients and food supply competitors who have no direct contract to ready meal manufacturers, so who won't include in food market micro environment to ready meal manufacturers.

Secondly, it includes the macro environment, it describes things that are beyond the immediate environment but can nevertheless affect an organization, so the macro environment of ready meal manufacturers which include the export countries' economies forces, such as unemployment ratio, GDP; technological forces, such as the export countries' factories food productive technology; social/ cultural forces, such as the export countries' people taste acceptance; political/legal forces, such as the export countries' import food quota numbers. Thirdly, it includes the internal environment, it describes ready meal manufacturers' employees and equipment and finance and functional responsibilities. Environment means everything outside influences the person, in contrast with individual or personal variables . The effects of change in the marketing environment on sales of ready meals can be analyzed by creating healthy food and eating environment changing factor and supermarket technological changing factor as below:

The ready meal manufacturers could not ignore threats to the natural ecological environment change Due to the food companies could have technology to manufacture good taste cooked ready meals to provide to supermarkets to sell. Thus, it might influence the consumers to decide whether restaurants or supermarkets or ready meals suppliers who could provide the most reasonable price and taste to satisfy whose eating needs every day. Thus, it caused the growing demand for ready prepared cooked meals bought from supermarkets. Due to it was possible that consumers felt to eat ready cooked meals in expensive restaurants or who did not like to buy foods to cook from food suppliers or who could not feel which could supply more good food taste and health food quality to compare supermarkets specially. Otherwise, although, supermarkets could provide cheaper ready cooked meals to satisfy who to feel good food taste and health food quality. Due to ready meal manufacturers had new techniques to develop ready meals which preserve taste and texture, which still making them easy to use to eat by the consumers. (consumer behavior prediction result)

Furthermore, great advances in distribution management, in particular the use of information technology to control inventories, has allowed fresh , chilled ready meals to be effectively and efficiently distributed to supermarkets or restaurants without the need for freezing or added preservatives. Creating healthy food and eating environments view describes an ecological framework for conceptualizing the many food environments and conditions that influence food choices, with an emphasis on current knowledge was been regarding the home, child care, school, work site, retail store and restaurant settings. The status of measurement and evaluation of nutrition environment and the need of action to improve health are highlighted in marketing environment. More processed and convenience foods are available in large portion sizes and which were supplied at relatively low prices at supermarkets. Parents are working larger hours, there are fewer family meals and more meals are eaten away from home. The school food environment is remarkably different. It seemed that it would be changed in the marketing environment on sales of ready cooked meals to supermarket more easily. Due to supermarkets' cooked meals should focus on selling high calorie and low nutrition foods are available in multiple venues throughout the school student client group target because it was possible that supermarkets could sell ready cooked ready meals prices were more cheaper to compare to restaurants or school canters' cooked meals provided prices.

The effects of change in the marketing environment on sales of ready meals which indicated that consumers chose prefer to buy ready cooked meals from supermarkets. It seemed that a restaurant market failure could be caused to arise. For example, there was poor information on the part of food (ready cooked meals) to provide to the restaurant about the foods that consumers in a location(place) would demand for a given price to compare to the supermarket sale prices. The restaurant would lose clients if which cooked the kind of meals to sell higher price to compare to the supermarket sale of the kind of cooked ready meals price possibly. Large size supermarkets could sell cheaper ready cooked meals to low income group clients. It could cause competition to constitute a market failure to small size supermarkets. If the small size supermarkets lacked good information on the true food (ready cooked meals) with concentrations to sell cheaper prices, then this ready cooked meal market failure was one potential reason why small size supermarkets did not locate to close to the large supermarkets. Due to supermarkets grew in size would influence clients' choice to buy the numbers of cooked foods (ready meals) products. Moreover, The advent of computerized logistics and inventory systems were integrated with the large size supermarkets themselves occurred between the 1980 years and 1990 years .

So large size supermarkets were reliance on their own distribution and cooked food (ready meals) inventory systems along with larger supermarket sizes to allow super center to change to sell ready cooked meals at lower prices. Supermarkets marketing can promote healthful eating by increasing availability, affordability or restricting / de-marketing unhealthy foods to sell cooked Food (ready meals) marketing strategy at supermarkets, including labelling, packaging, pricing and point of sale advertising. Consumers' cost saving efforts and income and ready cooked meals prices increasing or decreasing factors can drive the choice of supermarkets as well as cooked meal products use of coupons and loyalty cards bargain shopping is another factor to influence their choice. Private label or store (supermarket) brands are taking an increasing share of consumers shopping dollars as the importance of brands. Supermarket shoppers stated priorities are cooked food (ready meals) quality or taste and price and healthy cooked food (ready meals) choices. However, supermarket shoppers' buying behaviors don't always reflect on favor healthful foods. Due to demand for locally grown cooked food is increasing. Anyway, restaurant meals are changed to supermarket to sell, which decide what kinds of meals to stock and how many of different kinds of meals to stock and how much variety of kinds of meals to offer to any one supermarket as well as supermarket shoppers prefer fewer options, provided that their preferred brand or cooked food (ready meals) products are available. The designs of supermarket ready cooked meal products and packaging to supermarket to sell is the focus of unusual colors or shape which can be used to increase interest and is specially pervasive among fun foods to compare to restaurant meals. Package design, including where text and images are placed, which can influences cooked foods (supermarket ready meals repurchasing again).The influence of design differs by the type of display consumer segments seek (convenience, information or images) and ready cooked meals package sizes have a relatively strong influence on consumption; larger ready cooked meals packages might increase per-use consumption ,but smaller packages might not improve self regulation and might not actually increase total consumption. In conclusion, I suggest that this ready meal manufacturers need to give more attention to be paid to food sellers, such as supermarkets' competitive differentiation and understanding the way in which customers attribute value to its ready meal products choice. Moreover, many consumers have become increasingly concerned about the health implication of the food they eat, so ready meal manufacturers will need to continue responding to such concerns. For example, who have responded with a range of low calorie meals, and addressed specific, sometimes transient, health fads, with respect to trans-fatty acids and omega 3 supplements of these cooked meal ingredients. Many consumers have also become concerned about the ecological environment and some supermarket suppliers, such as Marks and Spencer have incorporated sustainability agendas into their ready meals, for example by reducing packaging and sourcing supplies from sustainable sources. Thus, it caused ready meal manufacturers why who needed to give more attention to concern how supermarkets helped them to sell cooked ready meals in this foods market.

Critically discuss the link between the economic environment and sales of ready meals in supermarket

How economic environment influences consumer behavior to ready meals choice : The macro environment, it describes things that are beyond the immediate environment but can nevertheless affect the organization. Such as the ready meal manufacturers in its macro environment, including the economic environment which can cause the manufacturers sell ready meal numbers whether which can sell more or less to different exported countries due to the exported countries' unemployment ratios, GDP and Government policies etc factors influence. Economic theory can help to explain why it can influence consumer behavior. In food sale market, it can include consumer behavior and demand side as well as retailer behavior and supply side two issues. Consumer behavior and demand side issue, such as the exported countries' consumer whose knowledge of the nutritional benefits of foods whether which prices were raised to choose to buy reasonably as well as retailer behavior and supply side issues, such as investing for developing a restaurant or supermarket in an underserved area whether the types of meals choices which are valued or which are not valued to buy to offer to clients from imports. On the other hand, economic environment factor, individual income can influence who chooses the type, quantity and quality of food that is purchased for a house holder and it also influenced the cooking and storage facilities available in a household to influence food choice.

On the other way, economic environment variation factor can also influence food access across areas. It is important to understand the economic conditions that may contribute to food deserts, that is the costs that food retail businesses face and the choice available to consumers who want to buy foods. Economic environment factor considers the consumer and demand factors, business and supply factors and the market conditions that interact to create differences in the food retail environment across areas and subpopulations. In general, high income meal client group can accept to choose to go to supermarkets or restaurants to spend than low income meal client group. The impact of the economic environment on sales of ready meals is such as an individual get richer, who can afford to buy ready prepared foods, rather than spend time and effort to prepare to cook them at home. It seemed that low income consumers were decreasing to eat meals at expensive restaurant to the alternative of relatively cheap ready prepared meals at home. Research could also consider how consumer knowledge and preferences and the time cost tradeoffs affect consumer decisions of which foods to eat and whether to make or to buy prepared foods from supermarkets or to eat at restaurant meals . Travel costs and time costs of acquiring foods as well as the time costs of preparing foods (meals) are also likely to affect demand for particular foods. Research on price variation at the local level and demand models could also be used to help determine which factors contribute to differences in access to food retailers. Price is also major determinant of food (meal) demand. The higher, the price of a food(meal), the lower the meal quantity demanded. On the other hand, the higher the price of a substitute food (meal), the higher demand will be for that food (meal) item. Given the budget constraints of low income consumers and the price of some specific foods (meals), low income consumers may substitute higher priced foods (meals) with lower priced foods(e.g. hamburger for steak or canned fruits for fresh fruits). Considering restaurants foods purchasing choice, such as economies of scale, which is when the costs of operating a restaurant decreases as restaurant size increases and economies of scope, which is when the costs decrease as more meals variety increases, suggests that larger restaurants that offer greater variety can offer lower meal prices. Both factors may account for the ability of larger restaurants to survive more easily than smaller restaurants. Considering supermarkets foods purchasing choice, it is possible that food retailers (supermarkets) actually have some market power, especially in setting where there are few competitors to close. It would have an incentive to increase food (ready meal) price and restrict foods(ready meals) supply quantities to increase profit. Supply side conditions, such as economies of scale, it could lead to (ready meal) food retailers (supermarkets) to have more market power, if it was not close between supermarkets. Individual behavior to make healthy choices can occur only in a supportive economic environment with accessible and affordable healthy food choices. Hence, food environment and sale strategies is needed to consider to adopt the exported countries' economic change.

Food marketing client target groups can include home parents, students and working people groups mainly and marketing and economic environment factors would cause food choices and these factors impact health and nutrition and the focus on the connections between people and their environments. In conclusion, macro level economic environmental factors play a more indirect role but have a substantial and powerful effect on what people eat. Macro level factors operate within the larger society, include food marketing, social norms, food production and distribution systems, agriculture policies and economic price structures as well as social environmental to influence within the home, such as model of healthful dietary intake by parents feeding style, frequent family meals may promote healthful food consumption among children.

Discuss the factors that might affect sales of ready meals in your country over the next five years.

Hong Kong people can choose to go to restaurants to eat or go to supermarkets to buy foods to cook to eat. Although, ready meal manufacturers had increased the sale numbersof the ready prepared meals in many western countries in recent years. However, there still had any factors to limit it's sale numbers to Hong Kong market over the next five years, so it needed to aware of what was changing in Hong Kong food market environment and appreciated how change in this Hong Kong food environment to lead to change patterns of eating cooked ready meals demand to attempt to win its similar food competitors in Hong Kong market next five years. Hong Kong food environment related to Hong Kong people eating behaviors, include social environments and physical environments and macro level environment. The cooked meal quality and quantity of available can influence food numbers to produce meal to supply to Hong Kong food market. Hence, Hong Kong natural climatic change can influence the overseas food supply numbers to be imported to cause meals prices to go up or go down. If next five years, Hong Kong climate was good to grow plants and feed animals e.g. pigs and cows etc. meats. The restaurant meals or supermarket meals sale prices can be cheaper due to farmers who have much foods and vegetables to supply , so who can sell cheaper price to these restaurants or supermarkets to cause whose production cost to be decreased next five years in my country. Hence, ready meals prices could not sell more higher than Hong Kong meals prices. Hong Kong people eating behaviors are often changed over a lifetime. In general, Hong Kong people want to eat to satisfy physical hunger and psychological desires and yet want to be healthy, which may enquire adopting eating patterns that conflict with these desires. My country people make decisions about food several times a day: when to eat, what to eat, with where to eat and how much per meal prices and how much per meal numbers . In general, Hong Kong people like to eat Chinese foods , but who also like to go to restaurants to eat or supermarkets to buy western foods, such as liking of specific tastes are important influences. However, these can be modified by experience with food from various intrapersonal and interpersonal factors to influence Hong Kong people to choose to buy uncooked or cooked meals from Hong Kong supermarkets. The next five year, food retailer behavior and supply factors of food access might affect overseas sales of ready meals numbers imported to my country. In general, supply is driven by the costs of input foods. The land, materials, machines and labor costs are needed to build and operate a restaurant or supermarkets. If these costs are increased to these food suppliers in my county next five years, overseas food demand shall be caused to be decreased if Hong Kong economy had changed to be worse and the new restaurants and supermarkets which costs were changed to be higher to much as well as Hong Kong unemployment was caused to be raised and many people lost jobs to have efforts to go to supermarkets to buy higher prices ready meals or go to restaurants to eat higher price ready meals.

How HK social environment and physical environment influence consumer behavior: My country's social environment and physical environment which also might affect sales of ready meals numbers next five years. Social environment includes interactions, with family, friends, peers and others in the community to impact food choices through mechanisms as well as physical environment includes the different places where people eat or buy food, such as whether the supermarkets or restaurants locations which are close to the buyers, e.g. schools, offices, houses. Hence, food suppliers' locations choice can influence who (target client groups) choose to buy more or less ready meals numbers. Foods prepared at home factor there may be relatively greater time costs than those to buy cooked foods(ready meals) from supermarkets or takeout foods. Hong Kong consumers may value the convenience of a fast food or takeout cooked meal more because it doesn't require spending much time to prepare to cook at home. Hence, Hong Kong people whose taste is for different kind of cooked foods (ready meals) and who feel the food suppliers' locations whether are convenient and Hong Kong economy whether is better or worse to cause unemployment numbers next five years, these factors can affect sales of imported ready cooked or uncooked meal numbers to my country Hong Kong next five year.

Case study of Ryanair airline-applying environment protection psychology to predict consumer behavior

If you are the marketing manager of an airline, such as Ryanair, how would you address the ecological concerns?

In recent years, social, economic and environment pressures have pushed airlines to accept their social responsibility. Closely tied to this acceptance is a corporate policy that aims at raising social and environmental standards on a voluntary basis and that means beyond legal and contractual requirement. It means that corporate social responsibility is not just an optional consideration to core airline business activities, such as airlines industry fuel consumption pollutes sky air to cause global warming problem. Rather, Ryanair airline needs to concern social responsibility because it's fuel emissions would cause negative influence to stakeholders. e.g. causing bad negative climate to influence farmers to grow rice and vegetables etc foods successfully, so global warming will make farmers stakeholder can not earn more income and food buyers stakeholder won't eat rice and vegetables etc. foods easily, even global warming will damage natural environment to cause strong wind or strong raining or water natural hazard to damage any countries' houses to make house owners stakeholder who lose their houses to live. Hence, in the long term, if Ryanair airline still continue consume too much fuels to use to fly to cause emissions to pollute air to any countries as well as other airlines do not achieve any actions to reduce to consume to use more fuels together efficiently. I believe that global warming will become very serious to influence human living and eating problem occurrence in our earth as soon as possibly. Hence, such as Ryanair airline is among of global airlines, which have responsibility to consider how to reduce fuel consumption to cause too much emissions to pollute air in our earth. Such as, I was Ryanair airline marketing manager , I ought need to let Ryanair airline to measure whether it ought only concern how to sell cheaper air fares and buy many airplanes and consume much fuels to fly to raise income or it ought concern it's fuel emissions to pollute environment to cause global warming to influence global human stakeholders encounter living and eating problem to face natural foods resource shortage to supply in the future.

The ecological concerns global warming problem is serious nowadays, it brings the possible long term harmful consequences of executive emissions to the atmosphere. The developed countries, such as Northern Europe and United States people needed often to play travel entertainment by airlines transportation choice. However, scientists proved airlines used fossil fuels to harm excessive emissions to natural environment which would cause global warming problem to cause devastation of low lying areas to influence natural environment danger, even the developing countries people life and their houses would also encountered to be hazarded in the long term. If I was the marketing manager of an airline, such as Ryanair, I must concern socially responsible needs to Ryanair airline. Although, Ryanair aircraft had become more efficient in use of fuel during 1990 years, but Ryanair airline's passengers were booming demand to cause to increase aeroplane numbers to supply to satisfy passengers' travel needs and to pursue raising profit aim every year.

How ecological concern can influence travel consumption behavior: In fact, Ryanair airline used fuels to give energy to push aeroplanes to fly and it also polluted sky air during it's aeroplanes often were flying to cause global warming. For example, Ryanair airline marketing strategy was low fare prices to attract to increase many passengers to choose to attract to increase many passengers to choose to sit it's aeroplanes and it designed a cheap weekend break by Mediterranean travel to increase the unknown and remote possibilities of global warming. Hence, Ryanair would increased many new airplanes to increase to use fossil fuels of excessive emissions to the atmosphere to cause the effects of aid rain, poor climate change , destructive winds, rising sea levels and devastation of low lying areas by global warming bad consequences. Hence, it seemed that Ryanair airline had responsibility to concern how to protect natural environment due to its airplanes numbers and passengers were increasing to cause to increase to use more fossil fuels to cause the possible long term harmful consequences of excessive emissions to the sky to bring global warming occurrence nowadays. As I was this Ryanair airline marketing manager, I shall recommend Ryanair airline needed to consider this global warming socially responsible issue due to its airplanes spent too much fossil fuels to cause harmful consequences of excessive emissions to the sky. It would bring threats to developing countries people life and houses by global warming, so it concerned only how to raise itself interest marketing behavior of performance, but it neglect the serious global warming to cause bad influence to any developing countries people life danger, it was possible that passengers would feel it was not a socially responsible airline company, so it could not build a good image to whom in this airline industry and its further passengers would choose its other competitors (socially responsible airline companies) to substitute its airline service provision.

Discussion

I should suggest Ryanair airline needed to control fossil fuel numbers to reduce to harm excessive emissions to natural environment seriously and it could spend much expenditure to buy good quality of fossil fuels to active the reduction of too much emissions to damage natural environment aim and it could shorten the sky flying distance to fly to other countries' airports from its airport to aim to attempt to reduce to use much fuel to pollute sky air per day and it could cancel some long flight flying routes and increased short flight flying routes to reduce flight spending hours to attempt to reduce to use fossil fuels to provide every airplanes to fly to pollute sky air every day.

Although, these marketing strategies would be possible to reduce airline income, but it would also attract many further passengers to choose to sit to its airplanes to go to travel if it could build good image to prove it was a socially responsible airline to serve passengers to let them to like to choose to use its flying service to go to travel willingly, even it could lead other airlines to follow it to use its marketing strategic methods to reduce to spend too much fossil fuels to pollute sky air to raise global warming problem seriously together. Hence, if Ryanair airline could attempt to achieve to reduce the fossil fuel numbers to use to airplanes to fly , it was possible that the other airline companies should follow it to do the same behaviors to aim to do social responsible organizations to concern how to reduce the global warming problem to cause to harm to our natural environment seriously for long term in the future.

The case study refers to apparent hypocrisy of clients who may claim to be concerned about the environment, but nevertheless continue to fly what might bring about a narrowing of this gap between what consumers think and what they actually do?

In fact, some apparent hypocrisy of consumers who may claim to be concerned about the global warming harmful natural environment problem due to airline companies, e.g. Easy Jet,
Ryanair etc. western countries' airlines which allowed fossil fuels produced harmful consequences of excessive emissions to atmosphere, but nevertheless continue to fly. However, I might recommend these methods to bring about a narrowing of this gap between what consumers think and what they actually do.
I think to bring a narrowing of this gap between consumers were happy to carry on airplanes to fly and it would not influence them to concern about climate change problem at the same time.

There was certainly a possible that governments would intervene. Such as the UK government and European commission had floated the idea of taxing aviation fuel and brought aircraft emissions within scope of the European emission trading scheme. Thus, if these western countries governments raised to charge aviation fuel taxing, it would possible to threaten any western airlines to shorten any flight routes hours and flight flying distance to fly to destination of the countries' airports from these airline companies' every country's airport, so which would not need to use more fuels for its airplanes to use if it had shorten flight flying routes distance to arrive other countries' airports. Hence, the airlines did not want to pay higher aviation tax to government, so which would attempt to shorten some flight flying routes from long distance to be short distance when their airplanes needed to fly to some other countries' airport to aim to buy less fuel numbers or which would not buy more airplanes.

Due to they needed to pay high aviation tax expenditure to their countries governments every year. Thus, it was possible that high fuel tax expenditure would cause airlines to shorten flight routes time. The most important, when some airlines decided to buy less fuels. These airlines might bring about a narrowing of this gap between what consumers think and what they actually do and these airlines were possible to raise their competitive ability, due to which would possible to persuade the concerned environment protective passengers who would choose to buy these airlines air tickets to more than to buy the other airlines' air tickets. Due to some airlines could not reduce to buy more fuel numbers to provide their airplanes to fly and which would increase air pollution to sky seriously, those airlines' spending excessive long hours (time) of every flight flying routes to fly to different countries' airports which would use more fuel to fly to cause air pollution to harm natural environment seriously and which would let these clients to feel unhappy to choose to buy air tickets to sit their airplanes possibly. Hence, different governments raised aviation tax would cause many airlines to reduce to buy too much fuel numbers to use possibly. It seemed that airlines needed have a social responsible duty to concern they needed to buy more fuels if they increased airplanes numbers, then they would raise air pollution to cause global warming problem seriously. Hence, I think passengers would not buy air tickets to fly to travel by airplanes when who would have long days of holidays. Otherwise, who would choose to stay at home or who would choose to go to travel by cruises on water transportation on their holidays. However, in western developed economies, legislation to enforce environmentally sensitive methods of productive is increasing, so airlines might adopt environmentally sensitive flight service processes to gain a competitive advantages. The challenges of using fuels resources in more efficient and less polluting way has achieved research and development, e.g. wind power research, solar panels, heat pumps and carbon capture technology have presented opportunities for airlines to improve the efficiency of fuels and airline marketing to business and individual group passengers.

Legal actions to place control over the emission of air pollutants have been instituted in several ways, such as the form of a public nuisance low. This is when conditions cause discomfort, inconvenience, damage to property or injury from airlines fuels to cause air pollution. The governments have also intervened in the protection of the public to threaten the airlines' fuels emissions pollute air in the sky. As a result of much research, devices for pollution control have been developed, guidelines for air quality were established fuels tax increasing incentives were introduced to enforce ordinances for restricting the emission from airplanes' fuels. For example, governments can pass the clean air act, legislation to reduce air pollution in their countries. In conclusion, airlines can co-operate environmentally friendly management to prevent global warming, it is as a part of its corporate social responsibility and makes company wide efforts to do by saving energy and reducing aircraft fuel emissions. Hence, global airlines ought plan to achieve to reduce to consume excessive fuel emissions to reduce a narrowing of this gap between what consumers think and what they actually do concerned about the environment pollution was caused by airlines if which still wanted to make travelers who prefer to choose to go to travel by flying more than other water or ground transportation etc. methods.

How would a company , such as Easy Jet airline measure and monitor consumer's attitudes?

Easy Jet airline has created environment problems, e.g. harmful chemicals sift down from smoky trails of low-flying jets. The scream of Easy Jet airline engines is constantly heard by people who love near big city airports. It's aircrafts produce air pollution with consequent changes in climate.

It is a fact that many people prefer air travel rather than ground or water transportation, This has promoted a critical look at safety and quality control. Contributions to air pollution is a chief concern because of this revolutionary change in public transportation in the United States and around the world. The government must also establish standards for exhaust emissions. Thus, Easy Jet airline measure and monitor consumer's attitudes which needs to indicate to let them to believe that which suggests which airplane manufacturers are forced to develop low pollutant engines. Due to the problem of air pollution from its airplanes involve a complex set of interactions among technical, social and economic factors. Hence, it also needs to measure it's emission from Easy Jet aircrafts, particularly on landing and take offs, are a source of bitter complaints from nearby residents. In a few airports visibility has been dangerously restricted by particulate emissions and photo chemical smog. Easy Jet airline also needed to have energy savings activities to its operations, ranging from procedural and flight plan improvement to reduce flight distance and attitude and weight management and it also needed to create energy through maintenance to achieve to continue to reduce co2 emissions by introducing high efficiency aircraft and through other measures to monitor consumers' attitudes . In line with its aim to be an environmentally friendly airline that harmonizes the needs of natural , humans and airline businesses. It aims to be respected by society , live up to its social responsibilities and make a contribution to society. Although emissions from aircraft are not included among greenhouse gas reduction targets, but it also needed to make systematic efforts to improve energy efficiency and reduce emissions by creating a road map to actively participate . Furthermore, Easy Jet airline also needed continually to pursue a management style that concerns nature, people and fellow corporations, even under the most severe conditions as a major practice toward implementing its environmental policy. Easy jet airline achieves environment goals to measure and monitor consumer's attitudes, such as minimizes energy and resource consumption and introduces up to date and fuel efficient fleet and engines and develops and apply energy efficient operation technique, it establish strict internal environmental standards to set internal standards that are stricter than general environment laws applied worldwide and minimize pollutants through systematic management and observance of standards. It systematically analyses the airlines' environmental impact and make the outcome to carry out reductions and evaluates the environmental impact of its aviation operations, maintenance and service and improves environmentally friendly processes and it continually improves environmental systems through feedback .

In conclusion, Easy Jet airline can increase the recycling of waste to reduce fuel consumption of resources and it can make systematic efforts to reduce emissions by creating a roadmap and actively participating in global warming by saving energy and reducing aircraft emissions through engine washing to aim to consume fuels efficiency and reduce emission to pollute air.

What might be the consequences for the marketing of a budget airline of Government policy measures which have the effect of doubling air fares in real terms?

How flight fuel tax policy influences travel consumption behavior: If the country Government decided to raise higher flight fuel tax charge policy to budget airline. Due to the country Government hoped budget airline to reduce fuels consumption to provide to airplanes to use to reduce sky air pollution to cause global warning problem. In fact, budget airline needed to increase to use much fuels to provide to many flights to carry on passengers travel needs. Generally, budget airline would not like to choose to reduce to consume much fuels due to it's passenger numbers had been increasing. If budget airline decided to buy less fuels to reduce much fuels to consume for its flight needs. It would lose many passengers if it had not enough times of flights to provide airplanes to fly to different countries' airports to satisfy passengers' different flight route choices. However, the consequences for budget airline would also be passengers to choose to buy budget airline air tickets possibly if it decided to raise doubling air fares in real terms. Due to budget airline hoped to compensate its loss if it's country Government raised higher fuels tax to cause budget airline needed to pay high cost expenditure every year. Hence, budget airline needed to raise to spend two kinds of expenditure every year, such as purchasing more fuels expenditure and paying more fuels expenditure both. For long term, budget airline would choose to raise doubling or more air fairs in real terms in order to reduce to need to pay too much feel tax expenditure to compensate it's loss every year. In result, it's passengers would feel it's air tickets fares were not reasonable raised to compare it's other airline competitors, but it's flight services were not excellent to compare it's airline competitors specially. Hence, it's increasing air fares would cause many passengers to choose other airline competitors possibly.

Critically discuss how the marketing manager of a budget airline might respond.

Marketing manger might use cost benefit analysis to let budget airline to know how to invest in intangible asset, such as corporate social responsibility to give long term benefit to itself budget airline. I suggest this marketing manager needs to explain the reason why reducing fuel consumption is an investment in intangible asset to budget airline as below:

Airline transport has increasingly become a global technologically and dynamic growth industry. However, airline companies need to remain committed to satisfy the clients' growing demands in a sustainable manner when at the same time maintaining an optimal balance between economic progress, social development and environmental responsibility. The concept of corporate social responsibility is a challenge for who to face today's risky, competitive and complex airline business environment. There has been a need for airlines in the airline industry to develop an environment agenda and take measures to minimize the ever increasing environmental impacts created by their activities. The forms of corporate social responsibility in the airline sector includes working in partnership with local communities, socially sensitive investment as well as involvement in activities for conservation of the environment. The fact, airlines are spewing 20% more co2 into the environment then previously estimated and there is a tendency for amount to increase to 1.5 billion tons a year by 2025 year. So, airline industry must need to innovative, environmentally responsible industry that drives economic and social progress. It has risks (social, environmental, operational, threat, strategic and financial risks) that they have to deal with marketing managers airlines, such as budget airline marketing manager is responsible for the optional decision making about corporate risks in its daily business. Adrian, (P. 2012) indicated that the marketing manager of budget airline needs to indicate the benefits can be categorized into three namely to let budget airline to feel as below:

(a) Regarding the economic view, budget airline is essential for facilitating world business and tourism, it needs to create jobs and enables the expansion of trade across the global by opening
up new market opportunities. It also attracts businesses to locations all over the world, hence satisfying the mobility requirement of a growing portion of the world's population. It also aids in the movement of products and services quickly over long distance facilities economies and social participation by remote communities.

(b) From the social perspective, budget airline forms an unique global transport network that links people in different countries safely and efficiently. Air transport is increasingly accessible to a large number of people who can now afford to travel by air for pleasure and its business purpose.

(c) Lastly, in terms of the environmental perspective, there is a need for budget airline to minimize or contain the impact in its environment through the continuous improvement of its
fuel consumption, noise reduction and the introduction of new technologies. Budget airline marketing manager can enquire this question to whose company, such as how budget airline can quantify the benefits derived from such investments to do with how to quantify the benefits, so budget airline can be compared to the cost of investments. Through budget airline has be different over the years to value many intangibles, such as corporate social responsibilities. Budget airline marketing manager needs to make choices among several alternatives: it is important to adopt a tool that with allow choices to clearly weigh and distinguish between the options available. So, budget airline marketing manager needs to persuade whose company to believe to maximize the gain, which may be either economic or social and may be beneficial to an individual, a group or society at large, e.g. reducing fuel cost can maximize economic or social benefits for long term. The measurement of benefits from corporate social responsibility policy includes gains from additional income to an increased quality of life or a cleaner environment. On the other hand, the costs are made up of the opportunities forgone, internal and external costs and externalities. For instance, increasing the flying route for budget airline, the noise and air pollution are the externality when the secondary effect could be an increase in the cost operations. In this case, the pollution creates the new cost (externality). The budge airline business cost is the increase in the cost of operating the additional route. The budget airline's fuel consumption causes air pollution will influence whose client stakeholders' powers of seeing and thinking, cultural setting, experience is from the past and motivation at the time of sensing to the airline image to be poor due to who will feel the budget airline is not a social responsible organization. It aims to earn profits from passengers, but it neglects to take care other stakeholders benefits due to its fuel consumption to pollute environment to cause global warming problem. It seems that budget airline needs to considerate to use more fuel consumption to cause global warming problem more than doubling air fares in real terms if Government decided to raise more fuel tax charging to it to reduce its income.

I suggest marketing manager of a budget airline to reduce to use more fuels to pollute air, so budget airline does not decide to increase double air fairs charges to clients due to Government raises fuel taxation expenditure. Because it will cause clients to cancel its air tickets if who feel its air fairs are not reasonable to raise prices to compare other airline competitors. The marketing manager of a budget airline might respond to promote this navigation system to persuade budget airline does not choose to double air fares if Government raised fuel taxing charge. Innovation of flight operation on the optimum routes using (RNAV) Area navigation, as conventional airways and routes between airports were built by connecting ground navigation aids to the destination, the budget airline often became rather inefficient. On the other hand, RNAV can build routes connected any points with almost straight line by confirming aircraft position by means of global positioning system etc in addition to radio navigation destination of fuel consumption and CO2 emission through shortened flight time and distance. Other reducing fuel consumption include reduction of aircraft weight, use of new type point for aircraft painting to reduce emission of polluted to air . Hence, budget airline will spend less fuels to avoid to pay high fuels taxation expenditure to its Government and it does not need to charge double air fairs in real terms to cause many passengers who will choose to find other airlines to buy cheaper air tickets or who will cancel their budget airline air tickets due to who feel budget airline charges unreasonable air fairs. So, if budget airline did not achieve as above any methods to attempt to reduce fuel consumption, I believe that it will lose many passengers due to it decide to charge doubling air fares in real terms to compensate its fuel tax increasing expenditure .

How can ethnographic research predict consumer emotion ?-Applying video recording method to predict consumer behavior

Critically assess the role of ethnographic research as a means of learning More about buyer behavior. To critically assess whether the role of ethnographic research as a means of learning more about buyer behavior. I shall indicate what the marketers who use general methods to learn more about buyer behavior to compare to ethnographic research difference. In general, marketers learn buyer behavior who shall follow the simplified stages in the buyer decision process , such as the beginning is from need recognition to information search to evaluate to decision to the end of post purchase evaluation stage. Hence, the any buyers behavior shall be cycle stage to decide whether who shall repeat to choose to buy the company's product or use it's service if who feel the product or service had achieved their satisfaction after who spent. The marketers shall use questionnaires or marketing researches to enquire consumers to gather their ideas to analysis to get evaluation to assess whether how whose companies need to produce what kinds of new products style, design, color, price level and sale channels to achieve the most suitable marketing strategy to raise their sale competition. Otherwise, the role of ethnographic search is one different method to learn more about buyer behavior. In general, companies shall not need to arrange questionnaires to enquire participants to fill to answer questions to gather data to carry on evaluation and which do not need to follow the simplified stages to assess target client groups purchase decision process to carry on the sale and post purchase evaluation cycle to evaluate whether what are their product criteria or weaknesses which need to improve to raise their sale competition in their market. I think ethnographic research can get closer to the truth about consumer behavior. On behalf of companies' clients, which can seek to uncover hidden truths about the way their clients' lead their lives, by paying volunteers to be followed for days on end, being filmed and having their every more recorded. Companies will pay their target householder participant group to carry on an observational survey by digital cameras to be filmed record at home. One essential feature of ethnographic research is that it must not have any predetermined agenda. There is little value in undertaking this type of research if the mind set of the researcher is expecting to see preconceived phenomena, it is the unexpected that is often of most interest, and which is so difficult to pick up through more structured forms of survey. In fact, participants in a survey may feel self conscious when who are being filmed, and the more interesting insights are likely to be observed when participants are feeling relaxed and off their guard .It is not just what people actually do that can be interesting, but what they almost do, and the body language used when members of the household are discussing an issue. It can take several hours of filming to yield just a few moments of true insights into participants' true attitudes and behavior.

One example of the company's ethnographic research in action was provided by a project commissioned by the footwear brand Dr Martens. It wanted to understand how young people used fashion brands in their every lives . Why for example, did some brands, such as Nike trainers or baseball caps become popular in youth culture? The researchers identified groups of young people around the world who responded to Dr Martens' target market. In return for a payment, volunteers were followed for several days and their daily routines filmed with a handheld digital camera. In total, 180 hours of captured film was edited to just one hour of highlights showing the key drivers of youth culture which are relevant to the Dr Martens brand. It seemed that young people preferred fashions that allowed them to customize an item of clothing and in some way take ownership of it. The research drew the conclusion that iconic fashion items for young people had to have a distinctive label or style that made their wearers stand out as part of a tribe. Hence, ethnographic research seems to help this company to know why the young clients choose to buy other brand sport shoes, it is possible that they the other brands sport shoes' color or design can be accepted more to than to buy Dr Marten brand's sport shoes when they wear different style of clothing. Hence, it can use digital camera to observe the worldwide choice of paying target youth volunteers whose daily individual behaviors at homes to get the more actual evidence to evaluate what factors influence youth clients choose to buy other brands of sport shoes. Otherwise, if it use structured questionnaire surveys to enquire youth clients , it is possible that who can not give their feedbacks honestly. Otherwise, observable youth people whose daily activities can help this company to know it is possible that their design and color of clothing are one factor to influence their choice to buy preferable brands of sport shoes to wear if who felt the brand of sport shoe was suitable to wear to influence their clothing to be felt more smart in appearance. However, I suggest companies to avoid to tell householders what the research project is about, until it is over. That way, the chances of participants deliberately playing to the camera can be reduced. Hence, ethnographic researcher ought not tell to participants why who needs to record their daily activities at home till to the end of observable survey finishing due to it is possible that the participants will not perform their actual behaviors if who knew the researcher's observable intention. However, if marketers need to understand how whose companies clients actually make purchase decisions to their products, who shall use structured questionnaire surveys for collecting large scale factual data, but it will have major weaknesses when companies can not understand individual's attitude. Complex sets of factors that influence their buying decisions can only rarely be captured by a questionnaire.

Qualitative approaches such as those using focus groups can get closer to the truth, but participants often still find themselves inhibited from telling the full story to the companies to know.

Ethnography is one of many approaches that can be found within social research. Ethnography was a descriptive account of a community or culture. Ethnography usually involves the researcher participating in people's daily lives for an extended

period of time, watching what happens, listening to what is said, and/or asking questions through informal and formal interviews collecting documents. In more detailed terms, ethnographic work usually has most of the following features: People actions are studied in every contexts rather than under conditions created by the researcher, such as in experimental setups or highly structured interview situations as well as data are gathered from a range of sources including documentary evidence of various kinds, but participant observation and/or relatively informal conversations are usually the main ones as well as data collection is for the most past relatively unstructured in two senses and it doesn't involve following through detailed research design at the start and the categories that are used for interpreting what people say or do are not built into the data collection process through the use of observation schedules or questionnaire to analysis.

Generally, fairly small scale, perhaps a single setting or group of people. This is a facilitate in depth study and the analysis of data involves interpretation of the meanings, functions and consequences of human actions and how these are implicated in local and perhaps also wider contexts what are produced for the most part are verbal descriptions, explanations and theories and statistical analysis play a subordinate role at most. How ethnography can learn more about buyer behavior. It means collection of data to pursue an answers to these questions more effectively and to test these against evidence. Collecting data in natural settings, in other words in those that have not been specially set up for research purposes (such as experiments or formal interviews). Where participant observation is involved the researcher must have some role in the studied and this will usually have to be done at least through implicit and probably also through explicit, negotiation with people.

How video recording method predict consumer behavior:

The methodological model for social research is physical science conceived in terms of the logic of the experiment. Ethnography was sometimes dismissed as quite inappropriate to social science on the grounds that the data and findings it produces are subjective. Hence, ethnographic research is the role to learn more about buyer behavior through marketers may have been listening more to consumers (e.g. through qualitative research), efforts have almost always been directed at controlling consumers; ranges of products or services pre determined by producers have been pushed through with little real involvement of consumers in the process at a time in which consumers are ever more aware of what is being done to marketers. Ethnographic field research involves the study of groups and people as who go about every day lives. There has two distinct activities. First, the ethnographer enter into a social setting and gets to know the people involved in it; who participates in the daily routines; develops ongoing relations with the people in it and observes all the approach. But second the ethnographer writes down in regular systematic ways what who observes and learns when participating in the daily rounds of life of others. Thus, the researcher creates an accumulating written record of these observations and experiences. These two interconnected activities comprise the core of ethnographic search: firsthand participation in some initially unfamiliar social world and the production of written accounts of that world by drawing upon such participation. Hence, ethnographers are committed to get close to the activities and everyday people.

Getting close minimally requires physical and social proximity to the daily rounds of people's lives and activities, the field researcher must be able to take up positions in the midst of the key sites and scenes of other's lives in order observe and understand whom. In learning about others through active participation in their lives and activities. Finally, close continuing participation in the lives of others encourages appreciation of social life as ongoing processes. Through participation the field researcher sees how people do uncertainty and confusion, how meaning is through talk and collective action, how understandings change over time.

Consumer behavior refers to the behavior that consumers display in searching for purchasing, using, evaluating and disposing of products and services that who expect will satisfy their needs and it's behaviors that are directly involved in the action of obtaining, consuming and spending products/services, including the decision processes that precede and follow these actions. The knowledge of consumer behavior helps the marketer to understand how consumer think, feel and select from alternative like products, brands and the like and how the consumers' buying behaviors are influenced by their environment, the reference groups, family and salespersons. Most of the factors are uncontrollable and beyond the controls of marketers, but who have to be considered when trying to understand the complex behavior of the consumers. Consumers buying cycle processes involved when individuals or groups select, purchase, use or dispose of products or services or ideas or experiences to satisfy needs and desires.

In the marketing context, the term consumer refers not only to the act of purchase itself, but also to patterns of aggregate buying which include pre-purchase and post purchase activities.

Pre-purchase activity might consist of the growing awareness of a need or wants and a search for and evaluate of information about the products and brands that might satisfy it. Post purchase activities include the evaluation of the purchased item in use and the reduction of any anxiety which accompanies the purchase of expensive and infrequently bought items. The various factors include lifestyles and its impact on the consumer behavior.

On the first hand, ethnographic research can learn more about buyer behavior as below: ethnographic research described the dominant, positivistic consumer perspectives and methodological and analytical overview of the traditional perspectives. There are two factors mainly influencing the consumers for decision making. Risk aversion and innovativeness. Risk aversion is a measure of how much consumers need to be certain and sure of what who are purchasing. Highly risk adverse consumers need to be very certain about what who are buying. Whereas less risk adverse consumers on tolerate some risk and uncertainty in their purchasing. The second variable, innovativeness is a global measure which captures the degree to which consumers are willing to take chances and experiment with new ways of doing things. Hence, ethnographic research can learn whether the buyer's shopping motivation is abound with which various measures of individual characteristics, e.g. innovative, variety seeking etc. different factors to the buyer behavior.

On the second hand, perception is a mental process, whereby an individual selects data or information from the environment organizes it and then draws significance or meaning from it. Perceived fit is an attitudinal measure of how appropriate a certain channel of distribution is for a specific product. Consumer's perception of the fit between a service/product and channel is very influential in determining whether who will consider using that channel for a specific service. In fact, perceived fit was found to be more important than consumer's preference for the distribution method or service. Product quality and packaging and brand awareness familiarity with a channel is a measure of the general experience who have with purchasing products through special channels , e.g. internets, newspapers advertisement factors let consumers to decide to choose to buy or not buy the specific product. Shopping motives are defined as consumer's wants and needs as who relate to outlets at which to shop. Two groups of motives, functions and non functional have been proposed with time, place and possession needs and refer to rational aspects of channel choice. The functional motives included convenience, price comparison. Otherwise, the non functional motives entailed recreation and it related to social and emotional reasons. Hence, ethnographic research can assess whether the product or service is the functional motive or non functional motive to cause the buyer's choice.

On the third hand, economic theory holds that of largely rational and conscious economic calculations. Thus, the individual buyer seeks to spend whose income on those products that will deliver the most utility (satisfaction) according to his tastes and relative prices. It aimed to simplify assumptions and examine the effects of changes in single variables (e.g. price) holding all other variables constant. (e.g. low price of product is the higher the sales. The identified the impact of price differentials on consumers' brand preferences; changes in produces on demand variations; changes in price on demand sensitivity and scarcity on consumer choice behavior amongst many others. The consumer behavioral perspective in contrast to the economic view which underscores the importance of internal processes in consumer decision making, the behavioral perspective emphasizes the role of external environmental factors in the process of learning, when which it is argued causes behavior. The behavioral perspective therefore focuses on external environmental, such as advertisement that stimulate consumer response through learning. Consumers must be exposed to information, e.g. advertisement of it is to influence their behavior. Hence, ethnographic research can assess whether the product/service is consumer behavioral perspective or behavioral perspective to cause the buyer's choice.

On the fourth hand, consumers were suggest that high involvement with a product results in an extended problem followed by an information search, alternative evaluation, purchase and post purchase activities. The process is aided by an active information processing sequence involving exposure, attention, comprehension, acceptance and retention. The choice is determined by the outcome of the information process aided decision sequence may have satisfying or dissatisfying outcomes. Consumer's motivation and intention and that unpredictable factors (such as non availability brand or insufficient funds) may result in modification of the actual choice made by a consumer. This model assumes that observed consumer behavior is preceded by intrapersonal psychological states and events (attitude intention-purchase sequence). Hence, the events are as outputs of the processing of information, taking for granted that consumers seek and use information as part of their rational problem solving and decision making processes. Hence, ethnographic research can learn why the buyer doesn't choose to buy the product whether it is unpredictable or predictable psychological factors.

On the fifth hand, personality perspective means some purchases have more personal relevance than others. When this partly reflects on factors, such as price, it also bears on the way in which some products enhance the consumer's self concept , e.g. possessions are considered to reflect on a consumer's image of whom. Personality in general is understood as a concept. Personality has also been understood as the unique way in which traits, attitudes, when individuals might not always be uniform and predictable in their patterns of choice in different situations, it might be possible to make sense of and to forecast the general reactions of broadly defined groups and classes of purchasers.

It is the concept of consumer general behavioral response patterns that forms the basis for marketing's personality based segmentation strategies. The possibility of using measures of personality to guide marketing action, for example in segmenting markets , tailoring new brands of innovative consumers and repositioning mature brands has encouraged a large volume of research. Attitude itself is a learning experience and can lead to a change in attitudes before buyers enter the buying process. Thus, attitudes don't automatically guarantee all types of behavior. They are really the product of social forces interacting with the individual's unique temperament and abilities and social influences are not all of the behavioral variations in people. Two individuals subject to the same influences are not likely to have identical attitudes, although those attitudes will probably more points than those of two and cognition. Affect refers to the way a consumer feel about an attitude object, behavior involves the person's intentions to do something with regard to an attitude object and finally cognition refers to the beliefs a consumer has about an attitude object. Thus, ethnographic research can learn whether it is from external social factors more or internal personality factors more to cause the buyer's choice. The theory of cognitive information processing , attitudes are formed in the order of beliefs, affect and behavior. Attitudes based on behavioral learning follow the beliefs, behaviors and affect sequence and finally attitudes formed based on the experiential hierarchy follow the affect, behavior and beliefs route. A consumer who is highly involved with a product / service category and who perceives a high level of product/service differentiation between alternatives will follow the cognitive hierarchy (beliefs affect behavior). From the ethnographic research marketers perspective the sequence of attitude formation is from a communication point of views from a strategic point of view, such as it has proved useful in specifying the different elements that work together to influence buyers' evaluations of attitudes ; products or services may be composed of many attributes or qualities, some of which may be more important than others to particular people. So consumer's decision is to act on whose attitude is affected by other factors, such as whether it is felt other factors, such as whether it is felt that buying a product/ service would be met with approval by friends and family. The complexity of attitudes is underscored by multi attribute attitude models, in which sets of beliefs and evaluations are identified and combined to predict an overall attitude.

On the final hand, the situational influence perspective, a situation is defined by factors over and above the characteristics of a person and product or service. For example, situational affects may be behavioral (e.g. entertaining friends), experiential or perceptual (e.g. being depressed or being pressed for time). According to the behavioral influence perspective of low involvement decision situation, consumer decision making is a learned response to environmental cues, as when a person decided to buy something on impulse that is prompted as a surprise special in a store.

According to this approach, then ethnographic research marketers must concentrate on assessing the characteristics of the environment, such as the physical surroundings and product/service placement, that influence members of that target market. For example, point of purchase (such as product/ service samples) are particularly useful in inducing impulse purchases. Ethnographic research marketers focus on measuring consumers' effective responses to products or services and develop offerings that elicit appropriate subjective reactions and employ effective symbolism. Situational effects can also be perceptive, e.g. there could be a number of ways in which mood can influence purchase decisions. For example, stress can impact information processing and problem solving abilities. In addition, time poverty can impact buying decisions. An individual's priorities determine whose time style. According, consumer buying change is not something which consumers do for themselves, rather it is a result of something that is done to them by some internal ,e.g. trait or external ,e.g. environment force over which they have little or no control. Thus, ethnographic research can assess what is the situational influence factors to cause the buyer to choose to buy the product or consume the service. In conclusion, conditions of competition are changing rapidly today and companies need strategies to react to those changes promptly to raise competition. Due to technological developments, physical differences of products/ services have decreased. Differentiation should be on the meanings products/ services bear instead of on their physical features and a successful brand differentiation can be possible by building personality. Hence, understanding consumer behaviors are related to marketing natures in the product sale or service provision to every marketer who needs to considerate to win whose competitors.

Discuss the ethical issues that are raised by ethnographic research.

Consumer research has been important to the development of marketing theory and practice. Consumers are seldom, if ever, involved in the research design and analysis processes which raises issues that go beyond ethics. Particularly, problematic when participant observation is employed , as little is and little could be addressed by research guidelines and codes of ethics relevant to marketing research. Some of the relevant ethical issues to participant observation that arise from the lack of the consumer in the research process as well as the potential issues that may be involved in participatory research designs, the shortcomings of the available ethnographic marketing research guidelines and codes of ethics as for as participant observation is concerned. Some argument regards the real time and nature of ethical circumstances at the field where the ethnographic researcher must often respond to unexpected situations immediately.

Why ethical ways of thinking it is important to recognize that are raised by ethnographic research.

It is possible that the issues of power that can arise ethnographic research as well as it is from the consequences of simply doing
research , even if the intentions are good and it is from the fact that ethnographic research marketers' knowledge system is necessarily linked to other forms of structural power (e.g. gender, race, development, the system). The ethnographic research marketers whose emotional and power issues present in ethnographic research relationships are also acknowledged to influence ethnographic results, and this is where the key issues of using research participants for data collection comes in. Ethnographic research designs that objectify and don't include research participants in the conceptualization of the research study through to data analysis have been widely criticized by ethnographic researchers and these issues must be considered within the scope of the ethics of care.

Researchers (ethnographers) need have moral responsibilities toward research, included informed consent, confidentiality, reliability and validity. In sum, ethical guidelines and codes of conduct can be beneficial in alerting consumer researchers of ethical ways of conducting research. However, participants needed rules to be aided by researchers' own ethical reasoning in the field. The ethnographic researchers need to highlight the importance of constant negotiation of participation in the different stages of research, how participants may not be willing (due to lack of time or even personal circumstances) to help ethnographic researchers in the data analysis process and how researchers' own deadlines and academic constraints may get in the way of the idealized research process of involvement between ethnographic research participants and researchers are well to their discussed topic. In general, ethnographic researchers need to know what who need to understand about ethics, such as harm, consent, data protection etc. recap of ethical approval what it is and what ethnographic researchers need to do and what further sources of information and support need. In ethic principles, ethnographic research should be designed, reviewed and undertaken to ensure integrity and quality. Participants must normally be informed fully about the purpose, methods and intends possible uses of research, what their participation entails and what risks, the confidentiality must be respected research participants must take part voluntarily, harm to research participants must be avoided in all instances and the independence of research must be clear and any conflicts to interest or partiality must be explicit and increasing stakeholder demands. The mature of the ethical consumer is educated, middle class or over emotional to decide what kind products who needs to buy and how many numbers are enough to buy. For example, with the environment dropping out of media attention, ethic provided new moral ground and campaigns or opening of a chain of ethical supermarkets, ethical image became a desirable commodity for the big retailers. Some ethical customers need to satisfy with fair trade marked products to buy from the ethical supermarkets. How morality may play a significant role in the performance of buyers' actions. It is concerned specifically with how rules, responsibilities and values centering on right or wrong influence the character of consumption.

The idea that morality (ethicality) can have a considerable impact upon the consumption. Hence, I think business moral performance is needed to satisfy every buyer's decision of consumption and it is linked to the ethnographic research growing literature on ethical consumer behavior. Within psychology, for instance, morality can be seen as a process of cognitive learning where systematic punishment and reward help to educate individuals of their actions. Whether consumption is informed by at least some of the available moral perspectives to some of the available moral perspectives, so it caused ethical issues that are raised by ethnographic research. Ethical consumption is concerned with predicting market behavior, it included some kind of relationship between the attitudes, values and behaviors of a defined ethical consumer group. For example, ethnographic researchers have been interested in the effects of environmental concern on environmentally friendly consumer behavior. Depending on how ethical consumption is defined, it recognizes alternative forms of what are essentially moral values, attitudes and buyer individual behavior. Consumer behavior has been changed by external elements, such as economy, technology, cultures, religion etc. factors. It would be unfortunate to be great importance for an understanding of ethical consumption issues.

In conclusion, consumption behavior is the art of need for desire to, it could be thought of as directly influenced by certain core values held as sacred within society. For example, ethical buyer behavior may concerns about animal protection, environmental protection, human protection etc. life rights issue. Facts, knowledge and truth about morality in consumption are seen as being raised by ethnographic research. According, the relationship between morality and consumers behavior could be better through of as the products of a continued process of political, social, technological and religious re-organization of life. For example, capabilities of new digital , microchip technology enhanced many consumers with the delights of efficient, task-saving, small and shiny products. Simultaneously, and not unrelated turbo-charges cars, mobile phones, cock tail parties etc. high technological products are arguably reflected power, success and good living to influence buyer behavior ethically daily in our society. Hence, I believe ethical issues that are needed to consider by ethnographic research.

Discuss possible alternative approaches by which marketers may learn more about youth culture.

Market based trading -selling, buying and consuming has existed in our society. Human action and interaction and behaving in different roles in exchange markets and various trading situations which is a typical of consumers and market trading interplays of several actors in economic, societal and cultural contexts as well as consumer behavior and consumer culture and consumption which have close relationship. Individual youth consumer or a group of youth consumers who is described as humanistic economics where people, their values and culture are primarily analyzed. In general, research on brands and organizational issues of the marketing function defined the questions of how to sell more products or provide more services to speed up the general level of consumption in order to better the economic situation of a firm or a nation. Basically, individual youth buyer seeks to speed whose income on those products/services what will deliver the most utility, typically satisfaction, according to whose tastes and budget. In economic, consumer behavior is identified with rational decision making. Decisions are automatically translated into purchasing and consuming, The price and income constraints are generally accepted factors in an economic analysis of

consumer behavior. Consequently, consumers are seen as rational actors that purposefully optimize the production of their utility.

Sociological and macro and cultural perspective which focuses on consuming , emphasizes on emotions, multicultural new consumers aspects, cultural studies and the meaning of culture for consumer research surfaced also in the late 1980 years. For example, consumption symbolism, different aspects to property and possessions, political consumption, research and cultures and subcultures. In consumer studies can be traced to the mid 1990 years, when consumer culture was recognized as a distinct cultural entity. Consumption was seen as a society activity which above all others, unities economy and culture. The one alternative approach is that learning more about youth culture, there is a clear common sense about its influence on social youth consumption changes, and the importance of its analysis in order to understand modern youth consumption. For example, marketers may learn more how to make youth to cause excessive consumption nowadays. The influence of the means of mass communication and oriented medias has contributed to send promotion messages to different youth audiences, e.g. from children and teen ages to youths. To see themselves in real conditions why who need to buy products or need services before beyond their possibilities have been planned to buy electronics, cars and even a house etc. products.

The another alternative approach is that marketers may also learn what are youth consumer modern culture how to make them, such as symbol status and power how become habituated to consume familiar products/ services able to reinforce familiar image in youth cultural different target groups. The final alternative approach is that culture is sociological influence on client's needs, it is based on the individual's physiological and psychological needs, such as food choice. Maslow recognized that once individual have satisfied these basic physiological needs, such as foods and drinks, who may seek to satisfy social needs by cultural influence, for example, the need to have meaningful interaction with peers. More complex still, western cultures see increasing numbers of people seeking to satisfy essentially internal needs for self satisfaction, products therefore satisfy increasing complex needs. Moreover, food is no longer seen as a basic necessary to be purchased and cooked for self consumption with growing prosperity, youth people have sought to satisfy social needs by eating out with friend or family. Youth peoples' satisfaction of such social needs may influences on their foods sating basic needs. Hence, if the youth clients had afford to go to restaurant to eat more expensive and good taste foods. The high class food culture can change the youth client's food necessity to influence whose food choice. A young child is often considered society unacceptable, so such youth behavior is socialized out before the child reaches adulthood. The faculty cultural influences a child's perception of the world and the family cultural influences lasts into adulthood. For example of this effect on buying processes can be found in youth adults selection of a particular brand breakfast cereal because it is the one that who were brought up with youth individuals are surrounded by peer group/or reference groups with act as a guide for youth consumption of behavior peer groups can be primary and direct to influence their youth culture (e.g. colleagues at work and school), popular movie actors can secondary and indirect to influence to their youth culture (e.g. guideline or behavior provided by popular movie actors or media figures) ; youth individuals culture can also

identify with a social class and the values of this class can influence youth behavior, e.g. school culture or working class. However, culture in its widest sense influences youth buying behavior and deference to suppliers can differ significantly between different countries' youth culture to choose to sell their products or provide their services to the countries' youth markets. Youth needs are also influenced by the situation in which youth currently find themselves in their countries. The subjects of age and socio-economic status can have profound effects on youth buying behavior at different youth age market segmentation, such as youth client groups can divided to any companies to concentrate on selling, e.g. between 20 ages to 40 ages or between 10 ages to 20 ages etc. different age groups.

In conclusion, marketer may learn more about youth culture from different countries' family life cycle stages of change which have sought to take account of their increasing complexity to influence to estimate the countries' youth buyer numbers. The family relationships can include single parent family, married parent family, no children family youth buyer groups of family life cycle youth buyer changing numbers in marketers' target countries. Due to all different countries family life cycle youth buyer numbers can indicate the countries' youth individual needs changing numbers and the target countries' youth buyer numbers are likely to change their purchase tastes and needs as youth culture goes through life. Hence, marketers can measure the target countries youth age segmentation estimate numbers to decide how many products or how much services to supply to them to satisfy their needs accurately.

Marketing research methods -applying survey or questionnaire methods to predict consumer behavior

Critically evaluate the relative merits of quantitative and qualitative approaches to data collection for a large retailer.

The marketing research process needs to follow these steps: defining the problem and research objectives, developing the research plan, collecting the data, analyzing the data, then presenting the findings.

In general, the specific marketing research major activities include: Research into customer needs and expectation and a variety of qualitative techniques are used to study the often complex sets of expectations that customers have with respect to a purchase. For example, when buying a personal computer, what are customers' expectation with respect to reliability, after -sales support, design etc? Customer satisfaction surveys indicate customer areas of satisfaction or dissatisfaction; how spending money on various forms of communication, such as advertising, sales promotion, and public relations; researching similar industry studies about competitors in completely unrelated business sectors how to improve own marketing effectiveness; researching key client studies about number of customers how to make special efforts to ensure that these customers are satisfied with its standards of service and prices; researching into intermediaries, such as agents dealers are close to consumers to gather information about consumers' needs and expectation. For example in relation to reliability, delivery times and after sales services; researching front line employees their attitude towards the company and researching environmental scanning changing on trends to influence the company development in the future. Structure of market research includes spending on market research, types of market research and potential problem. Market research means researching the the immediate competitive environment of the marketplace, including customers, competitors, suppliers, distributors and retailer. Otherwise, marketing research includes all the above and companies and their strategies and markets of whose products sale or services provision and the wider environment within which operates (e.g. political, social, economic etc factor influences). Hence, marketing research means the systematic design, collection, analysis and reporting of data and finding relevant to a specific marketing situation facing the organization. In general, the ten most common market research activities for a large retailer data collection, include determination of market characteristics, measurement of market potential, market share analysis, sales analysis, studies of business trends, short range forecasting, competitive product studies, long range forecasting, pricing studies and testing existing products.

The reasons why a large retailer needs to conduct that research in new product development include the product must appeal to the customer, timely market research can help the large retailer to predict its client's needs/wants, market research tends to point out success and failure before its product is launched for real and it can save its money and time. A large retailer's market research can be sources by either primary or secondary or both and it can use either qualitative or quantitative or both methodologies and it can achieve objectives either exploratory or descriptive or causal experimental.

The primary source is collection of data specifically for the problem or project in hand and the secondary source is based on data previously collected for purposes other than the research in hand. e.g. published articles, governments etc.

On the quantitative benefits hand, it is cheaper to sample

size ; probabilities in depth motivations and feelings, it allows managers to observe real client reaction to the issue, e.g. comments and associations regard a new product fresh from the laboratory. It often used precursor to quantitative research, it can give the research department a low cost and timely sense of which issues in quantitative research. Quantitative research is designed to gather information from statistically representative samples of target population. The sample size is related to the size of the total population being studied, the variability within it, and the degree of statistically reliability required, balanced against time and cost constraints. It includes these skilful analyses such as below:

Correlation analysis means two phenomena are associated with each other. For example, whether change in household income is associated with the amount that a household spends on eating out of or firm's advertising expenditure on a product and sale revenue for it's relationship. Regression analysis means to use to build a model of causes (independent variables), which lead to an effect (the dependent variable). Companies shall use a historical database to test models that are assessed for the amount of variance in the dataset that they explain. Analysis of variance is used to test hypotheses about differences between two or more means. It is widely used in experimental frameworks where the researcher wished to examine the effects of two or more treatments on customers.

Conjoint analysis can provide valuable information for market segmentation, new product development, forecasting and pricing decisions and it can analyze the real life trade off that shoppers make when evaluating a range of features that are present in a range of product. Cluster analysis is frequently used in segmentation studies, but does not provide the marketer with a unique solutions.

Neural network analysis splits a dataset into a training set and a testing set. However, quantitative analysis techniques can suffer from a number of weakness , such as sampling error, measurement error, significant estimation of sample population error, inappropriate estimation of population may be validated statistical tests and inappropriate interpretation of results can highly subjective.

On the qualitative merits hand, large retailer can get merits, such as many sample size and questions and information per respondent and much application of questioner's skill, analyst's skill and type of analysis. Qualitative techniques essentially seek to recreate the listening ear and interpretative mind that so many entrepreneurs use so well. Qualitative marketing research involves the exploration and interpretation of the perceptions and behavior of small samples of individuals and the study of the motivators behind observed actions. It can be highly focused, exploring in depth, for example, the attitudes that buyers have towards particular brand names. The techniques used to encourage respondents to speak and behave honestly. However, it is difficult to assess the validity of qualitative research techniques, and the tests for significance that are available for most quantitative techniques are largely lacking for qualitative techniques.

The quantitative and qualitative approaches to data collection for a large retailer its merits can achieve objective is either by exploratory, it means preliminary data needed to develop an idea further, e.g. outline concepts, gather insights, formulate hypotheses; it is either by descriptive, it means to describe an element of an ideas precisely, e.g. who is the target market, how large is it, how will it develops ; it is either by causal, it means to test a cause and effect relationship, e.g. price elasticity is by experiment. Moreover, the quantitative and qualitative approaches to data collection can help a large retailer to find methods how to solve problems to raise competition confidently. In the beginning, of the market research process step, it needs to define the problem and objectives, such as it needs to distinguish between it's research type needed, e.g. exploratory descriptive or causal . Then, it needs to develop the research plan, such as deciding on budget, data sources, research approaches and instruments, sampling plan and contact methods. Next, it needs to collect information, such as information is collected according to the plan. Following step, it needs to analyze the information , such as statistical manipulation of the data collected, e.g. regression or subjective analysis of focus group. Final step, it needs to present the findings, such as overall conclusion to be presented rather than statistical methodologies.

Data collection gathers for a large retailer, it can gather syndicated data from householders, it is gathered either by psychographics and lifestyle, advertising, evaluation etc. styles of surveys and use panels or both sources. Primary data is originated by a researcher for the specific purpose of addressing the problem at hand, the collection of primary data involves all six steps of the marketing research process as well as secondary data has already been collected for purposes other than the problem at hand. These data can be located quickly and inexpensively. The intention to uses of secondary data for a large retailer, it aims to identify the problem and better defines the problem, develops an approach to the problem, formulates an appropriates research design, for example by identifying the key variables, answers certain research questions and test some hypotheses and interprets primary data more insightfully.

On qualitative merits to secondary data collection for a large retailer. The criteria aspect, this data collection method can give merits of response rate, quality and analysis data, sampling technique and size, questionnaire design, fieldwork benefits to a large retailer, so it's data should be reliable, valid to the problem; on error and errors in approach, research design, sampling , data collection and analysis and reporting, so it can assess accuracy by comparing data from different sources. On currency aspect, this data collection method can assess time lag between collection and publication, frequency of updates, so census data are updated by syndicated large retailer; on objective aspect, secondary data collection method can help large retailer to judge whether the data collected were needed to used for which parts of market strategies benefits for consumer research, so the objective determines the relevance of data; on nature aspect, this data collection method can define key variables, units of measurement, categories used, relationships examined, so it can reconfigure the data to increase a large retailer market strategies benefits usefulness and on dependability aspect, this data collection method provides expertise, credibility, reputation and trustworthiness of the source, so it's data should be obtained from an original source to raise market research benefits to a large retailer. Hence, internal secondary data collection can help large retailer department project to store project to analyze sales by product line, by major department, e.g. men's wear, by specific stores by geographical region, by cash versus credit purchased, sales in specific time periods, by size of purchase and trends in many of these classifications were also examined.

Secondary data collection can include demographic data, which is type of individual household level data available from consumers, such as identification, e.g. name, address, telephone , sex, marital status, age, income, occupation etc. as well as psychographic lifestyle data, such as consumer personal interest. Hence, a large retailer can get this quantitative and qualitative data to judge whether who is segmentation target to compete in its business market. For example, market research demands cooperation and trust between the client commissioning a study and the company carrying it out.

The reputation that a market research agency has built for itself
is particularly important where qualitative research is involved as well as qualitative research techniques are utilizing quasi quantitative technique in order to enhance their credibility.

In conclusion, large retailers are reliance on customer's view due to many experienced larger retailers are relying more on interactive development with lead clients. Because traditional market research for truly innovative new products have frequently proved misleading. Hence, quantitative and qualitative approaches must need to use to gather to assess how to achieve marketing strategies timely and objectively and relevant to win whose competitors nowadays.

Discuss the limitation of statistically based consumer databases of the type discussed here. Do qualitative approaches based on small groups offer any advantages?

Any large retailers need to follow this process to use marketing information system to gather data from consumer databases. First step, which need to gather data either from internal data or external data source or both. The internal data includes enquires, orders, customer complaints etc. as well as the external data is from customer panels, intermediaries etc. Next step, the marketing information system will carry on processes as data collection and analyzing internal data. Final step, the marketing information system will produce outcomes, such as input to decision support system and data for decision makers to evaluate and storage of data in a data warehouse outcomes. A large retailer can collect consumer data computerized database, from online bibliographic database or from internet numeric databases, full text database or offline directory databases, special purpose databases. Hence, computerized published external secondary sources can help large retailers to identify individuals or organizations to collect specific data, for example, consultants and consulting organization directory, directory of market research reports, studies and surveys and research services directory and gather indices to help in locating information on a particular topic in several different publications. Hence, large retailer can collect classification of computerized databases include bibliographic databases are composed of citations to articles, numeric databases contain numerical and statistical information , full -text databases contain the complete text of the source documents comprising the database, directory databases provide information on individuals or organizations and services and special purpose database provide specialized information. Hence, large retailer can get syndicated service to collect and sell common pools of data of known commercial value designed to serve a number of clients and syndicated sources can be classified based on the unit of measurement (households/consumers) and institutions two groups. Syndicated services of householders/ consumers include surveys, data collection is from psychographic and lifestyles, general and advertising evaluation as well as it also include panels data collection is from purchase and media of volume tracking data and scanner diary panels as well as it also include electronic scanner services is from scanner diary panels with cable television.

Potential problems to limitation with market research of statistically based customer data bases include, small groups do not know when and how to do research from database and problems exist with research buyers and suppliers and it needs frequent techniques and small groups exist problems with traditional market research effort. On limitation of when and how not to conduct market research issue, it includes lack of resources, closed mindset, poor timing arrangement in marketplace, research results are not actionable, late timing is process, unclear objectives and cost outweighs benefits limitation. On the lack of resources occasion issue, if quantitative research is needed, it is not worth doing unless a statistically significant sample can be used, On the research results, small groups' clients are difficult to get psychographic data from statistically based consumer databases to analyze to carry on market research. On the closed mindset limitation issue, when research is used as a preconceived idea. The statistically based consumer databases needs long time to gather data to analyze to carry on marketing research in its process. It cause poor timing to give clients to find marketing research result, if the client wants to know whether who ought to invest to develop the new product to promote to the marketing to sell from statistically based consumer database in the short time.

On cost outweighs benefits limitation, the statistically based consumer databases expected value of the information gathering time and resources spending cost should outweigh the cost of gathering the data from normal marketing research method.

On the limitation of problems with research statistically based customer databases , qualitative limitations include narrow concept of research, unrealistic view of timeframe, as well as variable quality of market researchers and it is possible that market researchers have not own sufficient technical to apply statistically based customer data bases. For example, market researchers will feel difficult to find facts from statistically customer data bases and who will spend much time to define research result from finding.

The qualitative approaches based on small groups offer any advantages from statistically marketing research customer databases only, but small groups can not offer any advantages from statistically market research customer databases. The reason is due to market research is about determining the characteristics of a market, for example, in terms of its size, requirements, growth rate, market segments and competitor positioning. Otherwise, marketing research is broader and is about researching the whole of a company's marketing activities. In most organizations, such search would probably include monitoring the effectiveness of its advertising, intermediates, and pricing position. Hence, small groups need to focus on marketing researching its company's internal marketing activities, such as pricing strategy, advertising method. Due to small groups are not large organizations, which did not focus on market research to external marketing environment, such as growth rate, market segment etc influences. However, statistically based customer databases also have these qualitative approaches to small groups offer advantages include, easy of completion, realism, comprehensive, per-testing, questioner training, respondent motivation, repetition, cultural issues, bias in formulation and sensitivity of question etc. qualitative approaches.

What effects do you expect the development of interactive electronic media to have on retailers' collection of marketing research information from consumers?Electronic media predicts consumer behavior

The effects that I expect the development of interactive electronic media to have on retailer's collection of marketing research information from consumers. Limited use of market research indicated formal market analyses continue to be

useful for extending product lines, but they are often misleading when applied to radical innovations. Problems, with traditional market research has allowed prominent product failures and wrong predictions; markets are increasingly becoming micro-segmented, e.g. sports shoes aimed at fashion conscious women specifically for aerobic, so mass market research becomes correspondingly irrelevant; it is helpful for improvements, but traditional market research method is less for radical innovations and is less for more accurate targeting. Thus, I expect the development of interactive electronic media effects to have on retailers collection of marketing research in formation from consumers. It may be advantageous to analyze continue to be useful for expanding product lines in the most short time and it will not mislead to businessmen when who applied this electronic media on retailers collection of marketing research method to get radical innovations accurately. For example, predicting whether who are major targeting segments for the sport shoe company to sell in the short time accurately, such as between 10 ages and 30 ages young male client group or young female client group or between 31 ages to 50 ages adult male client group or adult female client group.

On the evaluating internet resources for retailer's collection of marketing research legal hand, it needs to indicate the content of a resource must be reflective. If there is change, the resource must promptly reflect that change; if a law has been amended, any discussion on the web must reflect the law as amended. Otherwise, the internet resource is not qualified for citation in legal marketing research; research specialization and achievement, institutional and professional affiliation, medium of communication, e.g. professional journal and publishers are all useful criteria to evaluate credibility; questions to ask include: Is it a reviewed articles? Is it a law review journal? And does the author exhibit critical assessment of a resource? ; Copyrighted work means that an individual or an institution could claim ownership, responsibility and liability for the resource. It also publication and therefore users may have to comply with the principle of fair value; resources with citations journalistic ones. Researchers should therefore accord higher preference to resources with citations; many web resources disappear with the resources who contain. For instance, an electronically published law report must not only be current but also be continuous for it to be a dependable source for consultation, it is important to examine whether a resource reflects the attributed of misinformation half truths prejudice; a marketing researcher needs resources that can be connected to individual retailer or company's resources. In general, online market researchers know that search engineers vary in how who select ranking of results. With the advent of search engine optimization and the role of online marketing search engines, results are impacted by things other than returning results that are customized to rank higher sponsored links, with the page owner paying advertising dollars to get their site ranked higher. General search engines can be helpful when getting started or determining the scope of a particular question. Search engines like Google, Yahoo can be powerful tools. It is good practice to not rely on only one general search engine. General research engines, like Google, also have power helpful in narrowing large search results.

An old librarian advertisement page is that customers can have something quick, cheap and accurate but who can only pick two out three. Therefore, choosing the top two most important factors will help consumers decide between conducting an open web marketing search and using specialized commercial databases. However, law firm librarians need to play important roles in helping their firms and staff members locate, manage and use internet resources efficiently and cost effectively and who need to understand not only the needs of their firms and clients, but also the specific types of information available online as well as offline to meet clients' unique needs and who also need to help business firms grow and strength their client services by taking advantage of the rich information online. For instance, law librarians need to lead the form in creating the best and most comprehensive combination of knowledge and information re-sources, including capturing and preserving reliable free and low cost internet resources, that accommodates the firm's budget and user needs, maintain the firm's intranet, further enabling cost effective online legal research, promote free and low cost online resources and research techniques, whenever, feasible to help attorneys and staffs improve research efficiency and cost effectiveness, manage electronic subscriptions which now generally account for a large annual spending than books and newsletters, educate users and conduct training sessions on online research skills, provide tailored content for individual users or groups to facilitate intelligent filtering of the abundance of available information online, provide guideline on the usefulness and reliability of legal resources, guide attorneys as well as consumers in finding information from the internet efficiently.

On evaluating internet research surveys marketing research hand, there have advantages of internet research surveys, rather than mailing a paper survey, a respondent can be given a hyperlink to a web site containing the survey or in an email survey, a questionnaire is sent to a respondent via electronic mail, possibly as an attachment . Electronic media survey is as an alternative to conventional survey modes , e.g. the telephone, mail and face to face interviewing. For example, a web survey can relatively simply incorporate multi-media graphics and sound into the survey instrument, automatic branching and real time randomization of survey questions and/or answers into self administered web surveys. However, unlike when phone and mail surveys were first introduced, concerned exist about whether these internet based surveys are scientifically valid and how they are the best conducted. Because internet can offer possibility of multimedia and interactive surveys containing audio and video, convenience samples to respondents email address. As a result, quick polls and other types of entertainment surveys have become increasingly popular and widespread on the web marketing research.

On the web marketing based surveys had particular three of benefit assumptions to attract companies to choose to do marketing research: (a) internet based surveys are much cheaper to conduct, (b) internet based surveys are faster, (c) when combined with other survey modes, internet based surveys yield higher response rates than conventional survey modes by themselves. In general, companies shall consider the following key characteristics of surveys choices: Response rate, timeliness, data quality and cost .

(Adrian, P. 2012) indicated that in response rate hand, web surveys respondents that can or will answer via the web may not be sufficiently large to compare mail surveys possibly. However, a company AT& T employees surveys experiment indicated to report a 63% response rate via email (63 returned not of 100 sent by email) compared to a 38% response rate for postal mail (14 returned out of 40 sent by mail). Interestingly, it indicated the response rates to the fast that, at the time, At& T employees received a lot of corporate paper junk mail yet over the internal email system, they received little to no electronic junk mail. I expect the development of interactive electronic media market research survey can achieve responses from a convenience sample might be useful in developing research hypotheses. Responses from convenience samples might also be useful for identifying issues, defining ranges of alternatives or collecting other sorts of non inferential data.

On timeliness hand, survey timeliness is increasingly stressed. The length of time it takes to field a survey is a function of the contact, response and follow up modes. the relevant measure is not average response time, but maximum response time (or perhaps some large percentage of the response time distribution) since survey analysis generally does not begin until all of the responses are in. However, simply concluding that internet based surveys are faster than mail surveys ignores the reality that the total amount of time for survey fielding time is more than just the survey response time. A complete comparison must take into account the mode of contact and how long that process will take and the made of follow up allowing for multiple follow up contact periods. For example, if email address of respondents are unavailable and a probability sample is desired than respondents may have to be contacted by mail. In this case a web survey only saves time for the return delivery of the completed questionnaire and not for the contact and follow up, so that the resulting time savings may only be a fraction of the total survey fielding time. For example, a internet survey company, knowledge networks has indicated that to achieve 70 to 80 % response rates they must leave a survey in the field for about 10 days. This period comprises one workweek with two weekends because they find that most respondents complete their surveys on the weekend (Adrian, P. 2012).

In conclusion, the delivery time of an internet based survey is faster than the delivery of a survey by mail, it does not necessarily follow that the increased delivery speed will translate into a significantly shorter survey fielding period. Two points are relevant: dramatic possible for specialized populations and even for populations in which all electronic surveys are possible.

On the quality hand, the primary purpose of a survey is to gather information about a population , the information is useless unless it is accurate and representative of the population. When survey error is commonly characterized in terms of the precision of statistical estimated, a good survey designing seeks to reduce all types of errors, including coverage, sampling, non response and measurement errors. Data quality includes unit and item non response, honesty of responses , particularly for questions of a sensitive nature, completeness of responses particularly for open ended questions and quality of data transcription into an electronic format for analysis of requires by the survey made. Data quality is usually measured by the number of respondents with missing items or the questions, longer answered are usually considered more informative and of higher quality email surveys may incur a higher percentage of items missing than mail surveys. Other quality issues for internet based surveys resulting from some sort of sampling errors are generally the same as for conventional surveys. However, such accuracy may be misleading if non response biases are not accounted for and researchers need to carefully consider the trade offs between smaller samples that allow for careful non response follow up and larger samples with less or no follow up. Web surveys can be programmed to conduct input validation as a logical check of the respondent's answers.These types of checks improve data quality and subsequently save time in the preparation of the analysis file. This will eliminate errors and from the respondent's point of view, simplify the process of taking the survey.

On cost hand, designing a survey fundamentally involves making trade off between the quality and quantity of data and cost. For smaller research surveys that are not subsidized in any way, a major component of total survey cost is frequently the researcher's time for survey design and subsequent data analysis. The labour cost of the personnel who actually execute the survey. It depends on the size of the survey and the complexity of the design either researcher labour cost, survey personnel labour costs or a combination of the two will likely dominate the survey budget.When lower costs are often of the benefits, of internet based surveys, Couper et al. (1999) found no cost benefit in email compared to postal mail surveys in their work. In a large and comprehensive survey effort of different government agencies. Couper et al. compared an all email survey (contract, response and follow up) versus an all mail survey. They found that evaluating and testing the email software took over 150 hours almost 4 times as much as they budgeted.

For the mail survey, costs for printing and posting were $1.6 per reply and data editing and entry cost about $1.81 . For the mail survey , managing the email cost $1.74 per completed case. In addition, they handled over 900 toll free call of a technical nature when the printing and mailing costs were eliminated for the email survey. Couper et al.(1999) found that the cost of evaluating and testing the email software, additional post collection processing and the cost of maintaining a toll free phone line which was largely dedicated to responding to technical questions related to the email surveys offset any savings. For example, email survey was designed so that respondents would use the reply function of their email program so the resulting replies could be automatically read into a database upon receipt.

I expect web marketing based surveys can reduce errors to avoid to mislead companies to find the wrong marketing strategy to compare paper surveys from every time of individual group customer questionnaires researches from internet. Moreover, I also expect web marketing based surveys can reduce cost to compare paper surveys from every time of group customer questionnaires researches from internet. In conclusion, I expect the development of interactive electronic media to have on retailers collection of marketing research information from consumers, the internet companies need to consider the electronic surveys response rate and time and quality and cost and legal responsibilities issues to let any companies to use their electronic media to carry on marketing research from customers to feel more satisfactory to compare to traditional questionnaires market research media if internet companies still hoped business companies still chose to use whose service to do marketing research in the future.

England wine bar segmentation case study-applying wince bar consumer segmenation method to predict consumer behavior

Critically evaluate the bases that bars may use to segment their markets.

The United Kingdom bars market is a mass marketing, it means a strategy that presumes these is one undifferentiated market and that the bars wine drinking service provision will appeal to all consumers in that similar bar market. Marketing matching strategy divides segmentation, it means act of dissecting the marketplace into submarkets (segments) that require different marketing mixes, then targeting, it is the process of reviewing market segments and deciding which one(s) to pursue finally positioning, it needs to establish a differentiating image for a product or service in relation to its competition. segmentation variables may divide geographic, demographic, psychographic and behavioral variables.

In general, marketers may use a single variable or two or more variables. Geographic segmentation is based on the location of the target market, people living in the same area have similar needs that differ from living in other areas, climate, population, taste and micromarketing. Demographic segmentation is based on factors, such as age, gender, marital status, income, occupation, education, ethnicity. Psychographic segmentation is based on lifestyle and personality characteristics. Behavioral segmentation is based on attitudes toward or reactions to a product/ service and to its promotional appeals, usage rate, benefits sought from a product/ a service and loyalty to a brand or a store.

There are three basic market targeting strategies, such as undifferentiated, differentiated and concentration. Undifferentiated strategy ignores differences between groups within a market and offers a single market mix to the entire market and it works when a product/service is new to the market and there is minimal or no competition. Differentiated strategy means targeting two or more segments with different marketing mixes for each, concentration strategy focuses on one sub-market. Most British towns would had many small bars, all looking fairly similar to each other, with relatively few point of differentiation. Thus, if the UK bars do not use to segment their markets. I believe these UK bars will face much competition between themselves. In general, the market for drinking in pubs was fairly homogenous, comprising mostly male, who went to the pub mainly to drink and only very rarely to eat.

Now, UK pubs, clubs and bars continues to be a popular leisure activity in UK and pubs have benefits from a growth in eating out.

But, pub operators face challenges , including taxes on alcohol, growing competition from supermarkets for off sales, a smoking bad introduced. Pub operators have had to focus the design of bars on meeting the needs of smaller and smaller market segments. No longer is the pub market dominated by males going out to drink-professional women and families are among many segments and the professional and families segments, who seems dislike loud music or big screen television, who like to drink good quality coffee served more than beer, who like to enjoy bright and airy decorative in bars, who like to drink served to the table rather than queuing at the bar. These may have been design features that were unsought or unwanted by the traditional male heavy drinker segment. Hence, it seems that UK female professionals and families shall be the popular segment in this UK bars market. However, segmentation can not be based simply on where people live, and must recognize their mobility and movement patterns. Therefore, for some sites located in town centers or on busy roads, an understanding of people's work patterns and commuting habits can be crucial. Being near a train station may be crucial for attracting a target market or urban professionals who want somewhere to stop off to meet friends before catching a train home. I think the UK bars may use to segment their market. Segmentation is essentially about identifying groups of buyers within a marketplace who have needs that are distinctive in the way who deviate from the average consumer. Some consumers may treat satisfaction of one particular needs as a seek to satisfy any of needs from a car purchase total market, the possible factor that might influence and individual's choice of car, car market segment targeted includes status, safety for families, a particular image, a cost effective transport, seeking environment by buying a green car and a company buyer saves tax client groups. Hence, British bars are fairly similar to each other, with relatively few points of differentiation. The market for drinking in bars was fairly homogenous and British supermarkets can sell wines and the comprising mostly males who went to the bar mainly to drink and only very rarely to eat. Today, the bar scene in any British town centre is much complex. Hence, I think British bars ought to segment their markets if which wanted raise their competition.

On the first hand , the UK bar owner can choose professional women and family segment, in upmarket local, low density housing areas, it is likely to offer high quality food, no loud music or big screen television, good quality coffee served more than beer, bright and airy bar environment, drinks served to the table, rather than queuing at the bar, due to the proportion of women using these bars is higher than most of the locals.

On the second hand, the UK bar owner can choose male segment, in basic or mid market locals, that were unsought or unwanted by the traditional male areas; trade is focused on regular drinkers and tend to be met lead with little food. Beer, cider and spirits are the big sellers. Most show televised most offer some sort of food. There may also be themed evenings, quizzes, darts or pool. Customers tend to use the bar to meet friend and relax.

On the third hand, the bar can choose young local customers aged 18 to 30 secondary and university students segment. Amusements including pool tables and machines with feature and chart music and video screen will be prevalent.

On the fourth hand, the bar owner can choose city local to workers and shoppers segment, such as non office labors and supermarket buyers clients, it will offer basic bar food and snacks as well as centrally located in town centers but offering high levels of food, city dry led bars target the same customers as city locals, but focus on office labor clients mainly and it tends to be large and it may have function rooms and restaurant areas.

On the fifth hand, the bar owner can choose office workers and shoppers both segments. It may locate in centrally city location, but it needs to change from day to night to attract different types of customers. It can provide coffee bar attract in the day serving office workers and shoppers, but provide wine attract to young people's bar with loud music by might.

On the sixth hand, the bar owner can choose bar is located on or near the young non student people's circuit. Expect loud music, possibly a dress code and door staff and food is less important.

On the seventh hand, the bar owner can choose adults no children targets, in more upmarket areas. Restaurant quality food served for whose premium dining aim.

On the eight hand, the bar owner can choose family with children target, it again focuses on food these bar offers good value for money dining during the weekend and early evening.

On the final hand, the bar owner can choose to meet point for a specific customer group for example bikers, sport client segment in bicycle areas. It may be live music or entertainers to drink whose wine after who ride bicycle to need to find restaurant to sit down to relax and eat food needs. Hence, UK bar market is such as car sale market to follow family life cycle, gender and household composition, age, ethnic group, social class, individual income, lifestyles, individual attitudes, values benefits sought, the bar loyalty, the bar geographic location etc. the client internal psychological factors or the external environmental factors to divide different segments to sell in the market. However, I suggest the UK bars market segment ought to analyze to target young adult wine drinkers mainly. Bar consumer segmentation in the wine industry takes on many forms: demographic, geographic, behavioral and others. For the bar wine industry, this group currently fits the legal drinking age range of 21 to 28 ages. With the recent oversupply of wine bars on the UK local market, so UK wine bars competitions are very high. Due to this situation, I recommend who need to focus efforts on finding new populations of wine existing consumers, rather than just redoubling efforts with existing clients.

I think wine bar marketers in the United Kingdom have primarily focused on the existing population of wine bar old consumers, which are the very large baby boomer young generation. This was an effective strategy for many years, when the wine supply and economic conditions were stable. Now, however, one of the most promising of the new wine bar consumer segments in the UK is that of the boomer generation. Generally viewed as children of the baby boomers. This segments group is considered whose consuming power and represented the future bars market for most wine brands drinking in UK bars. The children of the boomers who are young and who ought like to meet friends to go to bars to drink different kinds taste of wines and play entertainment in bars during who have school holidays. UK bars market segmentation means the process of dividing which different drinking wines taste into meaningful, relatively similar and identifiable segments or groups. In general, UK bars market segmentation is useful for two major reasons. First, it assists bars marketing searchers in analyzing the needs of a specific customer segment. Second, the resulting data, it allows bars marketing campaigns to be focused on these identifies needs. In the long run, this allows bars to spend their marketing and advertising budgets wisely when at the same time meeting the needs of the drinking wine customer. Ideally, this should result in efficient, effective and profitable bars marketing and sales efforts. There are multiple types and levels of segmentation used in various industries, but those used most frequently by the wine bar industry are those that also fall into for four classic marketing segmentation bases. There are geographic, which is based on where the customer lives, such as big cities or small cities, demographic, which is based on age, gender, income, social class, psychographic, which is based on lifestyle and personality and behavioral which is based on occasions, benefits, usage rate , readiness to purchase stage.

In bars business, the wine taste is main factor to influence the clients choose to come to the bar again. In general, there are five consumer segments, such as conservative, knowledgeable wine drinkers; image oriented, knowledge seeking wine drinkers, basic wine drinkers, experimental, highly knowledge wine drinkers and enjoyment oriented, social wine drinkers. Anyway, psychographic factor can influence people choose to go to bars, the psychographic wine segments identify five major wine lifestyle, such as relaxed lifestyle, dining ambience, fun and entertainment, social aspiration and travel lifestyle. Hence, psychographic factor and wine taste knowledge factor are reasons why people choose to go to bars to drink wines instead of who choose to go to supermarkets to buy wines to drink. Regarding geographic segments in the wine industry, it includes individual wine bars or organizational wine bars or supermarkets or stores wine sale methods in UK country. Regarding wine consumption behavior is another factor, it includes five segments: Super-core, who consume wine daily; core, who consume wine at least two or three times per month; marginal, who consume wine at least two or three times per quarter ; non adopters, who don't drink wine, but drink other alcoholic beverages and non drinkers who don't on the areas where are not close to supermarkets or stores and the living people who are super core to consume wine daily in the areas. The bar has more chance to increase client numbers, it is unconsidered whether the bar's wine taste can satisfy its clients needs. However, the young age market segment has very high consuming power. They don't only have a lot of money, but who influence family purchase. Many perform the grocery shopping for their families and have been given parent co-signed credit cards at a young age.

A key question in market segment analysis for this group is: What drives their purchasing behavior regarding wine? Young people can spend on average of 16.7 hours per week on the internet, excluding e-mail. They use it for shopping, in chat rooms, for research and to keep up is their primary source of information and who trust it. Because of this focus, wine bar marketers are urged to use integrated media to reach young people and not use only traditional channels. Online technology is a critical part of this,, but also offline locations where, such as music clubs, wine bars magazines, cable television and outdoor posters. E-mails targets at online interest groups and cell phone marketing are also useful. However, wine bars advertising that ought includes diversity of race and gender. In addition, young people are highly influenced by minority cultures in terms of music, sport, dress and language. The wine bars marketing implication is that advertising should show a variety of diversity in terms of race and gender. Another consideration is to emphasize values and focus on cultural values when targeting specific ethno-centric segments of young people population in UK. I believe why wine bars can attract more young people, it is due to their focus on wine brands and who like to attempt different new or old wine taste, young people are very wine brand conscious and seek wine brands that provide quality, but at a fair price. Anyway, young people market segment characteristics is their belief in fun and responsibility, who tend to believe that life should be fun and enjoyable, but at the same time who do want responsibility and challenge on the job, who want to make sure that who take time out to enjoy life and believe that certain activities, so I feel young people accept to drink wine in base , the possibility is more than old people or adult ages people.

(Marketing segment predicts UK bar consumption behavior): In conclusion, I think this UK bar market is an undifferentiated mass marketing, due to any bars characteristics can only give places to provide similar tastes of wines or coffees drinking or foods and entertainment for clients to enjoy to single formulation of its food provided services, to bars have traditionally offer one standard of food service delivery to all of their domestic or foreign customers. Due to UK small, middle and large size bars and supermarkets and restaurants are increasing to cause competition seriously. Overtime, however, bar consumers' needs tend to fragment into segments of different needs. Where UK bar markets are competitive, a bar may no longer to able to ignore the bar clients whose special needs of small groups of its customers, because if bar owner sold similar taste of wines, coffees drinking and foods to its competitors of bars and restaurants and supermarkets, I believe the non segment bar will lose many clients to compare the segment bar in UK bar drinking wine restaurant industry.

In the context of bars, discuss the relative merits of quantitative and qualitative approaches to market segmentation.

In UK bars market, I think it had the relative merits of quantitative and qualitative approaches to bars market segmentation. As UK bars market segmentation, the UK bar owners need to identify groups of bar customers who have similar needs and respond in a similar way to a given marketing stimulus to raise their bar competition. Hence, UK bar owner may use segmentation to measure whether whose bar ought to choose to locate where location (areas) to provide which kinds taste of wines, coffees, foods and entertainment to attract which kind of bar client group mainly, e.g. if the bar target client group is professional office female, it can locate at upmarket location in low density housing areas. It is likely to offer high quality food because there are many professional office female clients are in these low density housing living. However, bars market segmentation should be regarded as the bar wines and coffees drinking and entertainment service provision of critical thinking rather than as some pre-determined set of procedures. It shall follow that to let the bar owner to know what is an appropriate basis for the bar segment and one client group market may not be appropriate to all bar client groups in the UK bars market. To aware of the criteria by which the effectiveness of any UK bars segmentation basis can be assessed. I shall indicate those four important criteria to measure the relative merits of quantitative and qualitative approaches to UK bar market segmentation which can earn. The four important criteria include the usefulness to the UK bars marketing planning; the size of the resulting to the UK bar segment; the UK bar measurability and the UK bar accessibility four criteria. On the usefulness to the UK bar's marketing planning criteria hand, it needs to ask this question before which chooses who is whose bar target client group and location and wine and food taste. Is the basis of bar market segmentation useful to the bar owner? It is easy to develop bases for market segmentation when losing sight of the purpose of the exercise. Essentially, the exercise is worthwhile only bar segmentation allows the UK bar owner profitably to penetrate a greater proportion of UK bars market then would have been the UK bar market case if the exercise had not been undertaken. UK bar market client groups identified as homogeneous bar market segments must be just that: Similar in terms of the needs of tastes of wines or coffees drinking and entertainment consumption behavior of the domestic or foreign individual client who contain. The UK bar shall fail in whose segmentation exercise because its assumptions about homogeneity within a bar segment, e.g. male or female or young student or young non student or family with children or family without children or bicycle sport client or office of non office segment, who overlooks some critical differences within the bar segment which leads to varied responses to the bar service offering that has been specifically targeted at the bar client segment. For example, a bar segment for the office workers target client group, instead of the bar owner needs to consider the location whether it is located to close to whose office, who also needs to consider these factors such as, what kinds of foods , wines, coffees drink taste and what kind of entertainment and service price charge and their habit consumption time. To be more effective, bar market segmentation must recognize the diversity of needs within this bar target client group. Hence, the bar can measure to quantify and quality its bar target client group to produce its bar market planning effectively.

On the size of the resulting to the UK bar segment criteria hand, the UK bar owner ought need to ask this question: Are the segments of an economic size to whose bar business? Any basic for bar segmentation should yield segments that are of a size that the bar can profitably exploit, because as the bar segments

get smaller who get closer to achieving the marketing philosophy of satisfying each bar client's needs as though each one were the center of the bar's attention. The problem for the uneconomic to provide for what a reasonable size of bar segment is varies from one UK bar market to another and is constantly changing over time. In the bar market , it is possible to provide quite unique tastes of wines or foods to target very small segments of the UK bar market. For example, if the bar target client group is professional female office worker clients. I think it ought need to locate its bar in the office areas location and the office and the office can not be close to supermarkets because supermarkets will have different style of wines and coffees to sell and its provision of cup of wines and coffees drinking and foods tastes must be different to supermarkets wines and coffees and foods tastes and the bar needs to consider what the entertainment is the professional female worker clients who need to enjoy in the quiet or noise bar environment. Because this factors will influence the bar's female professional workers' psychological needs and satisfactory needs. If who feel the bar's drinking and food and entertainment service provision which can't satisfy whose demand, who can choose another bars to close to office areas to cause the bar female client numbers will reduce. On the UK bar measurability criteria hand, the UK bar owner needs to ask this question: Can the bar market segment be measured? Ideally UK bar should be able to know the precise size of its identified bar market segment(s).

This is imported in order that the bar segment(s) can be compared and its profit potentials assessed. Unfortunately,

UK bars clients data are often not available to the UK bar quantity market segments. So the UK bar owner should believe the areas of bar clients exist but can't measure or the bar client numbers should define bar segments only on the basic of what it can accurately be measured, but the different areas (location) bar clients may have litter bearing on the homogeneity of bar consumers' needs and consumption aims or reasons. The UK bar market segments information have include, e.g. the age profile of an area, number of people per household etc. However, bar owner also needs to assess of individuals psychological subjectively factor, such as whose attitude and lifestyles, e.g. if the professional female worker who does not like to drink coffee or wine drinking, even the bar location is close to the professional female worker office client, it will not persuade who to enter the bar. Hence, the UK bar owner needs to find the areas where people whose lifestyles and attitudes to bar enjoyable feeling, then it may decide to measure whether the area (location) may have which bar target group(s) is/are the largest numbers to choose which kind taste of wines, coffees drinking and foods provision and which kind of entertainment to satisfy the bar's identified target client group(s) needs. Finally, on the UK bar accessibility criteria hand, the bar owner ought to ask this question: Are the segment(s) accessible to where bar business? There is little points to define the UK bar owner segment(s) of the UK bar market whose those bar segments are not accessible to the bar segments are not accessible to the bar owner or ever likely to be inaccessibility can come about for a number of reasons. Such as the UK bar owner may be prohibited by law from opening to locate whose bar in certain areas in UK geographic location (areas) or the UK law prohibits UK bar to sell some kind of taste of wines in whose country. Hence, the UK bar owner needs to know UK law prohibition to which kind of taste of wines drinking sold and where location (areas) to open its bars before who decides where to open its bar to sell wine to whose target clients segment(s) in British country. In conclusion, the UK bar owners can earn the relative merits of quantitative and qualitative approaches to market segmentation from these four criteria consideration.

P&G body and skin product marketing strategy case study-applying survey method to predict consumer behavior

How would you explain the success of the fairly brand?

P&G fairly brand which mainly sold low value consumer goods, such a household detergents from bar of soap washing products to sell in UK country supermarkets in the beginning. Then, it innovated to produce liquid soap washing products to sell in UK country supermarkets. Further, it continued to innovate to produce soap products, such as the power of four for price of one, launched this low bulk, high concentration soap product to sell more cost effective to sell in supermarkets, even overseas supermarkets. P&G predicted domestic dishwashing machines instead of liquid of soaps , so it innovated to produce dishwasher cleaning fluid detergents products to let housewives to clean their dishwasher after every family used dishwashers to clean their plates to aim to keep their dishwashers to feel more clean to compare to clean by hand washing. Even, P&G will continue to innovate to produce potential anti-bacterial food washes to satisfy consumers' increasing concern over resides on the surface of fruit and vegetables.

In fact, P&G can predict what the new washing products will sell in this washing market, who will be its direct competitors, which are generally similar in form and satisfy customers' needs in a similar way as well as who will be its indirect competitors, which may appear different in form, but satisfy a fundamentally similar need. Such as P&G sold bar soap washing products in the beginning, it aim to satisfy families wash body to feel more clean needs. But, P&G felt it's direct competitors can sell similar bar soap products, so it innovated to produce new liquid soap washing products to raise its washing unique products and was different to its body washing product competitors. On the other hand, P&G also predicted domestic dish washing machines instead of liquid of soaps , so dish washing machines shall be which indirect competitors. Due to housewives can use dish washing machines to wash plates, so who will not use hands to wash plates after eating, it will cause who reduce to use bar or liquid washing soaps to wash their hands. So, P&G innovated to produce dishwasher cleaning fluid detergents products to let housewives to clean their dishwashers after every family used dishwashers to clean their plates to aim to keep their dishwashers to feel more clean to compare to clean by hand washing.

Even, P&G will continue to innovate to produce potential anti-bacterial food washes to satisfy consumers' increasing concern over resides on the surface of fruit and vegetables. Hence, P&G had attempt to raise its competitive ability in fruit and vegetables food and dishwasher machines cleaning market instead of bar and liquid soaps human clean market. It seems P&G threats of new entrants and threats of substitute clean products. In fact, P&G considers it soaps or other washing products whether which will cause chemical harmful to human skin or foods or dish washers after consumers have used its washing products. In the absence of that safety relationship of P&G social responsibility, its brand can act as a substitute in managing buyers' exposure to risk. P&G branding simplifies the decision making process by providing a sense of security and consistency of buyers which may be absent outside of a relationship with a washing product supplier.

P&G brand addresses a number of dimensions of purchase risk which have been identified as: physical(Will it's soap or washing products cause consumer skin harm or foods harm or dish washers harm?); psychological (Will P&G soap products or washing products satisfy consumer's needs for safety of mind?); Performance (Do P&G soap products and washing products work in accordance with consumers' satisfactory requirement?); Financial (Will P&G soap and washing products provide adequate performance with consumers' budget?). Due to consumers will compare P&G soap and washing products to its competitors' risk level to choose which brand washing products can give the minimal risk to harm to their health to decide to buy from supermarkets. Hence, P&G brand needs be built objectively measured (bar or liquid soap products or washing products are such as unique shape and smell and reliability) and the subjective values that can be defined only in the minds of its consumers (such as perceived personality of P&G brand is unique compare to other washing products brands). It means that P&G will be recalled that its brand processes functional and emotional attributes. P&G brand has been variously described as having personality that are ' fun', 'reliable ', 'traditional' and ' adventurous' and it needs to let consumers to feel it can give no harm to whose health after who use P&G soap or washing kind of products. In fact, P&G developed a single strong P&G brand strategy to sell different kinds of washing products, such as bar soaps, liquid soaps, dishwasher cleaning fluid and anti-bacterial food washes etc products, It aims to let consumers who choose to buy to use these kinds of washing products, then who must remember P&G brand. One approach to P&G branding is to apply the same brand name to every washing products which produces. The big advantage of this approach is the economic of scale in promotion. Instead of promoting many minor brands through small campaigns, it can concentrate all of its resources on one campaign for P&G one brand. But, the main disadvantage of this approach is that P&G can pose significant risks of confusing the values of it's brand. If P&G positioned its bar soaps, liquid soaps, dish washing fluid
and anti-bacterial food washes etc. products range as premium priced, top quality, confusion may arise in consumers' minds if it applied the same brand name to a budget version of its washing products. Does P&G brand still stand for top quality? This is a particular problem for P&G new washing product, such as anti-bacterial food washes and dish washer cleaning fluid products which are of unproven reliability. Hence, P&G sells in low price strategy in supermarkets to let many families can buy its different washing products to do trial test whether its innovative washing products which are better quality to compare to other brand washing products to satisfy who to choose to buy P&G brand washing products for every families to use long term.

In fact, UK soaps product is a imperfect competitive market. The different soap manufacturing companies produce similar color and shape bar or liquid soap products and they build different brands and they are targeted at specific segments, such as family group and they need promotion to promote their brands and soaps price is premium sustained. Hence, P&G needs a differentiated product may have significant monopoly power in that it is unique, but if it fails to satisfy customers' needs, its uniqueness has no commercial value. However, P&G had innovated it different bar soap products to liquid soap products, even it also launched dishwasher cleaning fluid detergents products, due to dish washer machines reduce housewives to use hands to wash plates to use soap to clean whose hands after eating as well as it launches
potential anti-bacterial food washes to satisfy consumers' increasing concern over resides on the surface of fruit and vegetables. Hence, P&G aims to be any new cleaning products leader to raise its cleaning market share effort.

The soap and other detergents manufacturing industry of Procter & Gamble (P&G) trends and characteristics who its primary intended is target client group(s). I think families (householders) or student individual daily consumption are P&G main target client groups. Soaps are personal care products. Consumers will compare different brands of soaps to decide which brand soaps ingredients can give health to them to wash their bodies and skins. The soap industry includes (P&G) and other soap manufacturing companies primarily engaged in making soap, synthetic organic detergents, inorganic detergents and crude vegetable and animal fats. In general, skin care soap sales include bar soap, body wash and liquid categories which can sell in supermarkets and discounting retailers and drug stores. Traditional , bar soaps, which are considered a mature category, exhibit very low growth, when newer products (shower gels and body washed) substitute products are launched. However, natural soaps still have opportunities for growth if which can be launched to raise care to skins and bodies health to human. The soap and personal products industry is being driven to a large extent by the changing age composition of the population, specifically, baby boomers have established anti-aging preparation as the chief benefit of health products aimed at correcting or improving the physiological condition of the skin. They have led the broad personal care sector of the economy to focus on the potential in aging consumers. Growth is occurring in a variety of age-sensitive product markets from soaps and skin creams to massagers and body fat analysis machines. As baby boomers lives get busier, stress relief soap products will become more important to carry on launching their skin care health quality for human benefits in daily washing. The group composed of 45 ages old to 54 ages old females is responsible for the highest amount of sales of body care and bath products in mass stores, who can influence householder families members spending effort in soaps consumption. P&G soaps are displayed to supermarkets to retail, the supermarkets' shelves are remained unaffected by the changing population in the personal care products sale areas. Even retailers like Brook stone and Sharper Image expanded their interest in branded personal care items. Not only was more retail dedicated to the personal care products, but they were often placed in specific "spa shops" within the store, with displays used extensively to merchandise the personal care category. Body boomers are not, however, the only group important to the growth of this personal care industry. The number of personal care products designed specifically for children is increasing. Health and beauty aids suppliers are using licensing to tap into the growing spending power of children. The traditional soaps manufacturers must carefully review their marketing and other business strategies in order to adapt to the transformed market. The changes also create better opportunities for new personal care product companies to enter particular market segments. The mass bath and body care category has made recent introductions reflective of several trends that department stores, salons and special boutiques have been offering for years. The world consumers are changing their personal care demand to cause a result of soap product innovation, so P&G also needs to replace older well known soap products with newer ones that contain special formulations. New product activity and the increasing popularity and liquid soap increase competition in this personal care market. A growing perception among consumers that who must deal with problem skin and rising levels of concern about germs are helping drive sales of personal soap. Although, traditional brands such as Dove, Dial and Irish Spring still hold the largest portion of the toilet soap market smaller special soap manufacturers are increasing their market shares. Hence, P&G needs to focus on concentrating who its specialty soaps. In general, consumers want a soap that fits their particular needs and specialty soaps, often made with natural ingredients to protect bath and hand skin health. However, some competitors choose to sell soap substitute products, such as oils, bath blends, perfumes and fragrances in supermarket. Hence, these personal care products can also influence P&G company liquid soap sales in overall soap retail market. In soap manufacturer industry, the naturals trends is also evident in the ethic segment of skin care. Ethic consumers are seeking multi-functional products full of botanicals and vitamins butter natural ingredients. So, I think P&G needs to launch this kinds of new class of skin care product to raise its skin class of skin care product to raise its skin care health care to increase consumers' confidence. Due to personal care products market competition is increasing, such as one stop shopping stores can offer for a variety of health related items, healthy foods, dietary supplements, prescription and over the counter drugs, skin care products and other natural personal care products. In addition, smaller natural skin care manufacturers are staying competitive by targeting skin-related over the counter drug markets. Moreover, internet retailing of personal care products has grown rapidly. Web site can offer can be nearly limitless. One important advantage held by online sellers over stores with physical locations is the constraint caused by a lack of shelf space. The characteristics of online sellers allow them to stock a much wider variety of the products consumers want, if also provides an opportunity for small or large manufacturers audience of consumers. One of the greatest difficulties faced by a firm wishing to enter a consumer products market is persuading retailers that they will benefit by dedicating scare shelf space to the manufacturer's products to online selling reduces that problem.

A potentially important negative aspect of electronic commerce for personal products is that inability to feel and especially, smell the merchandise. Many personal care products list fragrance as an important characteristics. To the extent consumers are already familiar with a special products, this is not a problem, but such as P&G getting a new liquid soap products might be more difficult. Soap industry needs to launch to improve soap qualify to satisfy consumer need. It must need enough workers to help P&G to manufacture enough different kinds of soap to sell to different countries soap market. I think its workers include these kinds , such as packaging and filling machine operators, first line production supervisors, cleaning, picking equipment operators, hand packers and packagers, hand material movers and soap researchers because it needs these workers to help it to produce different kinds soaps in the manufacturing process in factory, so it needs to give training to raise whose proficient skills to prepare to produce any new kinds of soap efficiently and it needs to consider the labor supply to soap manufacturing market , e.g. who needs to know what the difference between chemicals and all natural ingredients to prepare to produce its soaps ethically. Because if they have errors in the manufacturing process to cause consumers feel to use P&G soaps to have chemical negative health response. These workers shall influence P&G health soap products image negatively. Hence, P&G needs to consider its workers' working attitude ethically. However, P&G was the largest soap maker and it did not own the most part maintain in house chemical manufacturing capabilities. P&G must therefore purchase new materials from other suppliers, so P&G needs to consider its raw materials suppliers market to measure whether who can give it the largest benefits and the cheapest costs both, Thus, giving the raw material suppliers global marker to choose who remain a greater incentive to provide superior service to P&G. I think P&G needs to spend time to choose who is its raw material suppliers who can provide the best natural health quality and the least chemical ingredients to cause consumers to use to feel uncomfortable response to their skins negative influence. Hence, I think P&G ought innovate its soap products quality to satisfy to avoid to use any cheap chemicals ingredients to produce its old or new kinds of soap products to sell to consumers unethically if it still wants to a sale leader in this personal care product market.

How do you think Procter & Gamble has been able to increase its market share at a time when competition from supermarkets' own-label brands has intensified?

Procter & Gamble operates mainly low value consume products, such as household detergents are among the most competitive and building successful brand is key to long term profitability. Differentiating one product from another in the minds
of consumers can be extremely difficult, with one packet of detergent looking very much like another and performing similarly. It seems that it can not be unique to sell in supermarket. However, then it innovated new liquid soap products, it seemed to adopt to change in consumer preference, and maintaining consistent standards when exploiting new market opportunities. Adrian, P. 2012) showed that Fairy liquid was rated as Britain's number one cleaning brand by Marketing magazine and in 2010 accounted for 3 percent share of the UK washing up liquid category by value. The brand has been a regular household feature since the name first appeared in 1898 year on a bar of soap. P&G first launched Fairy liquid in the UK market I think Procter & Gamble (P&G) has this marketing strategy to supply its soap products to supermarket retailers. A supermarket is not only supply to likely to encounter a massive range of products, such as food , drink, homecare, personal care, luxury products etc. Consumers can see categories and see how much the offering changes, the range , the packaging , the branding and advertising or promotion of any brand products sale at shelves. Hence, such as P&G manufacturer in 1960 year. At the same time, the market for washing up products was still in its infancy, with most consumers using solid soaps, and only 17 per cent of households using liquid soap. But P&G gained most from a change in consumers' habits. It educated the public of the benefits of using washing up liquid. The launch of Fairy liquid soap products involved distributing 15 million trial bottles to about 85 per cent of household in the UK. Creating early awareness and trial of the Fairy liquid soap innovative products led to Fairy gaining a market share of 27 per cent by 1969 year. It had a proud positioning as a slightly more expensive product which is better value and worth. So, it created brand values of a soft, caring, homely image by advertisement promotion. It also attempted to adopt in response to changing attitudes, for example, a commercial in 1994 year for the first time used a father instead of a mother at the kitchen sink. During the first

twenty years of the brand's life, product innovation had been relatively modest. However, an increasing competitive market, customers have forced P&G to innovate in order to maintain and strength its market share.

Adrian, P.(2012) showed that with emergence of many 'me-too' competitors from supermarkets, Fairy needed to offer additional unique advantages to raise its competition. In 1984 to 1985 years, P&G introduced a lemon variant of Fairy and its total market share increased to 32 per cent. By 1987 year the market share had increased to 34 per cent, with the newly introduced lemon variant accounting for one-third of sales. In 1988 year, a new formulation was launched , offering 15 per cent extra mileage, as well as more effective grease eradication. In 1992 year, the original Fairy Liquid was replaced with Fairy Excel, which claimed to be 50 per cent better at dealing with grease. This helped to increase the market share to 50 per cent . In the following year a concentrated version of Fairy Excel Plus was launched, with the slogan ' The power of four for the price of one'. P&G launched this low bulk, high concentration product to retailers, such as supermarkets, who were tiring of filling their valuable shelf space with more and more variants of basically low value products. Excel Plus offered supermarkets more cost effective and profitable use of their shelf space. Increasing ownership of domestic dish washing machines posed a threat and also an opportunity to Fairy. The threat came from a relative decline in sales of liquids used for hand washing of dished. The opportunity arose from increased demand for dishwasher cleaning fluid and the Fairy brand was extended to dishwashing detergents. In 2006 year, P&G introduced Fairy Active Bursts for dishwasher. Excel Plus was launched in the UK, Denmark, Finland, Germany, Holland, Ireland and Sweden etc western countries' supermarkets to help it to sell.

Innovation and reliability have been at the heart of Fairy's branding strategy, in a market which has been contested by other manufacturers' brands, and increasingly by supermarkets' own label brands. Preferences for new scents of detergent are continually emerging and provide an opportunity for innovation. Following a series of food safety scares, some observers of the market have pointed to a potential market for anti-bacterial food washes which would satisfy consumers' increasing concern over resides on the surface of fruit and vegetable.

Its innovative liquid soap products, it needs supermarkets where which compete with other soap product manufacturers for the attention and hopefully the purchases to shoppers choice. It's a soap products from bar soap to liquid soap kind of products. P&G brand have been a player in the household and consumer personal care products market for nearly 200 years. They started life making candles at a time when there were still a common source of domestic lightly. But they moved on from those to other related products, soaps and cleaning products. Today, P&G have around 300 brands, including Crest Oral Care brand, Pampers Nappies brand and Baby products, Tide and Arial brand washing powders, Tampax Sanitary products etc different brand in this personal care market. To keep a range as wide as this refreshed and to develop new and improved produce to feature on the supermarket stages around the world needs a powerful innovation engine. P&G had built a world wide research and development operation which involves some 7500 scientists and a spent of around USA$3 billion per year. It might be not as much as the high technology pharmaceutical industry, but still very impressive for its sector. P&G had some very effective systems and structures to ensure efficient soap products innovation project selection and progression . P&G had an impressive record on new product launches and many of their new categories billion dollars brands, products magic whose annual sales could be high as US$150 to US$200 million. But, in the late 1990 year, there were concerns about this approach to innovation. When if worked there were worries, not least the rapidly rising costs of carrying out research and development cost. However, I think P&G should not raise its new kinds of soap products sale price, such as liquid soap products. Even it had spent too much research and cost development expenditure. Hence, I think it still needs to keep competition to attract different countries consumers to buy from different countries consumers to buy from different countries supermarkets globally. Hence, low sale price is its major market strategy in supermarkets sale make. For long term, I suggest P&G chooses to outsource its research and development internal business department to one or more than more external technological research and development consultant company/companies to carry on researching any new soap products to avoid spending too much expenditure to raise soap products sale prices to reduce its competition to sell in supermarkets. P&G 's pioneering use of advertising, direct distribution , marketing research , brand management and produce innovation strategies to raise it's growth throughout the 20th century. Diversification, globalization of it's brands, innovations in distribution and supply chain management and P&G 's technological and product innovation strategy continues to drive its success into the 21st century. P&G had pioneered a series of strategic innovations had sustained its competitive advantage in a number of highly competitive market and its primary focus was process innovations in many areas.

Firstly, background on P&G was from its origin to 2008 year briefly reviewed. Next five strategic innovations were each reviewed along with its competitive implications in the areas of direct to consumer advertising, direct product distribution, marketing research, brand management and technological and product innovation. Hence, P&G soap products innovation was divided to two stages of two different periods to aim to satisfy consumers' body and skin health needs of bar soaps choice to use liquid soaps choice in this personal bath and washing care market.

Adrian, P. (2012) showed that in 1915 year, P&G opened a facility in Canada representing its international operations. A chemical division was created during 1917 year and 1918 year which was responsible for research and development of new products. To sell these new products. P&G created a market department in 1924 year. The purpose of this department was to study consumer preference and purchasing inhabits (Data monitor, 2008:7). In 1926 year, a perfumed bar of soap was introduced. By the end of the 1920 year P&G had no longer produced candles, thereby signal a major shift in its core business . Then, 1933 year, the acquisition lead P&G into hair care products. In the early 1940 year, P&G established a drug products division which also developed and sold a variety of toiletry items.Then, P&G introduced new products and entering new markets, it had not stopped innovating on its established products , such as tide liquid soaps was launched in 1984 year. During this time P&G also purchased Blendax a popular tooth paste brand in Europe. As the 1980 year, P&G made a significant move in Asia by entering into a joint venture to produce products in China. In 2007 year, it invested US$35 to US$50 million in its Gillette manufacturing facilities in South Boston, USA. At the same time, it announced a restructuring whereby P&G. Beauty and health division would be managed under the P&G purchased HDS cosmetics laboratory skincare line that focuses on specific skin conditions that require more attention than general cosmetics. P&G 's history of marketing innovation began in 1980 year with Ivory soap on what had been promoted around the world as the floating soap (Dyer et al., 2004). Ivory represented P&G 's first attempt to brand a product through the use of advertising to connect with customers. Direct to consumer advertising was an innovation P&G pioneered with its customers and as such was a major innovation versus the traditional practice of advertising to wholesalers and practice of advertising to wholesalers and other distributors. During the 1800 year's soap was cut from huge soap slabs at the local grocer. Soap was a classic commodity with each manufacturer's product virtually indistinguishable from others. It is believed that P&G 's technological innovation was making Ivory out of Palm and Coconut oils, both less expensive than olive oil that was the basis of better soaps of the soaps to be mass produced and felt of finer higher quality soap (Dyer et al., 2004).Unlike other soaps of that, Ivory ingredient was lathered, easily and floated in water without melting. The unique blend of the soap meant that P&G could sell the soap in a premium market, such as supermarkets. However, since it used less expensive inputs, this led to higher margins. Those higher margins provided the mass to pay for advertising to raise the profile of the soap (Dyer et. al., 2004), thereby creating the brand and the beginning of a product differentiation strategy to sell in supermarkets.

To what extent can the principles and practices of brand management used for fairy liquid be applied to other goods and services, such as televisions and package holidays?

I think the brand management principle used for P&G brand, fairy liquid soap products sale which is more similar to apply to any television brands management products sale. Otherwise, the brand management principle uses for P&G brand, which is not more similar to apply to any package holidays travel services. Firstly, televisions and liquid soaps which have similar characteristics, such as they are products and it can be touched, seeing it existence and they are needed to launch to adopt consumers' taste, e.g. consumers link to accept to use liquid soaps more than bar soaps popularly as well as consumers like to watch colorful and clear image of televisions more than black and white image of televisions. Hence, any soaps and televisions companies which need to launch high technological televisions or more health ingredients of soaps to satisfy consumes' needs seriously if which wanted to build their brands famously and which wanted to retain old consumers and attract more consumers to buy their products in this skin care and television entertainment markets. Otherwise, if some companies did not continue to launch their television or soap products. I believe these companies brands will be not popular, even consumers will forget their brands existence due to other companies continue to launch their televisions or soaps to build strong brands in those skin care and television entertainment both product markets competitively.

Anyway, any one travel agent's package holidays travelling service is not similar to P&G brand fairy liquid soap products characteristics. Due to package holidays travelling services which can't be touched and can't be seen, the package holiday visitors who can only feel the travel agency whether whose travel journey itinerary arrangement, e.g. travelling destination, travelling date and time, travelling living apartments, hotels, restaurants, leisure activities, air tickets prices, airlines choice etc. whether this package holidays travelling is suitable to him/her only or whose family or whose friends with her/him together. The most importance, package holidays travel services are not similar to soap or television products which need to often launch whose skin care and seeing entertainment products to adopt consumers' needs. Although, the travel agencies sometimes need to reorganize new travel journal itinerary , e.g. seeking England, United States fresh and unique travelling places or cheap hotels who travelers choose popularly. But, travelling industry is seasonal period leisure business, it means that public holidays will have many consumers. Hence, basically, the seasonal periods are limited to travel agencies to build whose brand easily. It means that the client numbers are influenced by the seasonal periods, their numbers will not have much changing, even the travel agent often spend much effort and time to seek any new and unique travel journey itinerary holidays package. Although, travel agencies do not need to spend much money to invest to launch its package holidays travel arrangement service. But, they are existence in one competitive travel market. Every travel agent package holidays travel service price is controlled by the seasonal period whether the period is holiday or is not holiday and what the travelers' feeling to the country, e.g. safety extent, shopping places and prices extent, air ticket prices extent, accommodations and restaurants prices extent. These factors are controlled by the travelling countries. Agencies are difficult to differ their packages holiday travelling services to win other travelling agent competitors to build strong brand management famously. Due to which cannot control external factors to influence their price competition easily, such as airline companies air tickets prices, the destination (country) which hotels, restaurants, leisure services and transportation prices which are controlled by the travelling destination country's businessmen directly. It implies any travel agencies are difficult to build unique strong brands to attract many travelers who choose to find which to help them to arrange packages holiday travelling services to earn more commissions easily. However, if the travel agency had owned only concentrated on arranging packages holiday travelling services experiences and it had many prior packages holiday travelling consumers who feel that it can arrange the most suitable packages holiday travel arrangement services to let them to satisfy all different packages holiday services. I believe who will only choose this travel agent to help them to arrange any packages holiday travel arrangement services again, even who will introduce its packages holiday travel arrangement services to their friends to know the travel agency's brand by mouth speaking individually. It seems that a new or an old travel packages holiday travel arrangement services agent who ought need more old customers who can speak to whose friends to know how it can give excellent travel packages holiday travel arrangement to them individually, so television or radio or newspapers media travelling advertisement channels do not need promote long time if whose old consumers feel which can provide excellent packages holiday travel arrangement services to make them to enjoy satisfactorily. Hence, it's old consumers' feeling whether who satisfy or who do not satisfy its packages holiday travel arrangement service which will influence the travel agent to build its brand successfully in this packages holiday travel arrangement market. Otherwise, a new or an old television products brand sale company needs more magazines, radios, televisions advertisement to promote which television products for long time due to every family who have different demand to choose to buy the television products, e.g. size, design, manufacturing history and manufacturing country's price. It implies the family can't influence to whose friends to decide to buy or not buy the television brand easily. Due to every family has different demand to choose which kinds of television company brand. The television brand's any different style of television products of the family to choose is not same to or influence to whose friends television brands, so the television brand's buyers speaking will not influence whose friends whether to choose or not choose to buy the television brand easily. Furthermore it will take a closer look at the motivational world of the travel agency staff and how both groups interact. These questions will be analyzed with regard to its significance and applicability in brand management. The results of a neuropsychological systems of package tourists and travel agents with a psychological test.

When investigating the travel market it must be taken into consideration that it is subject to considerable changes due to , for example new dynamic production processes, price comparing systems, the growth of online providers etc. Every travel agent needs to make each brand unique and distinguishable in its perception . The key issues discussed where: Why do package tourists buy? Which scopes and potentials are there ? When positioning style brands? How can potential customers be better addressed and won as a customer? Central question concerning travel agents where: What is there main motivation (commissions, incentives) ? How can travel agents be addressed more effectively? How can travel agents help to increase the sale? Sensing versus intuition concerns perception itself, thinking versus feeling are decision strategies based on perception and judging versus perceiving relate to the handling of these decision . Because individual travel agent needs explain why their choice of packages holiday arrangement is the best suitable to every consumer considerately when the consumer is the first time to contact the travel agent , so the travel consultants need have professional image to make whose visitors to believe whose packages holiday arrangement is the most right to satisfy them to travel in their journeys. Otherwise, one of television brand seller who does not need to build more professional image, due to who is only the television company brand representative, whose duties are needed to explain what the television features and functions to let whose customers to compare to other brand television products when who enquires any one of television brand seller. However, travel agent must need to seek any packages holiday travel informational to let any consumers to choose to let them to compare whether which packages holiday arrangement service is the most suitable to who from the travel agent immediately. Hence, a package holiday travel agent seems to be a travel economist, who needs to compare which packages holiday arrangement is the most right and the most reasonable price to follow travel data gathering to adopt to every customer needs after whose customer spends whose packages holiday arrangement to feel satisfactorily if who want to help whose travel company to build famous brand of providing excellent packages holiday arrangement successfully in this travel market. Hence, any packages holiday businesses which travel consultants seem to be individual mouth speaking advertising to every visitor when who enquire whose packages holiday arrangement ideas to achieve aim to let every visitor to feel travel consultant can suggest the useful packages holiday arrangement because who must not have confident to arrange their travel plan by himself or herself. It seems that a new or an old travel packages holiday arrangement service agent which needs more old customers who speak to whose friends to recognize its existence to build its brand for long term. So television or radio or newspapers travelling advertisement do not need to spend long term if whose old customers feel which can provide an excellent packages holiday arrangement service to them to enjoy satisfactorily. Hence, its old consumers' feeling whether who satisfy or who do not satisfy its packages holiday arrangement service from the first time, they shall influence whose friends or relatives who decide to attempt to enquire the travel agent successfully. Otherwise, any one of television brand sale persons who do not need to build more professional image, due to the sale persons are only the television company brand sale representative, whose duties only need to explain what the television features and functions to let the customers to compare to compare to other brand television products to decide whether who ought to buy the brand television or ought not to buy the brand television. However, any travel agents must need to seek any packages holiday information about airline air tickets prices, itinerary journey and hotels, transportation, restaurant meals, leisure activities of the travel destination country to let any consumers to choose the different packages holiday arrangement programs to compare whether which packages holiday arrangement program is the most suitable to their travel needs immediately. So, their satisfactory extent to the packages holiday arrangement from the travel agent's consultant who can influence their friends or/and relatives to feel whether the travel agent can help them to arrange packages holiday satisfactory. Otherwise, a new or an old television product brand company needs more advertising from magazines, radios, televisions to promote which television products for long term, due to every family who have different demand to choose to buy the television products, e.g. television size, design, manufacturing history and manufacturing country and prices etc factors which can influence every family choice. It implies the family can't influence to whose friends or/and relatives to decide to buy or not buy the television brand easily. Due to every family members who have different demand to choose which kinds of television company brand. Furthermore, it will take a closer look at the motivational world of the travel agency staff and how both groups interact. These questions will be analyses with regard to its significance and applicability in brand management. The results of a neuropsychological study, which measured the implicit personality systems of package tourists and travel agents with a psychological test. When investigating the travel market , it must be taken into consideration that it is subject to considerable changes, due to , for example, new dynamic production processes , price comparison systems, the growth of online providers etc. Every travel agent needs to make each brand unique and distinguishable in its perception. The key issues discussed where: Why do package tourists buy? Which scopes and potentials are there? When positioning style brands? How can potential customers be better addressed and won as a customer? Central question concerning travel agents where: what is there main motivation (commissions, incentives)? How can travel agents be more effectively? How can travel agents help to increase the sale? Sensing versus intuition concerns perception itself, thinking versus feeling are decision strategies based on perception and judging versus perceiving relate to the handling of these decision. Because individual travel agent needs to explain why whose choice of packages holiday arrangement is the best suitable to every consumer considerably when the customer is the first time to contact the travel agent , so travel agent is needed more professional travel knowledge to arrange the best packages holiday to serve every visitor to enjoy their holidays satisfactory to build their brand. Otherwise, any television brand company sale representatives who only need to introduce what the style of television product which feature to let the visitor to know to decide to buy or not buy it. So, any television product brands which need more different kinds of advertising to help them to promote to build their brands long term.

Survey predicts consumer behavior result:

In conclusion, P&G fairy liquid soap brand management principle, which is more similar to apply to television product brand management principle, which need to launch their different style products to satisfy clients needs. Such as P&G brand company needs to continue to change its product ingredient to let many customers to feel to use safely , e.g. it launches bar soap products to liquid soap products as well as any television product companies to launch how to change television images and colours to be more clear to attract many customers to choose to buy whose television brands products. Otherwise, packages of holiday arrangement tourism service, tourism consultants need to own professional travel knowledge to help whose visitors to arrange any the most reasonable price and the most safe and the most unique journeys to attract any visitors to choose whose packages of holiday services. In fact, travel agents who do not need to spend much money to invest to carry on launching their travel service to raise time to gather travel information to increase whose ideas to achieve to persuade every visitors to choose packages of holiday arrangement successfully. Hence, it seems P&G fairy liquid soap product brand management principle which can not apply to packages of holidays travel arrangement service clearly.

Mobile phone company marketing strategy case study-apply online (internet) technology data gathering statistic method to predict consumer behavior

Critically evaluate methods that mobile phone companies could use to assess buyer's likely response to new features, such as video on demand.

Mobile phone is a product to satisfy customers' verbal communication needs during who leave home to need to communicate with anyone urgently . Mobile products are only bought for the verbal communication benefit. In other words, a mobile phone product is of value to someone only as long as it is perceived as satisfying some extra need, instead of verbal communication, such as watching video demand from internet when people are sitting on buses, or trains , or drive cars to watch video entertainment from their mobile phones. So, a mobile phone can be a material product, it can also provide an intangible service, such as verbal communication and watching video or sending email from internet by an 3G or 4G telecommunication fast speed internet service provision channel when who leave their home, who can also enjoy to watch video and call anyone and send email such as staying at home. However, mobile phone is a high level of emotional involvement communication product by the buyer due to there are many different and similar style of mobiles to provide to customers to choose to buy, so I think the mobile phone can provide watching video from internet feature is prefer to buyer to choose more than the mobile phone can not provide watching video from internet , even it's price is more than the non video watching mobile due to young people like to watch video instead of going to cinemas to see movies, it is possible who have no time or who feel movie tickets prices are expensive. Mobile phone is low level of accessible product, due to buyers can use home telephone when who stay at home or who can use any restaurant phone if who is walking on the street , it's location is near to restaurants. Mobile phones are shopping goods, due to consumers generally put a lot more effort into choosing shopping different style of mobiles to buy. Their evaluation include price, credit facilities, guarantees, after sale service, email or video entertainment from internet service. Different brands of mobile products are distributed through fewer retail outlets and therefore there is likely to be a higher margin for the retailer. Customers are usually willing to travel to an outlet to find a brand style of mobile, rather than expecting it to be available on their doorstep. Large amounts of money may be spent on advertising to develop strong brands, such as 3G and 4G telecommunication provision service to watching video or sending email from mobile internet. In fact, mobile product needs to provide intangible service, such as verbal communication , watching video, sending email. Hence, many mobile users ought prefer to buy the brand of mobile company which can provide these kinds of services because who feel these services are whose basic needs, specially the students like to use mobiles to watch video entertainment or working people like to use mobiles to send email to their offices to keep communication when who need to leave offices to work outdoor. However, watching video on mobiles is one new idea to focus of whether who need this service, it can be unclear who the customer is and it can be difficult to conceptualize the exchange that takes place between the provision video watching service of mobile buyer and the mobile seller of the idea. Hence, mobile phone companies need to do market research to evaluate who are the preferable ages segment group and what factors which will cause who do not choose to buy their mobile brands of watching video mobile products. Mobile phone industry is a product innovation industry. Nowadays, mobile phones have these features, such as cameras, MP3 players and web-browsing. The life cycle of mobile phones as a broad product category is now at the mature stage, some would say saturated. But when individual product formats are examined, a pattern of continual development, launch, growth and eventual decline is evident. Mobile phone companies vision is to affect people, process and technology by enhancing workflow, improving access to knowledge, increasing the speed of business transactions and providing better modes of video watching feature. Some mobile phone companies are already using mobile applications to deliver video image to increased client matching feeling satisfaction. The mobile phone video watching speed convenient availability and price is factor to influence individual client to choose the mobile phone company's style video mobile or chooses another mobile phone to buy.

Some mobile companies have complex products that need to be maintained at the client's premises. Photocopies are a good example. The quality of field service and support is an obvious factor is establishing customer satisfaction as well as in building the kind of customer loyalty that leads to repeat business. The mobile companies have leveraged the potential of wireless support tools are gaining ground in the marketplace. I think mobile phone is not seen simply as a way to communication function. It ought to spend on carrying on researching and development on internet to deliver email message communication and it also needs to provide on line video watching entertainment service new features when every individual client is using every mobile phone company's different style of mobile phone if the mobile phone companies still wanted their mobile phones can sell to clients in this global mobile phone competitive market. Today, mobile phone is popular communication tool to every family. Due to beyond the rapid consumer adoption and usage of mobile phone is the opportunity mobile phone companies offer for brands to connect more meaningful and personally with consumers. Considering it every individual direct line and immediate connection with audience when who is leaving at home to communicate easily.

Most brands spend less than one percent of their marketing budget on mobile. The argument is that the one percent spend level is too low, given the fact that most consumers devote about 10% of their media attention to their mobile device.

During the 20 century, marketers employed mass-market media channels-Television , radio. The result was that brands created marketing massages that out of necessity had to appeal to a broad spectrum of consumers. It implied that watching video had been every person's habitual behaviour everyday. If mobile phone can provide video watching feature to satisfy every client's seeing enjoyment. I think the individual client will choose to buy the mobile phone, which can provide video watching feature more than the mobile phone which can't provide video watching feature, even the individual client feels the owing video watching feature of mobile phone which price is higher than the lacking video watching feature of mobile phone. Because there are many people like to bring their mobile phones to watch video when who are leaving at home.

I shall suggest to do one marketing research of open to close survey method to new features, such as video on demand by whose mobile phone.The survey questions can be conducted , such as whether the client will determine to buy mobile phone with video feature more or who will determine to buy mobile phone without video feature more when the client need to buy one mobile phone to use; whether the client shall compare all different style of mobile phone with video feature which price, size, design and functions before the client determine to buy one mobile phone with video feature; whether what the factor is the most importance to influence the client choose to buy the mobile phone style with video feature, such as function, design, price, colour, size, quality more durable use production of year; whether what factors influence the client to buy other companies' mobile phone with video feature, such as cheap price, unique indifferent design, attractive colour, smaller size or larger size, production of year, whose friends or family introduction, advertisement promotion, convenient availability more durable use and quality; what kind of mobile phone with video feature, the client won't accept to use, such as screen picture is small size, image lacks clear color, too big size or too small size mobile phone feeling difficult to control . Hence, after any mobile phone had gathered their questionnaire researchers idea, then which can analyze whose data to carry on evaluating to estimate whether video features on mobiles demand on the difficult countries' consumer numbers. For example, every country sample of 100 people whose ages were between 10 ages to 20 ages segmentation group, a sample of 100 people whose ages were between 21 ages to 30 ages segmentation group, a sample of 100 people whose ages were between 31 ages to 40 ages segmentation group, a sample of 100 people whose ages were between 41 ages to 50 ages segmentation group, a sample of 100 people whose ages are between 51 ages to 60 ages segmentation group etc. If the 10 ages to 20 ages segmentation group had 50 people out of 100 people who prefer to buy video feature on mobile. It can estimate the country's this age group whose people numbers whether how many population shall prefer to buy video feature on mobile in the country. Hence, market survey research method can identify to measure every country's different age segmentation of client numbers who prefer to buy video feature on mobile clearly.

In terms of a new product development process, how could the development and launch of Tele point services have been improved in order to avoid the problems that were experienced ? What lessons can be learnt for the development of 3G (or 4G services)?

Adrian, P.(2012) showed that Hutchison is not new to taking big risks in the mobile phone market. It was behind the Rabbit network of semi-mobile Tele point phones launches in the UK in the 1980 years. These allowed callers to use a compact handset to make outgoing calls only, when they were within 150 meters of a base station, these being located in public places such as railway stations, shops, petrol stations, etc. As in the case of many new markets that suddenly emerge, operators saw advantages of having an early market share lead. Customers who perceived that one network was more readily available than any other would all other things being equal be more likely to subscribe to that network. Operators saw that a bandwagon effect could be set up to gain entry to the market at a later stage could become a much more expensive market challenger exercise. Such was the speed of development that the Tele point concept was not test marketed. To many, the development was too much product led, with insufficient understanding of buyer behavior and competitive pressures. Each of the four companies forced through their own technologies, with litter inclination or time available to discuss industry standard handsets which could eventually have caused the market to grow at a faster rate and allowed the operations to cut their costs. The Rabbit network came with the announcement by the UK government of its proposal to issue licenses for a new generation of personal communication networks, these would have the additional benefits of allowing both incoming and outgoing calls, and would not be tied to a limited base station range. By 2006 year, the next generation of mobile phone services were under development, with Japanese trials of 4G faster than 3G telecommunication service. 3G phones were also challenged by the development of alternative wireless access services, notably Wi Fi. Many companies, such as T-Mobile had began offering mobile Wi Fi services, which allow users to log on a local access points and gain access to their email and browse internet. Subscribers to VOIP telephone services could also effectively make the free phone calls from a Wi Fi access point. For many business travelers, using their laptop, Wi Fi access seemed a more attractive and less expensive option than using a 3G phone connection to check for email. It was likely to become even more attractive, with development of longer range Wi Max services that extended beyond the very limited 50 meter or so range of Wi Fi. The pressure of 3G telecommunication services was intensified when the UK government announced in 2006 year that it would license the development of a national Wi Fi network.

It seems that 3G and 4G telecommunication service can be capable of speeds faster then Tele point Rabbit telecommunication in any places conveniently. It causes Tele point Rabbit telecommunication becomes obsolete to mobile to use. From 2003 year, mobile phones industry seemed that the new digital technology would be a third generation of mobile phones (3G). By 2008 year, work was well with the development of the next generation of fourth generation

mobile phone (4G) telecommunication service. In terms of a new product development process, the mobile companies need to consider the development and launch of Tele point services have been improved in order to avoid the problems that were experienced. The mobile product mix comprise range of mobiles that a company offers to the mobile market. Tele point service launching whether it is the individual mobile is with its core or secondary and augmented elements to influence consumers to buy mobiles essentially. I think the external factors, such as UK mobile phone companies whether which can sell the augmented mobiles or the secondary level mobiles or the core mobiles which can influence Tele point service demand, such as if the mobile company can only provide the core benefit, but it's style of mobiles which lacks the better characteristics in the secondary level to attract consumers, which shall reduce mobile sale numbers, features are such as mobile design, color, shape, reliability, texture, packaging , even if it lacks the augment level competitive effort, such as after sales service, brand name, credit facilities, speed of delivery and warranty. Thus, even Tele point service launching is useful to mobile buyers, if the consumers feel the mobile products prices are expensive and they are not valuable to attract them to buy mobiles. Tele point service is not the main factor to influence the buyers to choose to buy mobiles in UK mobile market when this mobile phones are launched to

sell in the beginning. The another factor is that Tele Point was new telecommunication service in 1980 in UK mobile telecommunication service market. There is likely to be a lot

of promotional effort by Tele Point service to promote to mobile markets to secure sales. It is likely that the network of semi-mobile Tele point phones telecommunication service needs have high costs in the development of its service, costs that in the early stages may not be covered by revenue. Potential customers for a new network of semi mobile Tele point phones telecommunication service may be few and far between and therefore sales in early stages may be quite slow. This stage is known as the introduction stage. However ,Tele point phones telecommunication network service had this limitation. It only allowed callers to use a compact handset to make outgoing calls only, when they were within 150 meters of a base station, these being located in public places ,such as railway stations, shops, petrol stations, etc. If it's service proved popular, more people will show an interest and start purchasing it. However, due to many other mobile network telecommunication competitors who copied Tele point network telecommunication service technology to launch more fast speed and no location limitation and they can make incoming and outgoing calls both functions, even 3G or 4G telecommunication internet service is provided to mobiles. Hence, Tele point telecommunication network can not adopt to consumers demands.

Although, Tele point is the first network telecommunication service to adopt to handset in UK, but it handset network innovation can't identified as a source to mobile users' long term competitive advantages in this mobile phone network competitive market. Due to other telecommunication network companies can improve or revise to Tele point network service to launch more advance telecommunication service to provide mobile users to use more conveniently. Tele communication network fails due to mobile consumers useful demands are raising, its existing telecommunication service may no longer satisfy their needs, telecommunication technological change may make Tele point existing network service obsolete, telecommunication network service competitors can provide more convenient telecommunication network to mobile phone users and the social and economic environment may have changed, creating new mobile users needs in the global mobile telecommunication network service market.

The development of information and communication technology (ICTS) with mobile can bring the benefits of within each of virtually all the world's people social communication, such as Japanese mobile phone focusing on 3G technology. Factors promoting it can be summarized as follows: Deregulations by government/ mobile number portability and collocation; competition among carriers, such as introduction of new change plans; technological development, such as connection speed and contents and applications. Dynamic models are based out only on the assumption, such that carriers don't instantaneously adjust to satisfy their long term demand but also on network externalities. The Japanese mobile market has shown a remarkable growth with more than 106.2 million 3G subscribers and 4.4 million 2G as of Dec. 2009. The 3G diffusion rate accounts for 90% followed by that of Korea and this implies the market is almost saturated. Another remarkable transformation is found in its usage: Data communication exceeded voice services. Japanese 3G(4G) mobile phone originally had much variety of functionality other than voice service, being based on supply and demand side of the services: The founder is 3G technology which enabled new services, such as m-commerce and e-entertainment while the latter is due to existence of consumers who are willing to utilize various services. Although, the global mobile phone market has reached to the saturation stage and the growth rate of subscribers has been slowing down. Moreover, the recent development is found in the fact that data communications exceeds traditional voice communication and being the first phenomenon in the world. However, the effects of price elasticity and product differentiation of various carriers and network externalities increase the demand for mobile phone. Hence the technological innovation , such as electronic payment, high speed access and consumers' attitude toward entertainment and m-commerce are important factors for the success of 4G telecommunication service need is more than 3G telecommunication service need to every mobile phone users popularly. Moreover, new business models including a flat rate charging plan can play an increasing important role. Operators under these circumstances are confronted with competition due to the short product life cycle and the pressure to differentiate. Although, 2 G networks are adequate for voice, there was a growing interest in shifting from 2G to 3G even 4G based on a number of important drivers. First, the higher speed of 3G technologies translates into added convenience, capacity and functionality for the user. Second, there is much excitement over adding internet protocol (IP) capability and hence internet access to the mobile phone. In developing 3G standards, international telecommunication union worked with regional organizations and industry associates to reduce a large number of initial proposals to a smaller number of global standards.

In accordance with the development of mobile technology services already provided on 2G mobile phone , such as upgraded and consumers needed not feel difficult when using those services including email services (electronic mail, phone mail and video mail), web access and download music, movie and game. Moreover, carriers provide their customers more innovative functions, such as video mail, video-clips, video phone , broadcasting type video program, walk navigation, ringing tone songs, high speed internet connection, digital television broadcasting etc. via 3G mobile phone. In short, 3G services add multimedia facilities to 2 G phone by allowing video, audio and graphic application. Since 2G mobile had technological limitation of networks and handsets data transmitted via 2G was mainly text when due to development of networks and handsets, pictures and flash moving pictures are available and some handsets enables to view HPS for personal computer. Google and Yahoo started mobile search engines. Thus, 3G mobile becomes platform to use mobile contents, such as games and mapping services etc. Data communication , such as viewing web showed remarkable increase in 3G mobile phone, but monthly changes also increase and this became serious problem. In case of the internet in fixed
communications, the flat rate changes are already introduced.

In addition, mobile carriers don't adjust to satisfy clients' long term demands and than dynamic model approaches are available . Especially, network externality or network effect has to be considered in telecommunication. Mobile telephone is the most widely used form by communication in the world today. Mobile communication boost the earnings of many users change the local economy and even significantly, raise the GDP of many countries. The mobile phone has a number of benefits but there is a huge gap in 3G mobile phone why there is the case only two countries . Japan and Korean have more 3G than 2G subscribers. Similarly, why do leading nations like the USA, UK and Germany have 3G penetration rates of less than 30%?

The conclusion, we obtained technological innovation were achieved first, than based on this various service innovation were followed. It should stress that the former includes innovations in handsets as well as those relates to networks and IP technologies. The diffusion on new services depends on how they meet clients preference and needs, but behind services innovations those always technological innovations. On the other hand, some other social backgrounds, such as consumer's attitudes, economies and businesses systems are required. For example, the Japanese and later other service providers solved the first start up problem for mobile internet (mobile internet uses 3G with entertainment content that was supported by a micro-payment system) . In conclusion, Tele Point telecommunication service failure was due to it felt it was the telecommunication service provider to Unite Kingdom people to use mobile, it believed UK people, even any countries' people ought only chose to use its telecommunication service monopoly. So, in this mobiles market, it did not continue to develop and launch its telecommunication technological service. However, due to its telecommunication service had geographic location distance limitation and out calling only limitation to every mobile UK and overseas users in different countries. Hence, many mobile users who would feel inconveniently. However, then other telecommunication service providers copies it's telecommunication technology to launch and research to develop 2G, even, 3G and 4G telecommunication technology, its competitors can provide no geographic location distance limitation and in calling and out calling both to every mobile user who can use conveniently. Finally, Tele Point telecommunication service was not accept to choose to use to its old mobile customers popularly, even the new mobile customers would choose to use any telecommunication service providers, due to which telecommunication service could give more advantages to compare it's telecommunication service.

If Tele Point telecommunication could spend time and technology to continue to launch to improve its telecommunication communication time speed, raised incoming call function and reduced no geographical location distance limitation difficulties (weaknesses). I believe that Tele Point telecommunication ought attempt to continue to launch to improve its weaknesses of such as above weaknesses to adapt mobile consumers' demand easily, then it ought continue to keep its competitive position in this global telecommunication market till to nowadays.

Consider how the launch of 3G services in a less developed country with a less sophisticated telecommunications infrastructure may differ from a launch in a western developed county?

The growth has 3G telecommunication service in less developed country risk for the companies involved, especially where new technological displace the technology which went before them, calling for ever increasing capital investment, and no chance of a return from customers until long after the initial investment has been made in new capacity. Mobile phone companies need to predict the less developed countries, such as Africa country which has how many people who need mobile phone usage whether Africa has high businessmen who can support place, promotion, people and service to assist mobile phone companies to launch 3G or 4G telecommunication service. I think mobile phone companies need to let Africa country people to know mobile phone 3G telecommunication service technology is as the key to a whole new world of mobile telephone in which the mobile phone would be positioned not just as a device for voice communication, but a vital business, leisure, and information tool. So, mobile phones can assist Africa people to communicate in any places conveniently. A less developed country is a planned economy, the government makes all decision for society. Producers only make what they are instructed to make. The main benefits are that most workers are employed and most people enjoy a similar basic lifestyle. The problems cause to launch 3G mobile telecommunication service include that a planned economy gives little capacity for development, so growth and investment is limited, the infrastructure is usually under-developed as government spends on other areas, such as defense, wages are state controlled, so people have less motivation to perform at higher levels, mobile charges are fixed by government, consumers often can't afford luxury products, such as computers or mobile pones which are taken for granted in developed countries. Otherwise, a western developed country is in market economies (also known as free enterprise), the government's role is limited to providing legislation to protect businesses and consumers and making sure or organization restricts competition. It also provides essential services (like policy defense) and ensures the developed country's money supply is stable . Thus, businesses are motivated by profits to make products that clients will buy. Customers' demand for products and services affects the levels of supply and the pricing, if clients don't less be more efficient or produce on alternative product. For example, During 2003 year, the Hong Kong based Hutchison Whampoa became the first company to launch a 3G service in the UK, with its 3G telecommunication network. The launch was accompanied about the wireless internet and video capabilities. The world was going to be transformed by streaming of video and football matches live to customers' mobile phones and a whole new world of mobile advertising media would open up. However, launching 3G or 4G mobile telecommunication service to developed country , such as United Kingdom or less developed countries, such as Africa , I think the mobile phone companies need to consider what kinds of needs are the country people who prefer to get needs mostly. UK is a developed country, the people will need to get video entertainment, internet extra service from their mobile. Otherwise, Africa is a less developed country, the people live very far. It seems that location technology was value added data services. Even the emergency services stood to benefit from 3G's ability to precisely pinpoint a caller's location. By 2004 year, 60 per cent of calls to the UK emergency services were made mobile, but in instances callers did not know exactly where they were and ambulances and fire brigades only had very approximate locations. A less developed country is developing economy . It often face great difficulties in improving its economy. For example, in a planned economy, assets like land or property are owned by government. Individuals and businesses are not used to make decisions and operating to make a profit. Developing economy likes a less developed Africa country may also be market economy. But share features, such as the population lives on very low incomes, poor infrastructure , such as transport (roads or railways) or local government, poor communication systems, low levels of basic health and education and a low gross national product (GNP). Over 75% of the country's workforce is in agriculture which can be affected by the climate. Telephone landlines are scarce, expensive and difficult to install . It has less bank branches which are based in cities and tourist areas. Many Africa people are self employed business people, such as small farmers. The impact of mobile telecommunication technology on developing countries. The connectivity provided by mobile phone technology supports economic development. Its impact on a developing country likes Africa country has been extremely positive. Many families live in remote areas of the countryside . Installing landlines over those distances is expensive and difficult families are often separated as the main earners are forced to live in order to earn enough to keep their families. Many are self-employed small farmers or trades people such as plumbers and builders. For small business, better access to mobile technology means that who can advertise to a wider audience and don't have to rely for work on word of mouth. They can be sure that clients can contact them with ease. Due to far remote distance between houses and mobile phone companies, to launch in less developed county, any a mobile company must need a mobile network is quick and easy and secure to install and less expensive than landlines. For example, in a less developed country as Africa country, any mobile phone companies need to provide 3 G telecommunication service to any customers when who go to an accredited shop and in return for cash which has credit registered on their mobile to pay rather difficult than a pay as developed country mobile clients top up their mobile card. So developed countries mobile clients must pay their charge more convenient to compare to developing country mobile clients. Hence, mobile phone companies need to locate mobile card payment stores in developing country, such as Africa country's petrol stations, supermarkets and retail bases stores places. Hence, any mobile phone companies ought need to spend more capital expenditure to launch rapid commoditization of 3G or 4G telecommunication equipment and rising separation of network and service provisioning are pushing the operators to adopt multiple strategies with network infrastructure sharing in the core and radio access networks to improve network costs to a less developed country, such as Africa country more than a developed country, such as Hong Kong country. However, Africa is a potential mobile phone market. Due to limited land line availability, the cell phone is becoming Africa's computer of choice. Never before has a technological innovation been adopted as quickly as the introduction of cell phones in developing countries. Africa county mobile market will be larger to compare to fixed telephone lines, broadband, computer in home telecommunication markets.

By international telecommunication union (2011) source indicated that global mobile usage, 2011 yr. of mobile subscriptions per 100 inhabitants statistic, Africa region had 53, Asia & pacific had 74, America had 103 and Europe had 120 inhabitant numbers. It implies Africa, less developed country had the least inhabitants to compare to any developed countries, so its mobile market will be large (Sullivan, 2007). In conclusion, extensive cell phone networks already are in place throughout the developing countries. These networks constitute and infrastructure providing clear solutions to many problems with building mobile transaction systems. These networks are not exist, but the majority of those in these nations, such as Africa country now uses cell phones for conventional voice communication and text messages to availability of inexpensive handsets and reasonable industry pricing structures. The features of mobile phones transaction systems in developing countries, include interface, network type, date, storage, power source for recharging cell phone, telecommunications provider, financial institution transactions of cash in/out receipt service.

England NHS public hospital patient price structure of marketing strategy case study-apply pricing concept method to predict consumer behavior

What do you understand by the concept of a pricing model? Critically discuss their relevance to a public sector service ,such as the NHS.

A price model reflects the fact that companies can generate revenue through a variety of combination of the basic price and prices charged for optional additional items. Some price models may be sustainable by giving away a product at very low price initially, but then charge higher prices for essential items that are needed to make the product function. Sometimes, the dominant pricing model in a market is challenged by a new entrant, with the result that consumers' expectations are changed. The price model can occur in perfectly competitive market or non perfectly competitive market. A perfectly competitive market characteristics include there are many producers supplying the market, each with similar cost structures and each producing an identical product. No single supplier on its own influence the market price because it is not monopoly, water and electricity is managed by government to control the public utility company which can not charge high fee to every householder user at the reasonable price ; both buyers and sellers are free to enter or leave the market and there are no barriers to entry or exit and there is a ready of information for buyers and sellers, for example about competing alternatives, e.g. oil products and stock markets where shares are bought and sold are exist in perfectly competitive market. In perfectly competitive markets, firms are price taker and their ability to set prices is limited by the level of demand and supply within the market they serve. If the total demand go up, all other things being equal, the going rate of prices in the market for their product will rise. Likewise, if there is a drop in total supply for whatever reason (e.g. because of bad weather, there will be further pressure for prices in the market to rise. The final price paid in the market will reflect the balance between supply side and demand side factors.

The model of perfect competition presented the forces of competition may be ideal for consumers because the tendency of market forces to minimize prices and/or maximize firms' outputs. But in such markets, suppliers are forced to be price takers rather than price makers. in a perfectly competitive market, firms are unable to use marketing strategies to affect the price at which they sell. At a higher price, buyers will immediately substitute identical products from other suppliers. Lower prices would be unsustainable in an industry where all firms had similar cost structures. Otherwise, an non perfectly competitive market, firms are able to use marketing strategies to affect the price at which they sell. Such as UK medical service market , private hospitals and public hospitals and clinics which can raise their service fee to their patients to follow their patients demand due to their doctors and nurses service performance, medicines quality and price and patient beds supplies factors to influence their service charges to their patients in UK. Hence, NHS needs to provide different and excellent medical service to its patients to make them to feel it's service is better to other private hospitals and clinics if it wanted to apply price model to its car parking or hospital phone system service charge to its patients because it is a public sector medical service organization. It ought not charge extra service fee to its patients in its hospitals. If it charged extra service fee, such as car parking and hospital phone system service which are same or higher or lower than other private hospitals or clinic , which need to ensure which medicine quality, doctors and nurses performance which are better than private hospitals and clinics and its patient beds need have enough supply to any patients when who feel need to sleep in its hospital. Because NHS image is a non profit medical organization to any UK poor patients, who choose NHS medical service are due to its medical service charge is cheaper than private hospitals and clinics and who feel it can provide free car parking and free hospital phone system service.

A market is defined here need not be a physical location where exchange takes place (as happens in retail and wholesale grocery markets). A market in the economist's sense refers to all individuals and firms who wish either to buy or sell a specific product. A market is defined in terms of products or service and geographic description, so the UK soft drinks market refers to all individuals in the UK who seek to buy soft drinks and the suppliers to that market. The UK medical service market structure can describe as the number of consumers, such as patients and medical providers , such as private hospitals and public hospital , such as NHS (National health service) and clinics; the barriers that exist to prevent new private hospitals or clinics or public assistance hospitals from entering the UK medical service market (or prevent UK patients do not prefer to choose NHS medical service); the extent to which the supply medical services is concentrated in the UK small number patients normally and the degree of collusion that occurs between patients and/or private or public hospitals or clinics medical service providers in the UK medical market. Governments often seek to regulate the prices of key products and service, such as electricity and telephones and public hospitals medical services, so it is important to understand how firms can reconcile the sometimes conflicting approaches of market forces and regulation, such as NHS public sector medical service in United Kingdom. Of course, if NHS public sector medical service planned to charge some non major service fees, such as car parking and hospital phone calling service to its patients and hospital visitors and staffs which are same to private hospitals, it needs to consider pricing model should never be seen as an isolated element of hospital's marketing decision making. It needed to consider its service performance of its doctors and nurses, its social responsibility of public medical service image whether it is better or worse than private hospitals that it had created and NHS 's distribution strategy whether it's patient beds supply numbers are enough to patients and whether it's medicine quality and supplies and prices which are reasonable to compare to private hospitals or clinics in this medical service market in United Kingdom. Private business organization with a broad range if products or services are often price different with their portfolio in quite different ways. They may have developed a price model, which describes the way that it uses pricing of its portfolio to maximize its overall revenue. Hence, one product or service may be charged at a very low price, on the assumption that it can raise higher price if many clients choose to buy its product or consume its service. In some sectors, a number of different pricing models co-exist. For example, in the emerging multi-channel television broadcasting market, some channels are provided free of charge to users, but make revenue from selling advertising space, when others charge to users, either on a monthly/annual basis or a pay to view basis. The idea of a pricing model is familiar to private sector organizations, but do they have a role to play in the public sector? In the UK, pricing models are increasingly being discussed and developed for services which have previously been considered a vital service and available freely to all.

Adrian, P.(2012) showed that the National Health Service (NHS) has a long and proud tradition of providing health service to all, according to an individual's need, paid for out of general taxation, according to individuals' means. Pricing has historically had very little role to play in the NHS. However, from the mid-1990 year, individual NHS trusts began exploiting charges for ancillary services as a means of boosting their revenue. One of the first targets for charging was users of hospitals' car parks. Trusts argued that providing car parks was not central to the mission of NHS trusts, and conveniently, government was encouraging more people to use public transport and leave their cars at home. Critics argued that patients were essentially captive and public transport was not a realistic alternative for most people. However, it showed that at one hospital in London, a patient who attended A&E on the advice of her GP, was charged UK$3.75 for the first two hours' use of the hospital car park and UK$7.5 thereafter. She was ten minutes over the two hour period and therefore had to pay higher charge. She also questioned the fact that charges were reduced to UK$1 per hour after 6:00 PM, when many hospital departments were closed. For private sector service, a lower evening price, when there is not much demand from customers, and plenty of spare capacity, it quite common. But is it right that a hospital should only charges lower prices at the not busy time when much of the hospital itself is closed? If lower prices are designed to stimulate additional demand, it this a realistic prospect when many hospital departments are only available between 9:00 AM to 5:00 PM? Another source of revenue exploited by many hospital trusts from the use of bedside telephones by patients. Many trusts entered agreements with private telephone service providers which allowed incoming and outgoing patient calls only through the officially appointed system, which used a premium rate number. A proportion of the revenue was retained by the hospital. Conveniently, hospital trusts pointed to evidence that mobile phones could harm sensitive medical equipment , and therefore used this to eliminate competitive pressure from patients' mobile phones, forcing them to use the hospital's own telephone system. The ethic of hospital telephone pricing was challenged by the House of Commons Health Select Committee, which accused some trusts of using excessively outgoing call, adding to patients' costs, and boosting hospital revenue. It cited a hospital in Essex where people wishing to telephone patients were being charges 49p per minute at peak time and 39p off peak. By comparison , a typical household rate for a long distance phone call was around 7p in the peak and

2p in the off peak. The select committee also expressed doubts about whether a ban on mobile phones in hospitals was actually a result of possible interference with medical equipment and recommend visitors should be able to use mobile phone within certain areas of hospitals. So, it seems that UK private hospitals patients phone calling service fee is below than householder phone calling service fee and it is not every patient must need to use phone when who stays in hospital as well as the visitors should able to use mobile phones and who should not use hospital phones within certain areas of hospital, who will not interference with medial equipment. Otherwise, by banning mobile phones, had private hospitals been more concerned about creating a monopoly environment for pricing their telephone service, than any possible risk to their equipment? However, I think National health service (NHS) which is one public government assistant hospital, it can not be same to private hospital to charge unreasonable car parking fee or hospital phone service fee to its patients, due to these ancillary services is not hospital main income source and it is one non profit hospital, it needs to provide the fair and non expensive medial charges to its poor patient segment because who are not rich, so who will prefer to choose NHS medical service to compare to choose private hospital services in United Kingdom.

National health service (NHS) is a privatization, fragmentation and market competition of health care provision supposedly to cut costs and improve the efficiency of the health service in England. The NHS was set up in 1948 year to be a free and accessible care, publicly owned and funded sector service in England. NHS needs to consider to redefine its relationship with health service, limiting the quality and quantity of care it can expect to receive, how it access that care, who is delivering if and even how it is paid for. The result will be poorer, fragmented services with larger differences in quality and access. Services/treatments will cost more and the public will increasingly have to pay for aspects of its care that used to be free at the time of treatment. Traditionally privatization has been through the sale of public assets and services to private owners through the mass sale of shares, e.g. the sale of telecoms, railways, energy or water services. These companies than own the services and are able to make profits from them like any other are able private businesses. In the NHS until now, this model of privatization is taking place through a combination of the reduction of the role of government in regulating health provision, the transfer of services to the private sector through commissioning from any qualified providers, such as independent sector treatment care centers, outsourcing of parts of services to the private sector, the creation of market mechanisms for the distribution of funding within the NHS (e.g. commissioning, payment by results mechanisms, the purchaser-provider split and so called patient choice policies). The use of private finance initiatives that use private money to build new buildings and infrastructure and then the state has to pay, the creation of foundation trusts that are run much more like private businesses and have the ability to raise funding through private patients that pay for services, allowing services to become not for profit organizations, such as social enterprises, cooperatives or mutual and thus leave public ownership, limiting access to certain services previously provided by the NHS. Provided healthcare tends to cost more. It requires a large bureaucracy to operate, with huge transaction costs that come with contracts, billing and litigation. In general, as the proportion of private spending on health care rises, so does the overall cost. The creation of healthcare market can also impact upon the continuity of care people receive. There is always the threat that the private sectors or other providers who take on a service that doesn't secure the expected financial returns may cut losses and withdraw from the provision of that service. NHS is under increasing financial pressure. For example, surgery like hip and knee replacements are more expensive areas of care, the results cause the loss of training opportunities for junior doctors expenditure spending and other health professionals as ever large shares of routine surgery and medical procedures are diverted away from the NHS. Centers for research and medical innovations are also threatened. This can lead to service being out. NHS hospitals will therefore fail financially and be pushed into greater debt. This could lead to hospital mergers, closure or the private sector coming in to run the service on profit making contracts. NHS will bring poor health care service if it will not increase its service charge price to patients. The poor service will be caused, such as permanent damage may have been inflicted on patients with serious conditions due to the lack of follow up care after treatments. In a second worrying example dangerous delays affected the patients of a privatized out of hours. A competitive market system leads to greater rationing and gradually drives patients to take on more responsibility for funding their own care. It seems this already in the privatization of long term care and dentistry. Patients may soon have to top up the cost of their hospital care in the same way that many already do for community health services. The concern is that the NHS will provide a less comprehensive range of treatments. For the private sector, the aim is to make a profit from every contracts, which is not the same as providing the best service . For example, Southern Cross, where the need to make profit lead to the rapid closure of care homes, leaving old people with no home. Hospital people with learning disabilities and challenging behavior were subject to physical and psychological abuse. Privatization will lead to fragmentation of the health services. This is a process on a commercial footing and redesigning the system along market lives. With different organizations delivering different service in different locations, it is also likely to lead a new health service with some area receiving much better care than others, hardest, leading to greater health inequalities. Fragmentation of services leads to worse clinical outcomes as staff have less opportunity to work in a fully integrated dynamic multi disciplinary team. Patients with complex needs can be particularly considerable. The impact of privatization on current NHS staff, who are transferred from NHS employment to non NHS organizations would be changed terms and conditions at the time of transfer. These terms and conditions could be changes at some time in the future, staff would no longer be covered by the national negotiating arrangement in the NHS, meaning they would not be entitled to any future pay uplifts or agreed charges to the change terms and conditions of service . If staff moved from this employer to another outsourced community service, who would lose their entitlement to access the NHS pension scheme and would be treated as new staff rather then former NHS staff, the new service provider could argue that the service who will be providing is so different that they will not be requiring staff to transfer. Those staff will than be made redundant. In conclusion, NHS is one public medical service non profit organization. It's pricing model ought be public service price model, such as no price discrimination and non competitor based pricing aim. It may be difficult or undesirable to implement a straightforward price-value relationship with individual of public services for a number of reasons: Such as NHS public sector medical service pricing can be actively used as a means of social policy, subsidized prices are often used to favor particular patient segment groups, such as car parking fee charges to visitors or hospital staffs only as well as hospital phone system service charges to visitors only or prescription medical service charges favor the very ill and unemployed patients and low income patients and students patients.

What factors should influence the level of charges at an NHS car park?

Principles for fair hospital car parking, such as NHS is important because its car park service represents the hospital reputation. Charging for car parking is often necessary, but needs to be fair, providing a travel plan for users of all types of transport, controlling parking fairly, with concession for those whose health conditions or work commitments mean they have to park frequently or at anti social hours, showing car park and transport costs and how charges are invested, thinking about the environment and how transport can reduce the NHS 's impact , being open and involve patients and the public. It is important to get car parking and transport policy and it is communication, right to ensure fair access, good patient and staff experience and to protect hospital organization , such as NHS reputation. Clinical and social changes as car ownership to patients, staff and visitors to hospital sites has increased. For services with rural or urban , as public transport infrastructure is less convenient and reliable . When for specialist treatment, some patients need to travel greater distance and modern hospitals have often been located on the edge of population centres.

Car parking is also a factor in patient's experience of using healthcare. When much progress has been achieves to improve the patient environment inside the hospital, including cleanliness and new buildings, patients frequently report dissatisfaction with transport and parking arrangement. Visitors concerns both cost of car parking and also the availability of space for people with an essential need, illustrating the competing demands that managers need to balance. Patient experience is an important objective for hospitals; poor experiences can undermine confidence in clinical quality and stress can be worsened by poor transport and parking policies. Car parking can have a major impact on the local and national reputation of the NHS hospital . As patient choice increases, reputation and loyalty will be key drivers for provider's commercial sustainability. It seems car parking is one important factor to influence patients who choose hospital more than location/ transport/ easy to get to/ reputation of consultants factors. Ensuring that patients can access hospital when they need to is an important part of healthcare delivery. Many patients who need to travel to hospital by car, either because of mobility or illness, a lock of alternatives or through choice. However, providing a car park is not the only component of a travel plan. Access to healthcare should be considered in terms of service planning, decisions on location of services, building design, access routes and the other transport modes. One of the factor of the current changes to the way that NHS hospital services are delivered is that healthcare should be localized where possible. In many cases, people who used to have to travel to hospital are being treated in community health centers. The NHS hospital can also ensure services are accessible. Most notably, ease of access has recently been improved by reducing waiting times and by enabling patients to choose and book their appointment at a time and location that is convenient to them. Another of factor is whether NHS hospital had or had not ran a bus service from a nearby park and ride car park that runs every 15 minutes. The service has proved popular and is now run by the UK country council. The hospital is been to extend the shuttle service to the other three park and ride car parks which serve the city. The other factor influences NHS hospital charge includes the control parking fairly with concessions for those whose health conditions or work commitments mean they have to park frequently or at anti-social ours. In order to ensure that those patients who really need to access hospital by car are able to NHS often need to ensure that car parking space is available on site. Space is usually constrained, NHS hospital is in city or town center with high land costs and planning constraints. Charging some patients, visitors and staff to park can manage demand for space when ensuring that those who really need to park are able to access services. Where charging is required to manage demand, the overriding principle should be to ensure that where possible those patients who have the greatest need to park are prioritized. Where managing demand is a reason for charging for car parking, there may be scope for varying rates for different times of the day and the week, for example, increasing charges for non essential users in peak hours but applying a minimal charge at night when there is less reason to ration space. As well as prioritizing car access for those with greatest needs restrictions on car parking may also be required to deter non hospital traffic, particularly where NHS hospital is located in controlled parking zones, near shopping centers or other facilities that might need to illegitimate required use of NHS hospital grounds. In these cases , NHS hospital may be required to be charge the same as local car parks to avoid abuse by non visitors. However, alternative arrangement could also be explored, including day permits for people with appointment. NHS car parking fair policies should need to be fair application. This is often a cause of concern for patients and visitors. Concessionary schemes and season tickets should be well publicized and available, since a patient may not known in advance low frequently who will need to attend a clinic in the next month. Penalty charges, or towing away should only be applied extreme circumstances with a presumption of good faith that no patient or visitor chooses to stay in hospital longer than necessary and may how on arrival how long who will have to wait for treatment. Running a car park can be expensive. These are maintenance, security, insurance and running costs and the NHS hospital has to pay for the space the car park uses. Costs are particularly high where land prices are high or there is increased risk of crime. At the same time, patients and the public rightly don't expect healthcare to suffer to pay for parking. The transport costs of non car owners are not subsidized by the NHS budgets to provide subsidized free car parks . To make car parking fee would be to penalize those using public transport. Therefore, fair charging is often the most sensible answer to adopt these two demands. Climate charge and pollution and congestion factor also have health impacts. Reducing car dependency is also a public health objective in order to reduce traffic accidents and increase physical activity. These NHS organizations have a number of environmental and health reasons to seek to encourage people to use other modes of transport. Parking charge together with the expansion of alternative bus an cycling options to encourage a modal shift from cars to alternative transport. Patients , visitors and staff need to be made aware of these aims. NHS hospital can achieve a travel plan to develop to its car parking with the aim of during a period of busy time reducing single occupancy car journeys by 15% over three years, ensuring tat patients and visitors do not have to search for a space for more than ten minutes at peak times, encouraging the number of direct bus routes to the site to increase reducing staff parking spaces per employee by 10% as staff numbers grow. Car parking charges were introduced as part of the plan with certain categories of staff on exempted from charges (night and weekend staff, disabled staff, volunteers, car sharers and tenants of residential accommodation. From an environmental perspective, NHS travel plan supposed to reduce numbers of cars arriving at the site and the numbers of bus car raise. It aims to improve bus services to cause air pollution at the busy car parking period and cycle parking spaces and improved cycle facilities have encouraged staff to commute by bike. Additionally, a park and ride scheme aims to reduce car traffic of the NHS hospital in the busy time.

Moreover, it is absolutely wrong to charge cancer patients regardless of income, for unavoidable parking costs. From a staff point of view, NHS hospital car parking is an indirect tax on healthcare. However, most unions also support the aim of reducing car usage, as long as policies are fair. Because NHS hospital needs to develop transport policies for patients requiring regular cancer treatment. This approach has potentially negative publicity into a positive image to public. These ought be free parking for the duration of a cancer patient treatment or as often as is needed.

If you are studying at a university or college, critically reflect on the pricing strategy that it has adopted for ancillary services.

The development of a costing and pricing strategy will provide an university staff with greater access to price information, thereby providing a more accessible platform from which to base negotiations with commercial organizations. As prices will be informed by cost, the university will be seeking to apply

pricing strategies that maximize university as opposed to maximizing income. In fact, any universities is education industry which is different to common businesses which provide service or product to raise price when client numbers are increasing easily. Due to if an university which planed to increase school fee to charge students, which needed have unique courses to attract students to choose to study and its lecturers educational experiences and education methods needed to make student to raise learning interest and feel the courses are useful to choose to study the university subjects, so who shall compare the university subjects to other universities subjects, then to evaluate their school fees and lectures educational experiences and qualifications to decide whether who ought to choose the university or another university to study. So, I believe that the university can not raise its school fee easily if it has no more confident its subjects and lecturers which can make students to study to feel more satisfactory till to graduate. Otherwise, it will reduce student admission numbers if it still increase school fees, due to it has not researched what the subject contents are students who like to learn. Hence, any universities can't increase its school fee easily.

However, university ancillary services have primary paths to reduce internal cost to raise competitive advantages, such as services differentiation, low internal cost or internal span structural advantage. I shall recommend these price strategy to

adopt to reflect some university ancillary service (non major) service. The pursuit of a service differentiation strategy to an university advantages. The university needs truly understanding its unique core service (value) and then focusing resources on its ancillary services. An implicit part of having a focused

price strategy is not only defining what the university is going to invest in, but is also clearly articulating what the university is no going to do. For example, if the university investigated its students did not like to eat some foods taste, which ought to change some foods taste which could satisfy its students eating needs in its university canteens. Even the university could charge cheaper student parking fee to compare outside public car parks when they park their cars in university parks from the morning to afternoon studying busy time. It could only permit students to park their cars in its students private car parks. Hence, university staffs and visitors could not permit to drive whose cars to park in university private student car parks, so university staffs could park whose cars in university staffs car parks as well as visitors could park whose cars in university visitors car parks. However, who also needed to pay cheaper parking fee to compare outside public car parks to buy

car park tickets to park their cars in university staffs and visitors both car parks in any limited time. Even, the university book shop could sell lower second hand books and new books prices to compare other private book shops to attract students to choose to buy studying books from university bookshops. However, if the university tried to pursue too many areas of service differentiation, which was likely to invest too broadly and thus reduced the return on investment for previous capital possibly because it needed time to research whether which aspects of it needed to change to adopted students tastes to satisfy their needs, then it needed time to change its services and it also needed time to evaluate whether it's changed services which can satisfy its students demand to make decision to raise its service prices. Hence, it ought concentrate on changing one aspect of ancillary service to ensure it's changing was right to adopt students' taste to attempt to raise service price. Then, it could attempt to evaluate whether what ancillary services which needed to change to achieve price raising possibility. University recognizes that focusing on the core is hard to do, given the history and culture of university. But the worst case scenario for an university is to be relatively expensive and completely undifferentiated. Whether will who pay high school fee per year to go to an university that is completely undistinguished on any ancillary service?

An university looks to areas where which can make cuts and achieves efficiencies, an university should start farthest from the core of teaching and research ancillary services. Cutting from the outside in and building from the inside out. Growth in programs and research, increasing faculty and student demands and increasingly compliance requirements have all contributed to the growth of administrative costs. The reasons are often very legitimate. But as new programs are added, old programs often are closed down in some university ancillary services, e.g. unimportant administration internal service . The resulting breadth of campus activities creates too much complex it for staffs to manage with any efficiencies of scale in university. Units don't trust one another or the center to provide ancillary services. Data center management is a good example of fragmentation on campus. At the university, the central information technology group managed fewer than half of the servers on campus in its data center. For the servers located in the colleges, fewer than half were managed by college information technology groups, the rest were considered hidden at the department or faculty level. Despite the internet data and security risk of having too many unmanaged serves on campus in the university's central information technology department. In similar cases, outsourcing data centers would be a good solution. Third party data centers could provide more solutions, higher levels of securing, greater flexibility in capacity and lower cost than internal solution. Redundancy, an university is an many other campuses, it was managed at the department level, there were no product standards and each department negotiated its own vendor contracts. A sample of purchase order showed that the same item was being bought for as much as e.g. 36% more in some departments than in others. By centralizing end, standardizing more if its procurement to expect to save more expenditure. An university hierarchy, most campuses have too many middle managers. Before it reorganized , an university has average spans of control (the number of employment). Campuses engage to save cost. An university campuses engage in too many activities that require to broad a skill set to effectively deliver in house. Take information technology application management for example, not only does it need to support classrooms and research needs across a diverse set of disciplines (history, music, law, engineering, biomedical science etc. different subjects), it also has to cover functions (finance, human resource, research, administration, student registrar, libraries and student services etc. functions). It weren't enough, information technology also has to serve industries beyond the core academics, including bookstores, retail food, debt cards, total museums, publishing houses. A single IT group would have a hard time managing all it that well, given the expertise required, leading to either poor service delivery, sub scale and costly delivery.

Outsourcing more of non core activities would reduce campus complexity and cost. Third party provides have greater scale capability and skill because the outsourced service is their core business, enabling them to deliver the same or better service at a lower cost. In order to reduce aministrative costs without diminishing service and perhaps even enhancing it's campuses will need to subscale operations by creating shared service or outsourcing improve processes by eliminating low value work and automating much. Better manage university assets to whether it is real estate, physical assets or intellectual property, a number of activities where partnership with third party providers would allow for financial relief and improved performance. Hence, an university can also invest its intellectual property to build its build to raise its market value for long term to raise its sale price for long term.

In conclusion, an university can attempt to use these two kinds of price strategies to adopt to reflect to its ancillary services. Such as the first is competitors price strategy, the university can set its students and visitors and staffs car parking fee by examining what its competitors such as, it's close public car parks are charging their car parking fee services whether they are similar in terms of the university car parking service characteristics fee to satisfy its parking car users' needs as well as the university can set its canteens meals price by examining what its competitors, such as it's close private outside restaurants meals price whether they are similar or different taste and low meal price to attract students or staffs or visitors to choose to eat their meals . The another is demand based pricing strategy, the students are prepared to pay represents the upper limit book numbers to the university's every year studying books. Such as the university book shops can decide every years different subject second hand or new teaching books price to follow the students demand. For example, if the subject second hand or new teaching books supply numbers is less than the student demand numbers, the university can raise the subject books sale price. Otherwise, if the subject second hand or new teaching books supply numbers is more than the student demand numbers, the university needs to reduce the subject books sale price, even it needs to reduce their prices to be lower than outside other private book shops marketing price to sell in the year. Hence, it seems that any universities can adapt price strategy to reflect to their services or products prices.

Tesco supermarket value chain strategy case study-applying value chain strategy method to predict consumer behavior

Identify the elements of the value chain involved in the supply of fresh fruit and vegetables to Tesco stores.

The place(P) of the traditional marketing mix decides about channel intermediaries or middlemen to use an outdated, yet user friendly, term and the management of physical distribution. Placing products involves managing the process supporting the flow of goods or services from producers to consumers.

The process has sometimes been described as developing the best routes to market for a firm's products. Products must be made available in the right quantity, in the right location, and at the times when customers wish to purchase them. Marketing channels can perform an important role in the later stages of a value chain, in particular outbound logistic (e.g. order processing, storage and transportation); marketing and sales (e.g. market research, personal selling, sales promotion) and after sales service. However, it depends on which kinds of business to need outbound logistic, such as Tesco supermarket only needs ordering fresh fruit and vegetables from local farmers, then these foods need to be stored in refrigerate in warehouse and transport these foods to different supermarkets by vans. So, Tesco value chain only needs outbound logistic activity, but it does not need marketing and sales and after sale service to sell its fresh fruit and vegetables to its clients from its supermarkets (stores). In fact, Tesco stores is such UK farmer's intermediaries which can add value by breaking bulk. This might involve purchasing in large quantities of fruits and vegetables from UK local farmers and then selling smaller, more manageable, to keep volumes of fresh food stock in warehouses, then its vans will deliver these fresh fruits and vegetables to different stores daily. Discrepancies of fruit foods quantity are reduced by Tesco (intermediary) who provides every store clients with individual preferable fresh foods items that suit their needs daily. Tesco stores can offer superior knowledge of a target market compared with farmers, for example by ensuring which kinds of vegetables or fruits foods numbers are stocked in every store to match the economic and lifestyle needs of Tesco store shoppers who live in the area. Probably the most important gaps between Tesco store shoppers and UK local farmers in channel management are indicated at those of location and time. A location gap occurs owing to the geographic separation of farmers and the store shoppers of their fresh fruit and vegetables foods. UK farmers generally want to grow their fruits and vegetable food in one central location (farming), but farmers' food buyers typically want to buy their growing foods locally. A time gap arises when the UK local farmers' fresh foods buyers want to buy whose fresh growing foods at a time when a UK local farmer may considerate it inconvenient to make the available. UK local farmers may like to grow fresh fruits and vegetable foods at night from 8:00 PM to 12:00PM, then who will collect these fresh foods from 5:00 AM to 7:00 in the morning, but their buyers may want to buy in the evenings or at weekends afternoon. Tesco stores (intermediary) need to facilitate vans to transport these fresh fruits and vegetables foods from farmers' farming to its one central warehouse to deliver to different stores to sell the budget numbers of different kinds of foods to every local store consumers more exactly (Adrian, P. 2012).

Tesco stores is one of the world's largest retailers, it has social responsibility to protect fresh fruit and vegetable to sell to clients. It had attempted to predict customer behavior about hope much fresh fruit and vegetable and what kinds of fresh fruit and vegetable whose consumers will buy from data statistic in warehouse. It aims to reduce excess fruit and vegetable stocks in warehouse to cause perishable. In the winter might have seen choice reduced to basic items such as potatoes, cabbage, apples, supplemented by canned fruit and vegetables. Look in a Tesco supermarket today, and clients may find difficult to tell the season of the year or the distance from the countryside, simple based on the fruit and vegetables with are on display. In UK supermarket sector is intensely competitive, and has seen continuous innovation in the way it seeks to satisfy customers' needs. As consumers have become wealthier, the supermarkets realized that buyers would no longer be content with the staple foods such as cabbage and potatoes in the depths of winter-significant numbers of them now wanted excitement on a plate, and all year round. Furthermore, if they were planning a menu, they wanted to be sure that when they went to their local supermarket.

By and large, supermarkets have been key drivers of the value for the groceries that they sell. They have been close to their customers and identified their changing needs. They have built confidence with their customers, who can trust freshness and provenance of food they sell and the reliability of supply. It is therefore the supermarkets who have gone seeking sources of supply, rather than growers aggressively seeking to sell the produce that they have available. Before, the development of very large supermarket chains, retailers were more
fragmented. They did not have the power or resources to innovate with new product lines which they could then commission a grower to produce. Today, supermarket such as Tesco invest heavily in their food technology laboratories, and can then go to suppliers and place large orders with exacting standards with regard to price, quality, and delivery. Above all else, supermarkets have put themselves at the center of a slick distribution system which connects an international networks of growers through transport networks of trucks, ships and planes to put fresh produce in their network of stores, every day, all year around. The efficiency of the logistics, and the bargaining power of the supermarkets has often led to the price being charged at a British supermarket being lower than the price changed in supermarkets thousands of miles away where fruit and vegetables were grown. Tomatoes grown in Bulgaria and sold in Britain can be cheaper in Britain in local Bulgarian shops. The bizarre situation has occurred where the supermarkets import apples from France to be sold in Kent, the traditional home of British apple growing, plums from Poland to be sold in the grown product in Lincolnshire. Supermarkets argue that sourcing from overseas is not just an issue of cost saving more importantly, the supermarkets seek a continuity of supplies from large growers who can guarantee to deliver a specified quantity at a specified quantity at a specified time and place. The supermarkets capable of achieving this. British supermarkets are among the most efficient in the world, and their desire to ensure that customers can always get what they want may explain the mass transport of food. Local farmers' market may could environmentally friendly, but they rarely guarantee a continuity of supplies. As part of their drive for efficiency, supermarkets have a tendency to move food , such potatoes could being transported several hundred miles between distribution centers before they end up on a supermarket shelf just a few miles from where potatoes were grown. The environmental campaigning group Sustain has estimated that the average children travels 2,000 between the farm where it was grown and the supermarket shelf and furthermore the distance products travel from farm to end customer increased by an estimated 25 per cent between 1980 year and 2007 year (Priesnitz 2007).

Global warming had become an important issue with many clients and there was growing concern that supermarkets' practice of transporting fresh produce long distances around the world was irresponsibly adding to greenhouse gas emissions. Hence, distance travelled was one of value chain factor Terso supermarket needs to consider their fruit and vegetables food to keep fresh in refrigerate to transport to retailers to sell in UK. The most contentious food miles are clocked up by fresh fruit and vegetables flow in by plane from overseas. Although, air freighted produce accounted for less than 1 per cent of total UK food miles, it was the fastest growing way of moving foods around. One response By Tesco was to introduce a greatest proportion of local produce. To achieve this, it placed buyers and marketing teams in the regions in order to get a clear picture of local markets and to develop relationships with suppliers. By 2007 year, Tesco claimed to have 7,000 regional lines from throughout the UK, which were promoted as local produce, supporting local growers and reducing greenhouse gas emissions. Throughout its history, Tesco has demonstrated its ability to listen to what customers want, and this has been true in respect of its distribution system. The weaknesses of commodity systems are particularly for major customers, such as Mc Donalds, commodity systems do not lead to reliability in supply, quality, quantity or price nor high rates of innovation on which they can differentiate their offer from their competitors. The opportunity and challenge of fresh food product differentiation, so Tesco stores need to innovation to give rise to a number of strategic options to keep vegetables and fruits to be fresh in the short time to sell full numbers. If a firm, such as Tesco is the lowest cost producer than commodity market strategy can be an attractive strategic option. As Tesco stores fresh food sale that it's larger competitors shall find difficult to copy. Otherwise, Smaller size stores can sometimes be a competitive advantage.

Tesco stores (fresh food retailer) need to co-operate with suppliers and fresh food growers to align the whole chain to the changing needs of consumers. The food chain strategy aims to deliver superior value to specific groups of customers.

Tesco stores work closely with its fresh food suppliers to develop specific products for each range. Both the supplier and growers understand the Tesco marketing strategy and their role in the innovation process. Tesco is actively seeking new

chain ideas and is prepared to pay for such efforts. From a primary producer and supplier perspective the range of brands enables Tesco to work with suppliers to market the total crop .

Critically discuss the factors influencing Tesco's sourcing of fresh fruit and vegetables.

At a time when the media enjoyed the big supermarkets, such as Tesco, being seen to source fresh fruit and vegetables food locally and being good to the environment helped to restore. One observe from Friends of the Earth noted the local produce sold at a branch of Tesco in Excess had in fact travelled served hundred miles as it was moved from the grower to a regional processing center, then to a regional distribution center, and finally back to the supermarket where it was sold. There has also been debate about where sourcing fruit and vegetables locally actually reduces greenhouse gas emissions. There is an argument that Tesco supermarket would be better for environment to grow them in countries where fresh fruit and vegetables need less heating and fertilizers than if they were grown in British. The greenhouse gas emissions resulting from growing them locally in Britain may be more than the emissions associated with transporting them from warmer countries.

The first factor influences Tesco's sourcing of fresh fruit and vegetables is the main stages of horticultural value chain are as follows: The first stage is inputs elements needed for production, such as seed, fertilizers, agrochemicals fungicides and pesticides, farm equipment and irrigation equipment, production for export includes the production of fruit and vegetables and all processes related to the growth and harvesting of the produce, such as planting, weeding, spraying and picking, packaging and cold storage means grading, washing, trimming, chopping, mixing, packing and label are all processes that may occur in this packing stage of the value chain . Once the produce is ready for transport, it is chilled produce is ready for transport, it is chilled and placed in cold storage units ready for export, processes fruit and vegetables include dried, frozen, preserved, juices and pulps. May of these processed add value to the new foods by increasing the shelf life of the fruit and vegetables and the final stage is distribution and marketing means the produce is distributed to different channels, including supermarkets and small scale retailers and wholesalers and food services.

The second factor indicates several basic conditions must be for a country to enter the fresh fruit and vegetables value chain. These include climate allowing for year found supply, adequate road and transport infrastructure, such as ports and airports, essential for moving fragile foods to market efficiently, establishment of sanitary and to prevent disease spreading. The value chain needs to upgrading into the packing segment and processing segment. Upgrading into parking is dependent on understanding the market needs investment in capital goods and availability of supporting activities within the country, such as United Kingdom. Maintaining open lines of communication regarding demand preferences in fresh foods, quality, packing and fostering buyer involvement is critical in all stages of the value chain. For example, organize trips to key markets and they observe interactions at the point of fresh food purchase, a wide variety of equipment to attain very high standards of hygiene within the pack house operations as well as on site laboratories for fresh fruit and vegetables research and staff health tests, horticultural sector has been greatly inhibited in its upgrading along the value chain by the lack of fresh food quality packing materials. Much of produce destined for the Europe is shipped to neigh countries where it is repackaged, resulting in a significant of value. However, upgrading into the processing segment of the value chain has been difficult to achieve for low income developing countries since the processing of fruit and vegetables is cost prohibitive at low levels of crop production. Therefore, countries must gain a level of expertise during the production stage to increase output to a level that will enable the country to upgrade to the fruit and vegetable processing stage. For example, given the importance of ability to read pesticide labels and understand barcodes amongst others, standards have led to additional training initiatives to improve adult literacy. Skills training must be carried our in all job categories of value chain to maximize growth and upgrading opportunities. Investments in training are required for all job categories, from farm workers to managers, such as farming activities and the workforce within the agriculture sector, packing and storage positions and the processing stage in which workers are classified under the industrial workforce. Hence, fresh fruit and vegetables packing and processing services, such as washing, chopping, mixing as well as bagging, branding and applying bar codes are often carried out at the fresh foods source rather than at the end market destination. These processes which were previously based in the developed country, such as UK have created considerable new employment opportunities in developing countries.

The third factor influences Tesco's sourcing of fresh fruit and vegetables, which indicates today, the fruit and vegetables sector operators as a buyer driven value chain and large supermarket chains are the leading actors both in key export markets with controlling market and shares across the Europe and United States as well as increasing in emerging markets. These buyers including Sainsbry's Marks and Spencer and Walmart seek enhanced cost competitiveness, consistency and product differentiation, such as convenient, ready to eat fresh foods from their global supply chains. It causes considerable value chain method how fruit and vegetables are produced, harvested, transported, processed and stored to achieve how fresh fruit and vegetables characteristics of quality, size, pesticide use and the social and environment conditions of cultivation and post-harvest handling will influence buyer behavior decision. This ensures that the perishable food reaches its destination in good condition cold storage units are used throughout the chain to keep the produce fresh and both air and sea freighting supported by the cold chain are key elements to ensure timely delivery. Export is divided between production for fresh and vegetables and fruit consumption and production for processed fruit and vegetables that are not accepted for sale as fresh produce are as well as inputs for the processing stage, but in order cases, such as orange juice or preserved peaches a specific variety and grade quality is required and production occurs separately. The next segment is packaging and cold storage unacceptable low grade produce will be redirected to processing plants or the domestic market. Washing, trimming, chopping, mixing, packaging and labelling are other processes that may occur in this stage of the value chain. Once the produce is ready for transport it is chilled and placed in cold storage units ready for export. Packaging usually requires economies of scale due to the high costs of cold storage and other capital investment necessary at this stage .Processed fruit and vegetables include dried, frozen and preserved produce as well as juices. Processing plants purchase fruit and vegetables inputs from the producers. These firms may export their products under their own brands as well as under the buyer's brand. The last stage of the value chain before consumption is distribution and marketing. In this final stage, the produce is distributed to different channels including supermarkets, small scale retailers, wholesales and food services. Air freighting for horticultural foods and more cold storage segment of value chain in order to increase their access to key markets and avoid competition form new countries entering cold storage technologies allow suppliers to adapt to geographic constraints, such as size and distance to market.

Assess the level of power that Tesco exercises in the supply chain for fruit and vegetables.

The themes identified were the perceptions of freshness, having good relationships with growers and suppliers , good quality of fresh fruits and vegetables, competitive and pleasant environment for shoppers. Globalization of the fresh fruits and vegetables, retailer system has impacted on the distribution and marketing of fresh modern supply chain outlets now dominate the fresh food retail market. The increasing population and rising personal income is resulting in significant shifts in fresh food demand. Supermarkets are perceived to be the place where more wealthy consumers choose to shop. Consumers purchase almost everything there including fresh fruit and vegetable, meat, children and fish and other household supplier like dry food, bread, detergents, stationary and toys in supermarkets, such as Tesco stores, not choose to buy from fruit and vegetable markets or food retailers. The traditional markets and grocery stores comprise wet markets, fresh markets, farmer's markets are popular among consumers when purchasing fresh food are the oldest food distribution channel. The traditional market has been defined as a market with little central control or organization that lacks refrigeration and doesn't process fresh foods into brands foods for sale where each vendor specialized in one fresh food line (meat, fish, fruit or vegetable) or in a sub line (fruit and vegetable). A fresh market and/or wet market generally occupies one or two floors of a building that is located adjacent to a housing area where there is a high population density and high traffic flow. The ground floor is normally rented to retailers who sell fresh food or ready to eat items. The upper live level is occupied by retailers who sell ready to items or non food products/ These stores are family owned retailers that sell a limited variety of foods ,such as fish, fruit and vegetable, bread and milk, stationary , toys and household supplies. However, consumers may limit their purchase from these stores due to the high prices and limited product lines. Another distribution power level to Tesco supply its fruits and vegetable to deliver to its clients in the short time. Tesco faces its customers occurred with respect to its home delivery service. With the launch of its Tesco online service, it effectively extended the supply chain right through to customers' own homes, adding value to its product offer by avoiding the need for customers to even visit a supermarket. Was it good for the environment to have fleets of delivery vans around town and countryside? Simple evaluations were difficult to make supermarket buyers again, Tesco was keen to be seen as a good citizen in this final leg of its chain, for example by launching electric delivery vehicles which Tesco decided to reduce global warmth when its vans do not need to deliver fresh foods and vegetables to different supermarkets from its warehouse in the long distance. Tesco stores is a retailer to UK local farmers that buys their fresh fruits and vegetable for the purpose of reselling them to end consumers in its different local stores daily. The Tesco stores are large, self service stores carrying a very wide range of different kinds fresh fruits and vegetable foods to sell in its different local value chains from UK local farmers supply daily. For example, Tesco stores are often the first with new store shoppers initiatives such as loyalty cards and low fresh food prices are based on large scale efficiency to sell in Tesco smaller independent stores to match. Hence, the factors can influence Tesco stores channel selection power include that the expectations of store shoppers who expect to buy local stores or who prepared to travel to a retailer that the farmers' fresh fruit and vegetables keep to save more than one day or more days to buy. This might mean taking into consideration factors such as a geographical preference to buy locally, or a tendency to feel more comfortable visiting a particular type of store; Tesco fresh foods attributes can be important, fresh produce that is highly perishable requires fairly short channels. Bypassing channels, a UK local farmer may seek to cut out intermediaries , such as Tesco stores by dealing directly with the public and Tesco may feel difficult to open up any new local stores for the farmers. Over saturation, a farmer may be accused of using too many fresh fruits and vegetable food distributors within a given geographical area, making it difficult for any individual distributor to achieve a satisfactory level of fresh foods sale , such as Terco stores. Too many links, in the supply fresh foods chain, Tesco stores may be required to buy excessive fresh fruits and vegetable foods from any farmers daily, who may be perceived as a fresh food farming competitor, rather than a cooperative channel member. New channels, these can have a similar effect to bypassing an intermediary, for example, many UK local farmers have opened up internet sales channels, thereby taking fresh food sales away from established intermediaries, such as Terso stores. Cost cutting, in order to increase volume fresh fruit and vegetables food sales, a UK local farmer may seek to distribute through higher volume, low cost intermediaries, which may make it more difficult for a smaller, full service intermediary , such as Terso stores sell the farmers' any fresh foods and UK local farmers can give incentives and rewards to other intermediaries to help them to sell in UK any stores to raise Terso's competition in UK foods supply market.

A national chain of restaurant mobile advertising strategy-apply mobile advertising strategy method to predict consumer behavior

Critically assess the likely opportunities and problems
of mobile advertising for a national chain of restaurants.

A global crisis in the advertising industry largely linked to the impact of the internet is transforming the business models of media industries, the content they create and distribute, and the audiences who consume that contents. Such as consumers can use whose mobiles to find where the chain of restaurants are located and meal and drink prices and meal and drink types and
restaurant opening and closing time etc. information for the national chain of restaurants from internet advertising when who leave at home conveniently. The opportunity to mobile advertising for a national chain of restaurants, it can expand its national chain of restaurants brand to different countries visitors and instead of its self country visitors to let them to know whether where its chain of restaurants can provide what kinds of food or drink to serve to them to eat before they prepare to go to any one of the national chain of restaurants immediately. Hence, when visitors travel to its country, it will be more easy to let them to remember where any one of the national chain

restaurants are located in the nation when who enter the national chain restaurants website or enter yahoo website to type" national chain restaurants" word, then who can seek any one of the national chain restaurants from whose mobiles easily.

In fact, if a national chain of restaurants chose to use television advertising, due to the national chain of restaurants which locate at itself country locally. It is only concentrate on promoting it's country's domestic eating consumers target to know it's existence when its country's domestic eating consumers are watching television at homes. Usually, working people need to work and students need to go to school to study from morning 9:00AM to 6:00 PM at night. Hence, the national chain of restaurants can only advertise at night time. Furthermore, the overseas travelers watch the nation's television when who are staying in the nation's hotels at night time. Hence, the national chain of restaurants can only use television to advertise to attract the largest numbers of local and foreign visitors to watch its advertisement at night time possibly. Due to mobile advertising exists, television advertising is more difficult to attract the durability of audience segmentation models to build upon demographic and it also lacks new opportunities to implement psychographic and behavioral models for understanding audiences. Such as, many young people who accept to use mobile to communicate, so it implies every family usually has a mobile to use and mobile advertising will also have much opportunity to help any businesses to promote whose services or products to let many families to know whose advertising. In fact, mobile users can use mobile to watch movies or news, so who ought to link internet to watch during who are sitting on any transportations or walking, so when the nation's people who feel hungry, who can use their mobiles to link to internet to seek any restaurants to decide which restaurants are the most close to their locations to choose. As a national chain of restaurants, it is more effective to advertise it's different chain of restaurants' locations to let any it's different locations of national mobile users to seek its any one of chain restaurant conveniently when who are walking on the street if who feel hungry who can turn on mobile to find map to seek the national chain of restaurants immediately. In fact, the global households who the average viewing audience composition, the number of global households using the television set and the various times it is in use, the average audience (home viewing during an average minute of a program) and the total audiences (homes viewing the program in excess of minutes) which are decreasing. Otherwise, the mobile phone users view mobile advertising numbers are increasing. Broadcast channels as well as whatever is available on their various devices, including computer, mobile devices, gaming devices, time-shifting devices or internet enables devices. As such, it is providing more and more difficult to track the audience and known who they are and the best way to target them. Additionally, the rise of social media adds another dimension to audience research. Social media provides new ways of segmenting audiences that currently can not be done on television. Hence, a national chain of restaurants can get better ways of segmenting its viewers from mobile advertising over a variety of platforms.

So mobile networks can be better package to the nation chain of restaurants advertising programming and the national chain of restaurants advertiser can make a more effective to attract foreign visitors or domestic visitors to make them to enter its website to view its advertising from their mobiles. For example, car owners, such as those who own a BMW or Audi famous brands cars, which have very homogeneous demographic characteristics, but each car brand has a specific type of owner with a unique personality. A similar look as television audiences could allow advertising of those car brands (who attend the upfront presentations every year) to match their car buyers to specific television shows. Demographics have not caught up with these changes and presume that viewers are still watching in only the conventional way. For instance, there is not yet a way for the networks to get credit for online viewers and it is as more viewers more to online platforms, like a network in landing site.

Instead, a psychographic profile of the audience, one based on psychological segmentations , such as behaviors, attitudes, interests, values, opinions feelings which is a valid and valuable way of narrowing down the audience into segments for an advertiser. So, psychographic data can measure, such as peoples' activities how who spend whose time, their interests what they place importance on in their immediate surroundings, their opinions how their view of themselves and the world around them and some basic characteristics, such as their stage life cycle and income and education and residence location. The result of the research then provides a detailed profile that allows the marketer to be better visualize the target audience. Psychographics start with people and reveal how the people feel client specific subjects, which can lead to be more effective marketing. When psychographic segmentations are used, the consumers are divided into group based on lifestyle and personality, often with all of this in mind, the research questions proposed here as follows:

What psychographic measurements are being used right now to determine the television audience or mobile advertising ?

How are the various branches of the industry , such as restaurant industry adaptive to the new television landscape ,such as mobile advertising and what actions are they taking?

What are some challenges and resistances to psychographic measures between television advertising and mobile advertising?

What incentives or lack are there to change between television and mobile advertising?

What would be helpful for advertisers , such as a national chain of restaurants or networks , such as internet advertising to know or do in order to more towards wider use of psychographics?

A reason behind dividing audiences based on engagement can be illustrated with the Pod mobile phone, such as the national chain of restaurants organization has shown that audiences' attachment to specific the restaurants' brand corresponds directly to how much the audience will pay attention to the national restaurant brand's advertisements from mobile and how likely who are the actually to choose to go to the national chain of restaurants to eat lunch or dinner or breakfast more than its other restaurants.

The problem is how the national chain of restaurants to advertise it's foods taste, price and service and locations uniquely to win its other restaurant competitors from mobile specific program, providing the network to be best convenient that it's restaurant brand to advertise on that specific program. Another key problem is trend segments viewers based on domestic and foreign consumers' behavior are more specifically their viewing behavior mixed with their restaurants choosing eating behavior in whose countries, watching the national chain of restaurants television advertising from whose mobile , what who are watching to know its existence and on how to let them to know what their actual eating taste to the national chain of restaurants can provide. Hence, I suggest the national chain of restaurants can attempt to use surveys to carry on researching the different countries foreign visitors and domestic visitors whether what whose tastes are preferable to choose what kinds of foods and drinks who hope to eat in this national chain of restaurants from mobile advertising website. The problem is who may choose not to fill its surveys from its mobile website advertising. If they use computer to fill its surveys at home, it will have more opportunities to gather data from survey due to who can sit down to fill surveys in quiet environment. Hence, I suggest it ought use computer internet to do market research about what whose tastes are preferable to eat in its restaurants. When it estimates whether the foreign visitors and domestic visitors numbers, how many people choose to eat different kinds of foods and drinks to its identifications. After it can achieve mobile advertising to promote its restaurant brand more confidently in this mobile marketing advertising strategy.

Discuss methods that could be used to assess the effectiveness of mobile advertising.

Measuring social media marketing , such as mobile advertisement, effectiveness and identifying the target market. The use of social media sites as part of company's marketing strategy has increased significantly. Regardless its popularity, there is still very limited information to answer some of the key issues concerning the effectiveness of social media marketing , ways to measure its return on investment and its target market. The social media was started around ten years ago. It began with linked in, which was launched in 2003 year, followed by both My space and face book in 2004 year. You tube in 2005 year and Twitter in 2006 in year. The popularity of social media sites has also spread to companies as part of their strategies. Executives are concerned with their budget justification for a social media plan in computer or media online advertising, when there is lack of supporting materials to confirm the effectiveness of the social media platform , i.e. conversion rate, the relation between buyer-seller relationship and increase in sales and the rate of return investment that they can earn from this plan. Others also believe that their companies' performance are not affected by their lack of involvement in the social media sites.

Clearly, the fact that social media marketing is still relatively new among business practitioners has raised some major concerns , such as its effectiveness, the main purpose of including social media mobile advertising in a company's media platforms, it's relation to the existing platforms and the target audience of this strategy. The methods to assess effectiveness of mobile advertisement include that marketing research method is about target client segment of respondents' social media activities and buying decisions relationship survey. Survey questions can include whether how long time and how often who turn on mobile phone to use internet, such as a week is less than 20 hours average or a week is between 20 hours and 30 hours average or a week is between 30 hours and 50 hours or a week is more than 50 hours, why who like to use mobile to use internet and not use home computer to use internet, e.g. reducing to use home electricity, interesting, convenience, no computer at home, what who will seek to see from mobile advertisement, e.g. advertisement , news ,email , message, movie, whether who decide to buy products or consume services choice is from which kinds of channel advertisement influence mostly, such as television, radios, newspapers, magazines, computer internet, mobile internet. It aims to gather target client segment of respondents' social media activities and buying decision relationship to estimate whether there are how many numbers of target client will decide to buy the company's product or use it's service from mobile advertisement channel.

Hence, the survey result can indicate these five respondent groups, such as highly affected, somewhat affected, neutral somewhat not affected and not affected at all groups. Mobile phone advertisement is needed to any organizations to use internet to operate. Hence, to access the effectiveness of mobile advertising which may begin by using measures that were very easy to capture and understand, such as the number of website hits or percentage of users who clicked on an advertisement. These measures were very useful fro examining trends in traffic patterns, but the impact of this traffic on sale and other marketing objective was sales and other marketing objectives were little understand. Standardized approaches for capturing and summarizing websites behavior were eventually developed to help make sense of web traffic and patterns. Metrics, such as number of unique visitors and the amount of time who spent viewing web pages provided marketers with new insights into who was assessing the site and how who were using it. But even with a high level of detail about how customers were interacting with the company via the web, marketing manager often lacked the information how user behavior data translates into increased profits and business value. For example, organizations using websites primarily for after sales support have used exactly the same kinds of metrics as these selling directly from the site. This is not due to a lack of available data.

Many organizations using web analytics gather and store vast amounts of information and develop large, complex databases to house it. But much of that information is never used. Because organizations who first began to market over the internet often lacked a clearly formulated strategy. In addition, the rapidly changing internet environment made it difficult for marketers to formulate clear expectation about the impact of activities. Both the amount of returns and amount of investments are difficult to measure. I suggest organizations may estimate the value of a visit to a particular web page by estimating the number of visitors who will become customers and then multiplying that number by the average value of all clients to estimate returns. What the 'clicks and hits' and 'measurement driven' approached have in common organization's strategic objectives and provide quantified models that plan and track internet marketing investments from intermediate outcomes to financial results. Hence, it can indicate how marketing expenditures in mobile internet advertising method to lead to increase shareholder value aim. I think investment in internet marketing , organizations will need follow these stages. In the beginning is inputs stage: Organization and business unit strategy includes structures, systems, resources as well as marketing strategy includes structures, systems as well as information strategy includes structures, systems and market strategy transfers to websites, search marketing , advertisement and public relations, mobile marketing and marketing research. Next, it is outputs stage: It includes intermediate outputs, such as awareness and perceptions, attitudes and intentions, value provisions, channel optimization and market information as well as it includes final outputs, such as marketing assets: customer value, brand equity, knowledge as well as financial flows: increased revenue, cash flows, reduced revenue, lower cost, lower working capital, lower fixed capital and reduced risk. Finally, it is outcomes stage includes shareholder value, return on investment and corporate profitability. For example, Donald restaurant uses its website to promote lower calorie food and fruit options as well as its global campaign tied to the Olympics, nutrition (Business week 8-7-06). Each organization should carefully identify the outputs it seeks to achieve. How can process produce these outputs? Organization can attempt to enhance of website functional or initiation of an email campaign. The final question to organizations which will ask : How outputs contribute to the long term financial performance of the organization from mobile advertising ? Is critical for organizations seeking to enhance return on investment from mobile advertising? In addition, whether mobile advertising can give these benefits to any companies, such as market capitalization and shareholder value can be enhanced by increases in marketing assets (customer value, brand equity and knowledge base) that produce future corporate financial flows from mobile internet advertising method. Hence, marketing assets include customer value, such as using dynamic pricing to manage demand, supporting sales through online information sites, shipping directly to reduce need for inventory possession, shifting in store sales to online sales, eliminating clients with prior post sales problems from promotion lists; brand equity, such as additional revenue through brand premiums, using customer relationship to speed adoption of next generation products target marketing to loyal clients during predicted slow periods, reducing customer turnover and support costs, shifting responsibility and risk for inventory management to major suppliers, pool inventories with suppliers and clients to reduce warehouse space across the supply chain, using trust in brand to reduce unwarranted lawsuits, knowledge base, such as developing mass customization capability, reducing time to market through online concept trials, time promotions to smooth demand, eliminating product features that are not valuable to clients. Watching production timing to demand, direct in store sales to products that generate high contribution margin per square foot of fixed space and anticipating and respond to stakeholder concerns. Finally, customer value and brand equity and knowledge base shall transfer to financial flows aim, such as increased revenue, accelerated cash flow, reduced revenue volatility, lower cost, lower working capital requirement, lower fixed capital requirement and reduced risk. However, Metrics can be used to access effectiveness of mobile advertising, both financial and non financial metrics are needed to effectively measure performance. Some non financial items , such as market research activities are difficult to measure and companies often avoid measuring those items. However, if the item plays a critical role in delivering organizational value. Measuring it, preferably in quantifiable terms, such as monetary changes or percentages. Even when such measures are difficult to obtain or depend a rough estimates, they provide a basis for examining trends over time and can provide useful information to managers. For example, two metrics for the output awareness are: The number of emails opened recipients and the number of clients that clicked on a promotional mobile advertising. Those two metrics can provide different perspectives on the meaning of awareness, thus the choice of metrics helps clarify the objectives, just as clear objectives can help in identifying specific and to be relevant must be specific and to be relevant they must be customized to meet the unique dynamics of the organization . It aims to achieve the best to capture and reflect the organization's unique sets of activities and results some may be relevant to all organizations and many can be readily adopted to be useful for decision making.

Discuss the relationship between mobile advertising
and other elements of the promotion in campaign
planning.

Mobile advertisement defines as the use of the mobile medium, it is as a communications and entertainment channel between a brand and an end user. In basic terms, it is the process of planning and execution conception, pricing, promotion and distribution of products and services through the mobile channel. Advertising is a form of communication intended to convince an audience (viewers, readers or listeners) to purchase or take some action upon products, information or services etc. The relationship between independent variables elements and mobile advertising which are environmental response and emotional response with behavioral aspect of consumer buying behavior with mobile advertising. It is time that people purchase those brands with which who are emotionally attached elements. Almost every one grows up in the world which is flooded with the mass media, e.g. television, films, videos, magazines, movies advertising and internet channel is either mobile advertising or computer advertising. Advertising is a subset of promotion mix which is one of the 4'p in the marketing mix, i.e. product, price, place and promotion. As a promotional strategy, advertising serve as a major tool in creating product awareness in the mind of a potential consumer to take eventual purchase decision. Advertising, sales promotion and public relations are mass communication tools available to marketers. Telecommunication technology, such as mobile advertising enables business and industry to grow at a faster pace when contributing to the economic development and at the same time telecommunication infrastructure can be reliable. Cellular phone industry has been one of the profitable businesses in Asian. The country's growing population and huge demand potential have always been an attraction for many high-technological multinational companies. Societies used symbols and pictorial signs to attract their produce users. There elements were used for promotion of products. A company can't make dream to be a well known brand until which invests in their promotional activities for which consumer market have been dominating through advertisements. As the primary mission of advertiser is to reach prospective customers and influence their awareness, attitudes and buying behavior.

The major aim of advertising is to impact on buying behavior, however this impact about brand is changes or strengthened frequently in peoples' memories. Memories about the brand consist of their associations that are related to brand name in consumer mind. These brand cognition influence consideration, evaluation and finally purchases. The promotion in campaign planning to mobile advertising focuses on young people because who choose advertising information and characters as whose role models, who may not only identify with them but also intend to copy them in terms of how who dress and what who are going to buy. As the market is surplus with several products or services, so many companies make similar functional claim, so it has became extremely difficult for companies to differentiate their products or services based on functional attributes alone. Differentiations based on functional attributed, which are shown in advertisement, are never long lasting as the competitors could copy the same. Mobile advertising may differentiate companies' products or services promotion channel to attract client's attention, e.g. the company can use movable product images on internet video to show on mobile. However, mobile advertising time ought depend on the business nature, e.g. facial health products target segment is female, so it's mobile advertising time ought choose form 9:00 AM to 6:00 PM working time between Monday to Sunday, due to housewives or working women shall go back home to cook, who shall not turn on mobile phones at home. Hence, if the company had differentiated which brand and it had chose what time is the more popular to accept to let mobile users to turn on their mobile from mobile advertising. The company mobile advertising will have more promotion effort. For example, if the company sold toys, it's target segment would be 3 ages to 10 ages old. It's mobile advertising ought let every family to find its company website easily. If the family didn't know it's brand, but is was difficult to let the family to find what its toys sale from whose mobile phone because there are many toy companies were using internet advertising to promote which toys. So, it might let every family types " toy" word on yahoo, Google websites, then this toy company name would appear on their websites, the family only clicked its name on their mobile phone, it could show it' toys images, prices, which country manufacturing and which year manufacturing different kind of toys, sale payment and delivery method, e.g. visa card payment, air or land or shipping transportation flight delivery, toys manufacturing ingredients indication from website advertising and it's toys advertising time ought to choose family working time, such as between 9:00 and 6:00 PM , due to who shall bring their mobile to work usually. Hence, the toy company needs to consider family will choose what time to use mobile phone. It ought not choose night time to advertise its toy products from mobile due to family would not turn on whose mobile at home at night time usually. Economic theory has sought to establish relationships between selling prices, sales achieved and consumer's income, similarly before the company chooses to spend mobile advertising expenditure, it ought frequently compared it with sales actual income each month.
Social media marketing, such as mobile advertising effectiveness is highly influenced by three aspects: content quality, involvement and integration with the other media platforms methods to assess whether effectiveness of mobile advertising.

On the first aspect, content quality isn't quantity. It shows that managers should not totally reply on the monitoring software to measure and analyze their social media campaign. For example, the twitter website analysis show that some brands/companies, e.g. Microsoft used their Twitter account to connect and to
communicate with customers . Their Tweets were about communicating and connecting with their follows, through some personal conversations in subjects. That were relevant to their customers . As a results, Microsoft clients were able to
beat their main competitors in financial performances and Twitter activities. So, Microsoft can use twitter website to assess whether how many numbers of people use internet service to enter phone, then who decide to buy its software products . If Microsoft found the result of the number of buyers who decide to buy its software from mobile phone Twitter website advertisement channel which is more than mobile phone Yahoo or Google websites

advertisement channel after who turn on mobile to see advertising. On the another aspect, building trust and long term relationship to mobile advertising to indicate to how to persuade to increase many shippers to decide to buy any products or seek service, e.g. travel tickets booking service after who use mobile to seek advertising habitually. Today, media marketing is about building relationship and trust through effective two way communications, e.g. talk about something that customers are interested in and creating products or service that will help to solve customers' problems from mobile advertising. Some of today's social media marketing campaigns are still driven by the old fashioned marketing and focus on short-term effect sales, which is also known as incentive induced behavior. To assess trust and genuine buyer/seller relationships achieved through consistent and engaging conversation will increase the messages (SMM) level of influence. Trust is the key factor to get the followers to actually to something, i.e. change in buying decisions influence their peers and turn it into revenue for the companies. It is crucial to build a strong relationship with customers and enhance brand loyalty. Hence, it implies mobile phone companies need to build trust relationship to let them to pay extract internet charges to aim to read email, news, watch movie habitually. Then, it will increase chance to let potential buyers to prefer to seek advertisement to choose to buy and products or consume service from mobile websites habitually. Hence, assessment of mobile internet habitual users who use mobile internet time per week from survey is one effective method. Also, firms should start their involvement by inviting their customers or prospects to join their social media community. For example, firms can post the icons of the social media main websites or giving some special deals to customers who become their fans or followers . In the online community, firms should start writing more effective posts. An effective post should reflect honesty and conciseness, it is as key elements of an effective post. It should also be informative to satisfy clients' need for information and experts; opinions. Effective contents should be able to actions from the audience (conversion) so that by the end of this process. Followers will place on order, subscribe newsletter or participate on online surveys. In the offline community, managers should share expertise with their speaker in the local community, which will help to attract more followers or fans and to strength connection with the community. A debate has been going on whether or not consumers are willing to receive mobile advertising. America consumers seem to willing to accept mobile advertising to subsidize the cost of other mobile services , such as email and news services.

A study conducted by HRI Research on behalf of Nokia brand found that the core mobile phone subscriber market (16 to 45 year old) is not only receptive to experiencing mobile advertising, but also actively welcoming mobile advertising in the form of electronic coupons promotion. The relationship between mobile advertising and the four key elements contributing to mobile advertising's acceptance of the promotion in campaign planning. There were mobile advertising should allow users to decide whether or not to receive messages, users could bypass sales messages easily, users should be filter the message received and users want to get mutual benefits of something back. The SMA advertising campaigns of mobile advertising industry plays and consumers have been made afraid of the spam phenomenon deriving from negative email spamming experiences. The personal nature of the website phone markets spamming especially invasive compared to spam received via other channels and devices. Mobile advertising has the potential to be one of the most powerful one to one digital advertising mediums of utilized in the right manner. SMS trials across the would have show the power of mobile advertising in building direct one to one relationship. The online companies like AT&T, AOC wireless, Microsoft and Nokia to mention few companies that are focused on the potential of mobile marketing via mobile handsets. Factors contributing to the success of mobile advertising include that ability, setting up research. measurement, tracking systems, availability of specialist expertise in agency, service provide and establishing consistent rate mobile cards. Other factors impact of drivers on the development of mobile advertising include that personalized medium, users able to opt in , call to action , i.e. immediate response possible , location specific, interactive profiling, appeals to younger customers , one to many communication.

In conclusion, the relatively between mobile advertising and other elements of the promotion in campaign planning include as below: The first element is by utilizing mobile advertising, companies can run marketing campaigns targeted to tens of thousands of people with a fragment of the costs compared to other direct marketing mediums, such as direct mail or telephone and this in just few seconds of line. The advertising industry uses two types of cost calculation cost per thousand impressions (CPM) and cost per rating point (CPP). CPM is used for both print and electronic media when CPP is more popular for electronic media. For instance, if an advertising campaign costs

US$5,000 and has an audience of 300,000 consumers, the CPM will be approximately to the initial CPM measure in media selection , such as quality of the audience, audience attention probability and believability of media selection when the CPM for direct mail is between UA$500 to US$700. For email the CPM ranges from US$5 to US$7. However when email marketing is losing its efficiency, mobile advertising offers new ways to promote products and services. A significant factor contributing to consumers' willingness to accept mobile advertisement is the capability of mobile handsets to service certain type of messages , such as multimedia messages. Evidently, most consumers in the future will carry on smart phone with them. The smart phones allow advertisers to reach consumers in different locations with personalize messages at a given time. Another element is the industry of SG or 4G network service is faster connection speed is a obvious enables users to receive digital photographs, moving wide images, high quality sound for their mobile handsets. From advertisers; perspective this opens various opportunities to plan and implement more advance m-advertising campaigns and integrate those with existing marketing channels. However, to develop and provide applications, for example, interfaces to the carrier's wireless network need to be provided in multiple areas: location, presence, billing, personalization, provisioning, packet network, transport and messaging systems. Next element is location awareness cab be seen as the driving force of many wireless applications and suits also well types of mobile advertising. When mobile phones are almost always carried with and intelligent location awareness technical solution are available. The final element is personalization means building customer loyalty by building a meaningful one to one relatively by understanding the needs to each individual and helping to satisfy a goal that efficiently and knowledgeably addresses each.

Personalization is about mapping and satisfying of client's goal in specific contest with a business's goal in its respective context. Personalization means understanding different kinds of individual preferences , needs, mindsets and lifestyles and cultural as well as geographical differences. Mobile are already equipment with a profiting options, e.g. silent, meeting, outdoors. For example, the utilization of time and location awareness as personalization variables has the benefit that mobile advertising is a marketing medium has features that other marketing channels lack. Hence, email advertising needs to keep every mobile users' personal information to be confidential, solicited message, relevance to users need and the right frequency.

Reference

Adrian, P. (2012). Introduction to marketing theory & practice,
3 rd edition, London: Oxford press.

Couper, M.P. J. Blair and T. Triplet (1999). A Comparison Of Mail And E-mail For a Survey Of Employees In USA Statistical Agencies. Journal Of Official Statistics, 15, 39-56.

Data monitor (2008). The proctor and gamble company. Retrieved Nov. 15 2009 from http://www.datamonitor.com/

Dyer, D., F. Dalzell & R. Olegario (2004). Rising tide. Lessons learned from 165 years of brand building at Procter and Gamble. Boston, MA: Havard Business School Press.

Priesnitz, W. (2007) Counting Our Food Miles. Natural Life, 1 July.

Sullivan, Nicholas P(2007). You can hear me now: How Micro loans and cell phones are connecting the world, San Francisco, CA: John Wilsey & Sans, 2007.

FOUR

WHY SOCIAL BEHAVIOR MAY INFLUENCE ORGANIZATIONAL STRATEGY NEEDS TO BE CHANGED

What does human network job mean ? Why may human network job be popular? Why human network job behavior may influence economy ?

Nowadays internet is popular to use. We can apply internet to find data , search any new things, even earn money. Why does internet

may become huma network job source. For example, e-publish may be one kind of new human network job. Any authors may apply internet

channel to help them to sell electronic or paper books from e-publisher web store. They may apply facebook, you tub etc. any online

channel to promote themselves new books to let new readers to know whether when they may buy themselves favourable new topic books to read

from electronic publisher web store.

Thus, future electronic publisher industry may help any authors to build internet network platform to help them to sell and promote

ot advertise their any one new electronic or paper book topic to let global any one reader to choose to buy their any new topic books from electronic publisher web store easily and conveniently. However, it implies that electronic network platform author may be one kind of future new human network job in our societies.

How electronic network platform author job may bring economy benefit in macro economy view? A person can have few friends, contacts and still be very influential if these few

friends and contacts are themselves highly influential, e.g. one author must not need to know any one reader in global society. When they like to choose any electronic books from electronic internet network platform. They may become the author's any one topic book buyer, when they feel the author's any one topic book is fun and attract they make decision to buth the strange author whose the topic book from electronic book publisher's platform web store conventiently in short time. Although, they are strangers, they do not know themselves , but the reader can understand what it way that made Google from writing platofrm to create new creative mind and typing network job method to replace traditional hand writing book method for global authors. It will be one kind of new human network writing job.

Hence, global any one reader can apply an innovative search engine , such as google.com to find whether whom author personal new topic books are value to read from internet.

Then, the electroniuc publisher's web store may be new book store platform sale network to help the author to sell many electronic or paper books from electronic network platform
in short time. So, internet may be future new network plaform to help global any one author to create network writing job absolutely. Furthermore, internet may be popular social media
to help any one author to build goold relationship between his/her readers. It is one kind of new network, human network job. New authors do not need to buy many paper books to prepare to put in any one book shop warehouse. Their every book can print on demand to reduce out of book stock in any one book shop. They may choose to sell either electronic books or paper books both from any one book publisher web store. So, electronic network platform may be one kind of good writing channel to help human authors to create income and it can also help authors to bring new creative mind and new topic fun content books to let readers to know and buy to read from electronic publisher network platform.

Why does human behavior may be one kind of new human network job to bring global economic advantages. ALthough, it may be free income or without inocme, but the person does the network behavior, his/her behavior may be bring advantages to influence many other people's health. For this case, when a worker in a coffee shop in an airport gets a vaccination aganinst the flu, it does not only helps him or her stay healthy, but also helps the many travellers who might otherwise have been inflected if that workers caught the flu. So, the externality , the result implies the vaccination of even a part of a community conveys benefits to the whole community. For example, governments pay special attention to the vaccinations of school children, teachers, health mothers, and the elderly, categories of people particularly susceptible not only to catching, but also to transmitting a disease.

It is not accidental that governments are heavily involved with vaccination . When there are externalities, free market, fail to persuade individual incentives with society's
their the worker's decision of whether to get a vaccine ends up attracting whether other people get sick. The workers might not fully take all these other people's potential suffering into account when making her or his vaccination decision.

As Stanford University does many suggestions, understand this and tries to help them make the right decisions and so providers free flu vaccines for its staff and students.
Small pockets of unvaccinated individuals can allow a disease to gain a spread more widely well-being. For example, parent weighing the costs and benefits of a vaccine for their child is not always thinking of the consequences of that vaccination to other people. THese are markets in which subsidizing or regulating behavior can make everyone better off. Because the reason for requiring that a child be vaccinated before enrolling in school is not just to protect that child, because each child's vaccination affects others via potential contagions.

Robots take our jobs behavioral and economy influences

Robot job behavior brings economy influences

If one day robots can replace human to do simple, even complex jobs. They will bring what influences to our global societial economy.The popular economic refrain declares that the
global middle class is dying and robots will soon take our jobs, e.g. shopping center customer service jobs, library service jobs, cinema ticket sale jobs, restaurant kitchen cooker jobs,
even, bus drivers, taxi drivers etc. public transport driving jobs, accountant, doctors etc. professional jobs. Whether it is beautiful or petty matter if our future societies have many human jobs can be replaced to do from robots. Businessman must may reduce to employ employees and reduce to pay salary or wage, when robots can be replaced to do their employees tasks. But, societies must bring unemployement rate rises , due to societies will have many people loss jobs when their employers choose to buy robots to serve their clients or do any office tasks or customer service or cleaning etc. tasks.

In micro economy view, employers may save money in long term, but in macro economy view, it will cause unemployment ratio rises , even crime rate rises when there are many people lose
jobs in societies. These models of doom, though, fail to account for the hundreds of businesses riding the waves of change in their industries when robots may be invented to replace human to do many simple , even complex tasks in

our future societies.

WE may image that one small factory needs to manufacture fishes canes to sell to supermarket, the small , cheaper stuff and higher margin parts of the fishes manufacture industry. Before, this factory needs to employe many human factory workers need to help every fresh customer makeing the perfect fishing gear, designed for performance, durability, and cost in order to achieve to manufacture every fish cane in whole fished processing manufacturing stages. Every worker needs to spend about 15 to twenty minutes to finish every fish cane , till to delivery to any supermarket to sell. If this fish canes manufacturing factory can apply manufacturing robots to help them to finish any one working tasks , every robot can only spend five minutes to finish whole fresh fish cane manufacturing process. Thus, every robot can

help this factory save 10 to 15 minutes time to finsh every fish cane manufacturing process. IN fact, time is money, because when every robot can help this factory to reduce 10 to 15 minutes time to compare human worker. Then, this factory can finish about 20 fish canes in one hour if it can use robot to help it to manufacture fish canes. Otherwise, if this factory still use human workers to help it to manufacture fish canes, then it can finsh about 3 to 4 fish canes in one hour. SO, the manufacturing efficiency ensures that robots must help this fish manufacturing factory to raise fish canes number more than human workers. So, in robotic behavioral economy view, manufacturing robots must help this fish canes manufacturing factory to raise fish canes manufacturing number and deliver increasing number to supermarkets to prepare to sell every day. Robots can help this fish canes manufacturing factory bring manufacturing time saving, rising manufacturing efficiency, improving performance and reducing wages expenditure long time advantages in micro economy view. However, manufacturing robots can also bring disadvanages to society, e.g. increasing unemployment ratio, increasing crime rate,

this factory workers will lose jobs and income, they need earn social welfare from government and increasing government finance pressure in short time, even long time in macro economic view.

Stanford University graduate program in economics, Scott lecturer explained that "in demand and supply economic theory for robots supply and demand case, robots supply number increasing may influence human workers demand number decrease. It sometimes calls " the efficient frontier".

No specific human beings were mentioned in any of economics classes. As robots supply and demand in market case, They (robots) may be purely theoretical " agents" who reached to the most reasonable sale prices in order to persuade any one businessman buyer to make manufacturing robot buying decision whether robots can help him / her to bring how much saving time , saving money, saving cost, improving performance, efficiency economic benefit before he/she plans to reduce workers number when he/she decides to apply robots to replace human workers in his/her factory or office or any service department, e.g. cinema ticket sale service, shopping center customer service, shopping center cleaning , supermarket customer service etc. service or sale tasks. When robots can replace human to do any one of these tasks in any organizations. So, robots may be human worker agents who reached to prices the way robots would react to a software

command. There was nothing that explained why some people thrived and others did n't or why truly brilliant, hardworking people could fail when much lazier folks succeeded." Having been admitted to the Stanford University graduate program in economics, Scott lecturer hoped to get his answers there.

How robots influence our future social changing? Using the right technology can be a boon to your business in this economy. For internet example, it is easier than ever to find well-matched customers all around the world, to stay in contact with them, and to more quickly design the products they want. If you focus solely on being cutting -edge, though you risk letting the technology

take over what should be very robust relationships with your customers , employees, and colleagues. IN nowaddays society, technoligical advances and cutomation, personal

relationships in business are more crucial than ever. I mean that robots can not replace human to serve clients to let them to feel more comfortable and passion more easily. For shoe shop case example, if the shoe shop apply one robot to serve its clients to replace human shoe salesperson to serve its shoe customers. Robots ensure that they can not persuade every shoe potential buyer to make shoe buying decision more easily when robots need to contact every shoe potential buyer. The reason is simple, because robots can not touch any one shoe buyer individual emotion very easier.

If the shoe buyer needs the robots to help him/her to choose any right shoe styles when he/she can not feel himself / herself can make the most right shoe style choice decision. The robots can not replace human shoe salesperson to make shoe style choice judgement more easily. They must need longer time to analyze whether which shoe style may be the most suitable to the shoe buyer. Otherwise, human shoe salesperson may attempt to make the most right shoe style choice decision to help any one shoe buyer to chooce the most right style shoe because he/she owns shoe style sale experience, shoe style knowledge, the most important reason is that they can feel every shoe customer individual emotion to touch whether he/she will feel comfortable or happy when they attempt to help every shoe customer to seek the most right shoe style in every shoe customer whole shoe searching processing. Othwerwise, serving robots are only one machine, they can not touch or feel every shoe customer individual emotion whether he/she feel comfortable or unhappy or happy when they need to contact them in whole shoe searching processing. Hence, I believe that some tasks robots can

not repalce human staff to do very easily. Otherwise, robots may bring disadvanatges to let any one businessman to loss his/her customers, due to robots can not touch every customer

emotion to compare human staff in service tasks more easily. Robots serving customer behaviors may cause money lose and customers number lose to the shop in micro economic view.

Intellectual human economic behaviors

What does intellectual human economic behaviors mean ? I believe that when we choose or decide to do intellectual behaviors, then our societies will be influenced to bring economic growth in consequence.I shall attempt to indicate pollution case to explain how and why eithet our intellectual or foolish behaviors may bring economic growth or recession in consequence as below:

On one hand, for air pollution social case aspect example, if we only consider to buy cars to drive for working aimr or holiday leisure aim. Then, our societies air will be polluted. Our health will be influenced to bad. Our car driving behaviors may cause global environment air pollution serously. In long tiem, global air pollution will bring our bodies health to be bad. Although, ourselves car driving behaviors may bring our driving travelling leisure enjoyment and comfortable feeling in short time, also we so not need to pay public transport fare often, but we need to compensate ourselves health economic intangible loss due to air pollution , when cars number increases, dirty air will cause ouselves health to become bad.

In the result, we will need to pay more medical expenditure when we are old age, due to ourselves bodies will become bad, due to we breathe global dirty air every day, due to ourselves cars pollute air in long time, e.g. 10 to 20 years, even 30 more without limited air pollution environment. So, driving cars behavior may be one kind of human foolish behavior and our foolish behavior may bring ourselves future long time medical expenditure absolutely.

One the other hand, water pollution social aspect, if we often keep much rubblish to pollute sea, oil exploration porcessing pollute ocean , ships gas pollute ocaen, then fishes will eat polluted food and drive dirty water, due to global ocean is polluted.

In fact, because human only to conside how to buy boats to carry on leisure enjoyment activities, or catch cruises to travel on the sea. Also, oil manufacturers only consider researching anywhere to find new oil exploration places to manufacture oil product, when their oil exploration processes pollute ocarn . Consequently, global fishes drink polluted warer or eat polluted food. They will have poison. SO, human will have high chance to eat poison polluted fishes, due to fishes are poison or are polluted.

So, human is doing foolish activities, we only hope to find oil exploration places to pollute ocean or we only spend money to buy ticket to catch ships to travel anywhere in global ocean. All of these human foolish behaviors will bring pollution to global ocean. On consequently, we will need to compensate to eat polluted or dirty or poision fishes, ourselves bodies health will be bad. In long time, we need have high chance to pay medical expenditure when we are old. So, pollution case may be one good example to explain how and why human foolish behavior may influence ourselves future need to compensate serious medical loss.

All of these human foolish behavior will bring pollution to global ocean. On consequently, we will need to compensate to eat polluted or dirty or poison fished , ourselves bodies health will be bad. In long time, we will have high chance to pay medical expenditure, when we are old. So, pollution case may be one good example to explain how and why human ourselves intellectual or foolish behaviors may influence future long time economic loss or economic growth or recession in micro and micro economic view.

On another water pollution aspect hand, if we often keep rubbish to sea, oil exploration processing pollutes ocean and ships' gas pollute ocean, then fishes will eat polluted food and drink dirty water, due to fishes will eat polluted food and drink dirty sea water because the global ocean is polluted seriously.

In fact, because human only consider how to buy boats to carry on any leisure water activities, or catches cruises to travel on the sea. Also, oil manufacturers only consider any where to find oil exploratin places to manufacture oil products from ocean, when their pol exploration processes can plooute ocean. Consequently, global fishes drink polluted water or eat direty food. They will have poison. So, human will have high chance to eat poison fishes.

Otherwise, such as pollutin case, it can infuence inflation or deflation. Consequently, the reason indicates supply and demand theory. If air pollution is serious, then we will consider health issue, global cars demand number may be influenced to reduce, when global cars number demand will reduce, global car prices and supply number will need to change to fall down in order to attract or persuade global car consumers choose to make car purchase decision.

Hence, global car manufacture number and car price will be influenced to reduce, due to global air pollution issue. Consequently, deflation will occur because when the country citizen usually does not spend much extra saving money to buy car expensive goods. Money value will be low. Otherwise, if global cair pollution is not serious, human considers to buy cars to enjoy driving leisure lives. So, global car demand is influenced to increase , also global car price will also influenced to increase.

Consequently, gobal human will choose to buy cars to drive. Due to we accept to spend extra saving to buy expensive car goods. Car sale price and supply may be influenced to rise up. Money value is influenced to reduce. Inflation may be influenced, due to global car consumers number increases, we would not have extra money to spend easily. Car expensive goods expenditure influences our spending habit to avoid to make car purchase decision more easily. So, human intellectual or foolish activities may bring inflation or deflation consequency in possible indirectly in macro economic view.

On conclusion, above pollution case explain that how and why human intellectual or foolish economic behaviors may bring inflation or deflation consequency as wll as economic growth or recession consequency as well as any goods demand and supply increasing or decreasing consequency. It implies that human behavior may have indirect relationship to influence any goods demand and supply number to either increase or decrease result as well as any goods price will be influenced to increase or decrease in micro and macro economic view.

The relationship between social change and human behavior

Why does economic changes may influence human individual behavioral change? I shall attempt to indicate shopping behavior and staying at home behavior to explain their case and effect relationsip as below:

Human behavior can be influenced by economic change or economic change can be influenced by human behavior? Why does recession may influence consumers reduce shopping desire? In social recession suitation, it is possible that many people lose jobs suddenly, due to businessmen lose many customers. They need to make decision to reduce employees number in order to continue to keep businesses. Consequently, many firms (organizations) their employees may lose jobs. When they have much time, due to lose jobs, they will feel to avoid to spend too much time and money to go to shopping often. Many losing jobs people, they will often stay at homes.

So, they will reduce time to go to shopping, then non essential products won't their preferable choice purchase products. Hence, recession will change many losing jobs people their shopping or consumption desires to avoid to buy non essential products often . Usually when economic boom, many people have jobs to do because consumers number must increase when many people have jobs to do. Then, many people can accept to spend money to buy non essential products often. Many people feel spend time to go to shopping can satisfy their purchase of any kinds of new products useful psychology or desire. So, recession is one good example to explain it can influence many people do not like often to leave homes to go to shopping easily. Many people like to stay at homes, becaue they feel worry about spending too much shopping time when they leave homes. Their staying home time is one good negative shopping behavior example. So, economic change may influence human individual behavior changes , they have direct cause and efect relationship in behavioral economic view.

May human behavior influence economic change? Is it possible that human behavior may bring the country social economic change in macro economic or micro behavioral economic view ? I shall indicate publishing industry example. Do you feel that if there are many students feel learning is very important when they read many books or many of students feel interesting to read or they have reading new books in habit, then it is possible that the country will have many students like to spend time to go to any book shops to choose the books, they feel that they can help they learn new knowledge. Then the country will increase students number, they often spend time to visit any one book shop every week. Their visiting book shops behavior which may become their habits. So, the country will increase students number, they often spend time to visit book shops. Also, it implies that visiting book shops behaviors may be their behavioral habits.

So, when the country has many students often spend time to visit book shops , their visiting book shops behaviors may help any one book shop to raise books sale chance. So, the country's student individual often visiting book shop behaviors, their habitual visiting book shops behaviors must may assist help any one book shop to increase books sale number absolutely.

Consequently, any one book shop , its books sale bumber must be influenced to increase to increase because the country will have many students like or feel need visit book shops habit in order to choose any suitable books to buy to read at home in order to raise themselves learning effort. When the country has many bok shops often have many students visit their book shops, then their books sale number may be influenced to increase. It explain why student individual visiting book shop behavior may help any one book shop sale number increases also.

How human productive behavior may influence economic development

May any country which citizen behavior assist themselves country development? It is one cause and effect economic question. I mean that if the country itself citicen can not concentrate mind or energy to choose to do one kind of industry in order to let themselves country can bring the most benefit, then whether the counry itself economy can bring the most serious economic benefit. I shall attempt to indicate these countries themselves indistry choice to explain whether these countries themselves citizen productive behavior may help themselves countries to achieve the largest economic benefits. I shall indicate as below:

New Zealand farmer individual wine productive behavior

For New Zealand country example, this country concerns itself effort is foucs on farming agricultural aspect. So, this country has many farmers concentrate on farming agricultural aspect. May New Zealanders choose to spend time to produce different kinds of wines, e.g. wine or red grape wine is for the people are eating meat, or they are eating dinner.

When these New Zealanders their behaviors choose to do farming or agriculture to grow and produce different kinds of taste of white or red grape wine drinking products job. Themselves grape agriculture behavior will influence these New Zealanders themselves, they can learn how to improve different kinds of grape wine drinking products in order to achieve every kinds of white or read grape wines taste improving aim during their white or red grape producing process.

Why can New Zealander every individual white or read grape wine producers improve their white or read grape wine taste more easily? In behavioral economic view, it can explain that why any one New Zealander white or read grape wine producer can be encouraged or excited or persuaded to concentrate nervous and energy and effort to learn how to improve their white or red grape wine products easily.

In fact, New Zealand is one agricultural food export country. It has good natural environment resource , e.g. land, seed to provide any one farmer to produce themselves any kinds of agricultrual food products, e.g. fruit, or wine food products. Because New Zealanders know themselves country has enough natural resource . So, in common, many New Zealanders choose to attempt to do farming agricultural jobs in order to export themselves any kinds of fruit or meat or wine products to overseas or sell to domestic in order to earn profit.

So, when these New Zealand farmers number has been increasing every year. This country farmers will feel themsleves competition between this New Zealand farmers themselves are serious due to they may feel New Zealanders choose to do agriculture businesses in order to export themselves different kinds of farming food to overseas or sell to local to earn profit.

Hence, when many New Zealand farmers feel that farmers number has been increasing every year. They will feel themselves competition is serious. They must need to spend much time and nervous and effort to research what method is the best how to produce the best taste of white or red grape wine products in order to let local or overseas wine buyers to choose to buy his/her producing white or read grpae products to drink.

Hence, in competition psychological view, may influence many New Zealand white or reaad wine producers had been beginning to change their learning behavior on researching what method is the best in order to produce the best quality of taste red or white wine products to sell in order to attract overseas or local white or read grape wine drinkers to choose to buy his/her wine products. Their behavior will focus on learning how to raising or improving white or read grape wine taste method more than only focus on producing a large number white or red grape wine products. They believe wine quality is more important to compare wine producing number. So, New Zealand wine producers themselves wine producers behaviors have been changing on concentrating on researching wine quality method aspect more then wine producing number aspect in behavioral economic view.

America high technological productive behavior

For America example, US is one high technological country, it owns many high technological knowledge talent inventors, e.g. computer science inventors. Hence, US must attract many diferent countries owning high technological computer inventors choose to go to US to develop their computer science profession career. Also, it seems that when many computer science inventors or professions choose to go to US to develop themselves computer science new career. In behavioral economic view, due to their leaving themselves countries choice, which may bring influence themselve country job behaviors need to be changed. They must need to adapt US new live. Because they will forgive their past computer science job. These computer science professionals need to spend time to adapt US new lives. They " past computer science job behaviors" will need to be changed to their new US any computer employer's new computer science job model.

Because their traditional computer science jobs needed to be forgot in their themselves countries. They will feel their old computer science job knowledge and behavior needed to change in order to let their US any one new of computer company employer feels satisfactory to accept their new working behavior in any one US computer organization.

So, on the other hand, many US computer company employer will feel that they must need time to accept any one new overseas computer science professions their working behaviors, their working attitude daily, because these foreign comouter science professional, their past computer working behaviors and working attitude must be different to US domestic computer science professions.

In behavioral economic view, these overseas computer science professions, their working behaviors and attitude must be needed to change in order to adapt any one US new computer company itself domestic or local computer science professional stafs themselves daily working behaviors and attitude because these overseas and local computer science professionals must need to team work together.

In behavioral economic view, it is only one way that foreign computer science professionals must need to change themselves past country traditiona daily working behaviors and attitude in order to cooperate with these US local computer science professionals in teams more easily.

Consequently, if these foreign compute science professionals can change their past working behaviors and attitude to let any one US local computer science professional feels to cooperate with them easily in short time. Then, the US computer company itself whole computer professional teams themselves efficiencies will be influenced to raised or improved by the changing past working attitude and working behaviors of these foreign computer science professionals. So, in behavioral economic view, only if US any one computer company hopes itself computer teams themselves efficiency can be raised or improved when it decides to employ foreign computer science professionals and US domestic computer science professionals. They need to work in teams together. They must need to let these foreign computer science professionals to know how to change their working behaviors and attitude to let their domestic computer science professionals feel easy to work together. Then, the US computer company itself whole team efficiency must be rasied or improved easily in short time.

● China share market investing behavior

For China share market example, economic development depends on financial market. Because if many Chinese have interest to invest to carry on shares buying and selling activities in orde to learn how to earn shares interest and share profit when the China shareholder can make decision to sell himself/herself shares in the the high price, then he/she can earn money when he/she can sell the China company's shares in the high sale share price position.

If China has many Chinese like to spend time to carry on investing shares activities. Themselves shares buying and selling behaviors will influence China has many companies can increase fund from many Chinese shareholders in order to have enough money to expand or develop themselves businesses in China in long term.

Consequently, when China can have many Chinese like to attempt to carry on buying and selling shares investing behaviors in China share market. Themselves buying and selling shares behaviors can help many Chinese companies have effort to increase enough money or capital in order to continue to do their businesses in long term absolutely. So, it explains why when many Chinese become shareholders , they can assist China will have many companies continue to develop their businesses if many Chinese like to carry on shares buying and selling investing behaviors in long time in China financial investment market nowadays in behavioral economic view.

Why has any individual country have many people invest share behavior which can influence the country's macro consumption desire?

I shall apply shares market buying and selling investment behavior to explaiin why shares investment behavior which may impact the country's overal consumption desire as below:

In behavioral economic view, I assume that when the coutry has many people have interest to attempt to carry on shares buying and selling investment behavior, then their frequent shares buying and selling behaviors which may bring negactive consumption desire or shopping desire of these shares investors their consumer behavior.

The reason is simple, when the country has many share buyers number suddenly been increasing rapidly. Consequently, these large group share investors must need to spend much time to research any kinds of company shares variations, whether when their share prices will rise up of fall down in order to achieve buying the company's shares in the lowest price and selling the company's shares in the highest price level in order to earn profit.

Basic on this reason, they must need to spend much extra time to research share prices changing behavior every day, e.g. one working person will wait to leave his/her job, after he/she can spend time to gather data to research the day's share price changing behavior after dinner. So, the working person's right time may be his/her share price market research behavior. Before he/she may spend his/her night time to go to shopping after dinner, but nowadays, he/she will fogive to do his/her shopping behavior before dinner or after dinner at hight sometime. He/she will make decision to spend much night time to turn on computer to click on share market website to research his/her share purchase choice to investigate whether his/her share price whether it rises up or falls down at the moment in order to make his/her share buying or selling decision at ever night time.

I mean the when the country has many people are share investors, their shares investment behavioral spenging time which will influence many shops lose customers at might often because the country will have many people feel need to spend night time to turn on computer or watch television to investigate share price variation. So, the country will have many people / share investors choose to stay at home in order to carry on share price variation investigation behavior, they need to listen share market update news from radios or watch the share market update news from computer or TV at home every night. Consequenly, they must reduce times to leave themselves homes at night. So, their shopping behavior also will be reduced. Because these share investors feel need to spend time to investigate share price variation news at homes which can bring economic benefits (high opportunity benefits) when they choose to forgive to leave homes to go to shopping times (opportunity cost) every night.

On conclusion, it seems that when the country has many people are share investors, then their share price investigating behavior may bring negative shopping emotion at night. Consequently, the country's any one shop may lose many customers from this share investor consumer group in behavioral economic view. Hence, when the country's share investors number had been increasing rapidly, it will influence any shops lose many customers from this share investing customer group at night frequenly in short time, even long time in behavioral economic view, because their shopping desires or shopping emotion will be brought negative feeling when they make decisions to spend much time to listen radios or watch TV or computers share price update nes at night. Hence, share market will bring negative impact to influence consumer shopping desire or negative shopping emotion in behavioral economic view.

Can technology influence human shopping behavioral change?

Nowadays, technological development has reached mature stage, whether technological mature stage may bring positive or negative shopping emotion influence to global consumers. I shall aplly internet inventin or ecommerce shopping channel tool to explain whether internet technology can bring postive or negative influence to global consumer behavior in behavioral economic view.

Internet is a good technological tool, it brings e-commerce business chance. In fact, commonly, global has have many businessmen choose to use internet channel to carry on their products transactions between global online-buyers and their electronic websites. So, global many shoppers had begun to feel online shopping is more convenient to compare visiting shops shopping. Their shopping behaviors have been changed from internet technological tool. Global has many shoppers choose to buy any products from any overseas or local businessmen their web stores. They only need to spend time to find any businessmen their webstores to choose the most suitable products to pay visa to buy from their webstores. at homes. So, in general, global had have may shoppers had changed their shopping behaviors from visiting shops to visiting webstores at homes often.

So, it seems that internet technological tool had influenced global many shops disappear, but internet webstores will be replaced their actual shops on streets. Some of businessmen either they choose webstores to replace shops or choose websotes and shops both or still keep shops only. Hence, internet tool influences global businessmen have three kinds of products sale channels to let globa local and overseas consumers to choose how to buy their products. However, in fact, many of global shoppers, youngers and olders had begun to accept to buy any products from webstores. They feel to spend time to leave homes to visit shops , their shopping behaviors will be wasted time to not essential part to their daily lives. Hence, since internet technological invention, it had changed many consumers their traditional visiting shops shopping habit to change to buying products from webstores channel.

However, on the one hand, internet creates webstores ecommerce shopping channel to let global many consumers do not need to leave homes to go to shopping. It brings negative visiting shops shopping emotion to global general consumers nowadays. But on the other hand, it also brings positive visiting internet webstores shopping emotion to global general consumer nowadays. So, it seems that global many consumers feel that they often do not need to spend much time to go out shopping. Many global consumers feel convenient and enjoy to choose any products to buy from different internet webstores, when the online buyer chooses the most suitable product, he she only needs to pay visa card to buy the product from the online seller's webstore conveniently at home.

Hence, online shopping can bring economic benefit to online buyers, e.g. avoiding walking time or spending transport fare to visit the shop to go to shopping, shortening or reducing shopping time to do another important matter.

On conclusion, global many consumers began feel online shopping can bring more economic benefits on shortening shopping time, avoiding transport fare spending aspect. So, online shopping will be popular shopping behavior for future long time. It may encourage global many shoppers can make rapid shopping decision in short time in order to carry on any products buying transaction to global any one online shopper in short time easily in behavioral economic view. So, global many businessmen had begun to build themselves one attraction webstore in order to persuade different countries consumers to choose to click themselves webstores from internet channel to buy any kinds of products in short time easily.

So, internet technology had changed consumers traditional shopping behaviors to build positive online shopping emotion as well as raise online sellers' any products sale chance easily in behavioral economic view.

Why and how human behavior may influence the country's economic growth or recession?

When one country has many people choose to do the same matter for one period, whether their behavior may influence the country's pvera; economic growth or recession . I shall attempt to indicate cases toexplain their relationship as below:

For flowing rubblish behavioral case example, do you feel that when the country has many people often flow rubblish on the streets, instead of their flowing rubblish behavior may bring streets dirty? But, their flowing rubblish behavior may explain that this country has people may have enough money to buy food to ear, or enough cloths to wear, enough bottles of water to drink, even they may have enough money to buy new television, radio, refrigeraters , washing machines, desktops or laptops electronic home products from old to new to use in order to satisfy their living needs. So, when they flow old electronic home products, their flowing old home electronic products behaviors may seem that they have enough money to buy other new home electronic products to replace old home electronic products to use at homes.

However, it seems thaat this country ought have many people have jobs to do. So, many of them, they can easy to make purchase decison to flow any old home electronic products and buy any new home electronic products to use . Because this country has many people have jobs to do. So, they can often not use old home electonic products to become rubblishs to flow on streets after they had bought any kinds of new home electronic homes.

In fact, it also implies that this country's economy grows rapidly. So, many businesses can glow up rapdly. When they expanded their businesses, they must need to increase employees number in order to let they help themselves to raise productivity or serve their clients absolutely. So, when the country has many businesses can grow up, it seems that its economy must be better or it is improved to compare past. Due to many different kinds of home electronic products had been often bought to use by this country people in this period. So, this country's any streets can be observed that expensive electronic home products were flowed on streets anywhere. then, this country will have many electronic home products sellers can sell their home electronic products very easily. When this country has many people can find any kinds of jobs to do easily. So, due to unemploymen rate had been decreasing.

In behavioral economic view, as this many electronic home products rubblish country case, we can observe this country may have many people have jobs to do. So, consumption number has been increased long time. So, cheap food, or expensive home electronic products may be rubblish on any streets. This country's people , their flowing rubblish behaviors may be explained that many of people have enough jobs to do, so they have ability to buy any good taste food to eat or buy any kinds of expensive electronic home products to use. So, this country's economy may be improved for this long period. So, in behavioral economic view, when this country can have many electronic home products rubblishs are flowed on anywherer in streets frequently. It seems that this country will have many people have jobs to do, so it causes they often change old home electronic products or replaced them easily, when they have enough income to spend to buy any kinds of new home electronic products to use at homes easily. Moreover, their flowing old electronic home products behaviors also indicate that this country has many people their salaries may be increased in possible from their emplyers. When this country can have many different kinds of home electornic products are sold. It means that this country's electronic home products needs or demand had been increasing, due to many people have jobs to do and income increases to excite their living of needs also improve. Consequently, this country may seem have better economic improvement. We can observe from this country's electronic home products rubblish increasing income in theis period.

On conclusion, this country ought experience economic growth at this period. So, " flowing expensive electronic home rubblish increasing number " may seem that this country's economic growth is rapidly in this period, due to many people have jobs to do as well as salaries increase in this period.

Technology how impacts human behavior changing?

Technology how influences human behavior to bring changing? For example, online share purchase and sale transaction from smart phone brings share investor can do share buying or selling transation in any where and any time conveniently, non manual driving auto vehicle, bring car owner feels comfortable and spends free time to do other matter, e.g. reading, listening mucis in himself or herself car freely. electrical energy vehicle can help car owner to reduce air polluton and it can brings the drivers do not feel drive long time in any journeys in order to avoid air pollution for environmental protection responsible car drivers in our societies. Thus, they will drive long time in any journeys when they can drive electronic energy cars to replace oil energy cars.

However, online technology can also bring consumers can choose to stay at homes to buy any things from seller individual online webstore conveniently. Such as online technology can bring shoppers do not need to spend much time to visit shops to buy any things. They can choose any kinds of products from any online sellers individual online webstores conveniently at homes. Online technology excite busy consumers can make purchase decision easily as well as it can help online sellers sell any kinds of products from internet easily.

In behavioral economic view, technology can change human behavior to be improved, it can let human feels comfortable, more free time ro use, rapid making any decisions, such as apply smart phones to make share purchase or sale transaction decision, online shopping decision, even travelling any where decision in short time, when the traveller finds the most cheap hotel accommodation room price and air ticket price frm any travel agent online tourism webstore, then the potential travel customer can follow the online hotel accommodation price and air ticket price data to make decision when to buy the air ticket from the airline travel agent or make decision when to prebook which hotel accommodation room to go to the country to travel from online travel agent tourism webstores. So, technology can encourage global any country travelers to make anywhere to trvel rapidly. If the traveler can find the country's general hotel rooms and airline tickets prices had been decreasing more sightly. The traveler may make travel decision to choose the country to travel in short time, then he/she can prebook the country;s any hotel room and airline ticket to pay by visa fraom the country's any hotel and airline travel agent webstores., before one week, even one month or more easily. Hence, online technology can also encourage traveler individual frequent travel times to be increased, due to global travelers can find any hotel rooms and airline tickets prices from internet conveniently at homes. They do not need to spend time to visit any airline travel agent to enquire travel choice country's hotel rooms prices and airline ticket prices. They can compare global travel of countries choices ' all hotels rooms and airline agents air tickets prices to make prebook airline seat and hotel room decision before one week, one month even six months early.

On conclusion, online technology can encourage global travelers can make travelling any where and when traveling time desicions easily. It can excite tourism industry develops in long time. Also, such as electricity cars invention can encourage environment protection car owners do car purchase decision easily, because they can choose to drive electronic energy cars to replace oil energy cars in order to avoid air pollution occurs easily. So, electronic cars can increase electronic car purchasrs number, due to many of environmental protection attitude of car owners can choose to drive electricity cars to bring air cleans, even non -manual driving cars can encourage lazy driving and free time driving car owners to choose to buy non-manual (artificial intelligent) cars to drive , because they can spend much free time to read, listen music or do any matters in themselves cars, they do not need to drive cars, robotic (AI) auto driving machine is such one non-manual driver to help them to drive themselves cars confidently. So, non-manual driving cars can attract lazy and enjoying free time driving car owners to choose to buy to replace traditional manual cars to drive easily. Moreover, online share transaction can help any share investors to make share buying and selling decision in short time easily. When they can apply smart phones technological tool to carry on share buying and selling activities easily. They can observe any share rising or falling price suitation from smart phones in any where any any time easily. So, smart phone technology can help global any shareholders to make share purchase and sale transaction easily. So, technology can encourage human makes decision in short time rapidly.

How and why employees behaviors may influence economy development?

In behavioral economy view,I believe the country's any organizational employees behavior may bring indirect relationship to influence the country's long term economic development. I shall indicate past manufacture industry social development period to explain their relationship. For many countries' past business activities had belonged to manufacturing industry, such as US, UK past before 1980 year, it focused on steel manufacturing and steel manufacturing related machine products. So, US, Uk developed countries manufacturing industries may be past main country's economic income sources. I assume US , UK past had one million number different kinds of industries. They ought had about seven houndred thousand number organizational businesses were belonged to manufactured industry. They may include:

Steel manufacturing and steel related machine manufacturing, e.g. vehicle manufacturing, home appliances, e.g. washing machine, television, radio, refrigerate cooler, heater, air condition etc. different kinds of different kinds of steel -related manufacturing machine, they were manufactured from US, UK steel machine manufacturers. So, US,

Uk the other three hundred thousand number industry may be general service industry, e.g. hotel service, restaurent, cinema, public transport service, tourism lesiure , wine bar, supermarket etc. different kinds of non-manufacturing industries business organizations were operated in UK, US past before 1980 year.

So, in UK, US developed countries industry development history, they ought have high percentage of businesses belonged to steel related manufacturing machine and steel products. Also, in the past before 1980 year, US, Uk business employers , they employed many workers are manufacturing workers. They needed to spend long time to work in factories. They were skillful workers, and they are trained to manufacturing cars, washing machine, television, heater, etc. even steel itself different kinds of steel related products to prepare to deliver to their shops to sell to US, Uk local or overseas clients.

So, I believe that past UK, US ought employ many employees, they belonged to skillful manufacturing workers, manufacture increasing steel machine or steel related machine number of products rapidly daily. So, if UK, US had had many of these manufacturing factories owned high skillful workers, then their manufacturing steel-related machine or steel both kinds of products number must be influenced to raise rapidly. Consequently, their steel machine manufacturing products would been exported to overseas or would been sold to local both markets , they may be influenced to raise sale number. They (these manufacturing workers) needed to be trained to know how to manufactur these different kinds of machine products in the efficient teams and they ought to be trained to raise their efficiencies in order to shorten time to manufacturing many kinds of steel related manufacturing machine or steel itself products rapidly. So , if their efficiencies and manufacturing performance was improved, these US, UK any one manufacturing worker and their teams ought achieve raising productivities significantly.

Hence, when past UK, US manufacturing industry development period, if these two countries' any manufacturing factories could have many manufacturing workers could be trained to be skillful and proficient manufacturing workers. Then, in past every day to these factories workers, they ought help their steel or steel related manufacturing employers to raise any kinds of machine or steel products number in every team. So, when past in the manufacturing industry development, US, UK could have many factories' manufacturing workers themselves steel or steel related machine products manufacturing skill could be trained to to improve to any kinds of these machine or steel manufacuring products quality as well as their products number could be influenced to raise by themselves skillful improvement significantly every day.

Then, what would be influenced to occur to past UK, US manufacturing industry period? In behavioral economic view, when these two manufacturing industry developed countries, such as UK, US , if they had many factories workers can be trained to improve their skill in order to achieve any kinds of steel or steel-related machine products quality could be improved as well as products manufacturing number could be also increased absolutely.

In consequence, past UK and US both countries ought increase themselves any kinds of steel and steel related machine products number to be supplied to themselves local shops to let local clients to choose any one kind of machine manufacturing products to buy easily as well as they could also export to supply overseas any countries to buy their different kinds of steel or steel related machine products to let overseas steel or steel related manufacturing machine product buyers, they can have many of these different kinds of these steel or steel-related different kinds of manufacturing machine from UK and UK these both countries easily to compare other countries.

On conclusion, I believe that past US, and UK macro manufacturing industry income GDP would increase significantly. So, they would have good economic growth performance because when many of these manufacturing workers themselves manufacturing effort could be improved. So, it explained when employees manufacturing abilities can influence economic growth indirectly.

    Robots invention whether they can help organizations to raise efficiencies or inefficiencies?

In behavioral economic view, in any organizations, when the organization hopes its worker teams can raise efficiencies , the organization may choose to increase more workers number and/or it can provide training to improve these workets themselves skills in order to raise their efficiencies. For one warehouse example, when the warehouse increases many goods , they are needed to delivered these goods from the shelves to the delivering destination locations. If this warehouse supervisors feel these workers themselves goods delivery speeds are slow, which is possible due to this warehouse's workers number is not enough. So, this warehouse supervisor ought increase workers number in order to increase their goods delivery speed in order to deliver goods from the shelves to every indicated goods delivery destination in order to let any one lorry driver can transport the right kinds of goods and ensure the accurate goods number to transport to any one client home rapidly.

However, if this warehouse supervisor planed to buy several warehouse goods delivery robots to assist these warehouse workers to find the right kinds of goods from shelves and then deliver to the right destination location in the warehouse. So, these warehouse orkers can concentrate on counting the accurate goods number and ensuring the right kinds of goods in order to prepare to let lorry drivers to transport these goods to these goods of buyers themselvers homes rapidly. Consequently, in the first step, robots can concentrate on finding th right goods from shelves and delivers them to the right goods transportation of location destination. Then, in the second step, these warehouse workers can concentrate on counting the accurate goods number and ensuring the right kinds of goods in order to prepare to put them to the lorry. Consequently, when warehouse robots and warehouse workers can cooperate to work together, the most important, robots, can deal on finding the right kinds of goods and deal on delivering the accurate number of goods of job duty as well as these warehouse workers can only concentrte on counting the right kinds of goods number in order to avoid it has none any mistake of wrong kinds of goods and inaccurate goods of delivery number to be transported to the lorry and to deliver to any one buyer's home.

So, it seems that warehouse robots ought help any one warehouse worker to raise himself efficiency and avoid goods delivery of mistake occurrence easily as well as their help to warehouse workers that can let any one goods buyer feels their goods can be delivered to their homes rapidly. Moreover, warehouse robots can also help these warehouse workers to raise efficiencies because warehouse robots can help them to shorten goods delivery time between any one shelf and any one goods delivery destination of location in the warehuse because robots may help them to find the right kinds of goods from the right shelf in the short time. So, any one worker does not need to spend long time to seek anywhere is the right shelf location for the kind of goods when the kind of goods are needed to deliver to the buyer's home from lorry. Warehouse robots can help them to do this aspect of " finding the goods from the right shelf in short time job duty". So, any one warehouse worker only needed tospend less time to do the counting of any right kind of goods number and ensuring the right kind of goods job duty. Consequently, this warehouse 's any one worker, his any one kind of goods delivery time may be reduced, because robots' assistance and they may have more confidence to avoid mistake to deliver the wrong number of goods and/or the wrong kind of goods to any one goods buyer's home.

On conclusion, it seems that warehouse robots ought may help any one warehouse worker to raise efficiency for any one team in the warehouse as well as the warehouse any one supervisor does not need to spend much time to observe any one worker individual performance for " goods delivery job duty aspect" because their goods delivery job duty that had been replaced to do by these several warehouse robots. Robots can achieve the more accurate of right kinds of goods and the right number of goods delviery job performance to compare any one of human warehouse worker themselves right kinds of goods of delivery and right number of goods of delivery job performance. So, when robots can participate to cooperate with this warehouse's any one worker to do their goods of delivery job duty in this warehouse every day. Then, robots can raies any one of supervisor individual confidence in order to let they do not need to spend time to observe any one of worker individual whose goods of delivery job performane. They can concentrate on supervising any one worker whose goods transport to lorry in the final step in order to avoid to deliver wrong goods number and / or wrong kind of goods to any one goods buyer's home every day. Consequently, this warehouse's overall teams of their delviery of goods performance many be improved by robotss' participatin to goods of delivery task as well as this warehouse's oveall teams themselves efficiencies may be influenced to raise by robots' goods of delivery task participation.

Why social behavior may influence organizational strategy needs to be changed ?

Why any organizations need to know whether nowadays social behaivor how has been changing in order to implement the kind of the most right strategy to achieve the profit aim pursue in possible. I shall indicate nowadays ecommerce or online, customer shopping behavior to explain above question concerns they ought have close relationship between social behavior and organizational strategic choice or organizational behavioral changing need.

On nowadays ecommerce business, or online shopping model, this kind of shopping model in global many young and old age consumers like to apply internet tool to choose any country sellers website stores in order to stay at home to buy any kinds of products from themselves webstores in global societies.

In fact, online shopping model had been popular for long time above to twenty years. Most of global sellers will make decision to design themselves webstores in order to attract global many online buyers to choose to buy their products from themselves webstores. So, it seems that social consumers purchase behaviors had been changed to online shopping from internet invention.

Hence, social consumers purchase behavioral changes may influence any organizations' strategies need to be changed from visiting shops purchase strategy model to online purchase strategy model, if the seller still concentrate on concentrate on considerate how to design itelf , but neglects to considerate how to design itself webstore, e.g. how to design attract product photos to put on itself webstore, how to arrange sale price information location to be putted on webstore and visa card payment location on itself webstore in order to let any one online buyer can feel very easier to buy itself any kinds of products from itself webstore. Then, its potential online buyers will be influenced to increase number when they can find this online seller itself any kinds of products photes and every kinds of product sale price information and visa card payment channel locations easily from itself webstore.

So, it implies that nowadays any one seller ought need to design one webstore to let any one online overseas and domestic consumers can have chance to click itself webstore to choose any one kind of product to buy conveniently when he/she does not hope to leave him/her home to go to shop, because nowadays social shopping behaviors had been influenced to change when internet invention, them it gives another online purchase method to replace visiting shops purchase method to global any one buyer in nowadays societies.

So, if nowadays any one seller still concentrate on how to design itself shop display in order to put any kinds of product on shelf in order to let any one visiting shop customer to find the kind of product to buy, but it neglects to change to choose to pursue another new technological shopping method, such as webstore purchase method in order to implement effective strategy to design the most right webstore as well as in order to attract global overseas and local consumers to find itself webstore easily from website and find its any one kind of product phots and sale price and visa card payment button in order to choose to buy itself any kinds of products in the short time. Consequently I believe that the seller will lose many customers from overseas and local when its other same or similar product sellers choose to design themselves webstores in order to let global any one product buyer can buy themselves any one kind of product when they can pay visa card to buy their products from them webstores conveniently when they stay at home habitly. Then, the seller will lose many global potential customers in long time.

On conclusion, in behavioral economic view, any consumer behavioral social changing, which will influence any in order to avoid customers number loses significantly . In future time, organizations need to make rapid decision in order to implement the most reasonable and the most useful strategy in order to avoid global potential customers number reduces or lose them in long time. So, social behavioral changing environment ought influence any global organizations need to decide how to change themselves strategies in order to avoid customers loses significantly in future time.